The Metaphysics of Edmund Burke

The Metaphysics of Edmund Burke

by
JOSEPH L. PAPPIN III

with a Foreword by
FRANCIS P. CANAVAN, S.J.

FORDHAM UNIVERSITY PRESS
New York
1993

Copyright © 1993 by Fordham University Press
All rights reserved
LC 92-41383
ISBN 0-8232-1365-X (clothbound)
ISBN 0-8232-1366-8 (paperback)

Library of Congress Cataloging-in-Publication Data

Pappin, Joseph L.
　The metaphysics of Edmund Burke / by Joseph L. Pappin III; with a foreword by Francis P. Canavan, S.J.
　　p. cm.
　Includes bibliographical references and index.
　ISBN 0-8232-1365-X (cloth).—ISBN 0-8232-1366-8 (pbk.)
　1. Burke, Edmund, 1729-1797—Contributions in political science.
2. Burke, Edmund, 1729-1797—Views on metaphysics.　3. Metaphysics.
I. Title.
JC176.B83P28　1993
320.5'2'092—dc20　　　　　　　　　　　　　　　　　92-41383
　　　　　　　　　　　　　　　　　　　　　　　　　　　CIP

For
my wife
Gay
and
Gladden John and Margie B.

Contents

Acknowledgments	ix
Abbreviations	xi
Foreword	xiii
Introduction	xv
1. Metaphysics and Politics	1
2. The Problem of a Burkean Metaphysics	11
3. The Case for Burke's Metaphysics	52
4. The Philosophy of God and Human Nature	102
5. The Metaphysical Elements of Teleology and Natural Law	139
6. Concluding Reflections: Metaphysical Nihilism and Radical Individualism	160
Selected Bibliography	175
Index	183

Acknowledgments

Like others before me, my initial interest in Burke was occasioned by a reading of Russell Kirk's *Edmund Burke: A Genius Reconsidered*. This discovery of Burke came for me at a time of deepening interest in the thought of St. Thomas Aquinas, an interest which was first nourished by Professor Francis Kovach, a truly outstanding Thomist philosopher, and then enriched by Professor Leo Sweeney, s.j. Without their guidance and the example of their zeal for the Common Doctor I could not have approached the metaphysical riches of Aquinas. And, in turn, it is Aquinas who provides, in considerable measure I will argue, the framework necessary to comprehend the metaphysics of Edmund Burke.

Both Professor Francis Canavan, s.j., and Professor Peter Stanlis read portions of the text along the way and provided invaluable suggestions and comments. Others who assisted at various stages in the writing of the text include Professors Tom W. Boyd, J. Clayton Feaver, and Curtis Hancock. Also, the comments and recommendations for improving the text provided by the three anonymous readers greatly assisted in producing the final form of this work.

I am especially pleased to acknowledge the generous support of the Earhart Foundation, Ann Arbor, Michigan, for a fellowship in 1984–85, and for additional support in 1991. Their assistance came at crucial moments, enabling the completion of this work. Also, I would like to thank John F. Lulves, Jr., who introduced my work to the Earhart Foundation, and who is a true friend of Burke scholars.

I am most grateful to Dr. Mary Beatrice Schulte, executive editor at Fordham University Press, for her constant interest in this work. I cannot imagine working with a more encouraging and considerate editor. The close reading provided by Katherine Moreau led to many improvements in the style of the essay. I am pleased to acknowledge her cheerful assistance. The essential typing of the entire manuscript was expertly provided by my secretary, Stephani Franklin.

But my deepest gratitude goes to my wife, Gay, who alone made this entire work possible, and to our dear children, Gladden John and Margie B., to whom this work is joyfully dedicated.

Abbreviations

Citations of Burke's works appear, for the most part, as listed here.

C *The Correspondence of Edmund Burke*. Ed. Thomas W. Copeland, 10 vols. Cambridge: Cambridge University Press; Chicago: The University of Chicago Press, 1958–1978.

NB *A Notebook of Edmund Burke*. Ed. H. V. F. Somerset. Cambridge: Cambridge University Press, 1957.

W *The Works of the Right Honorable Edmund Burke*. 12 vols. Boston: Little, Brown, 1866.

The following individual texts appear in various volumes of *The Works of the Right Honorable Edmund Burke*.

ANW IV *An Appeal from the New to the Old Whigs* (1791), W IV
ISB I *A Philosophical Inquiry into the Origin of our Ideas of the Sublime and Beautiful* (1757), W I
LNA IV *A Letter to a Member of the National Assembly* (1791), W IV
1LRP V *First Letter on a Regicide Peace* (1796), W V
2LRP V *Second Letter on a Regicide Peace* (1796), W V
3LRP V *Third Letter on a Regicide Peace* (1796), W V
4LRP VI *Fourth Letter on a Regicide Peace* (1796), W VI
LSB II *Letter to the Sheriffs of Bristol* (1777), W II
RF III *Reflections on the Revolution in France* (1790), W III
SC VII *Speech on the Reform of the Representation of the Commons in Parliament* (1782), W VII
SCA II *Speech on Conciliation with America* (1775), W II

TPD I   *Thoughts on the Cause of the Present Discontents* (1770), W I
TPL VI   *Tract on the Popery Laws* (1765), W VI

Foreword

THIS IS A BOOK that has long needed to be written. In the period since the Second World War, a number of writers, myself among them, have drawn attention to the strong role played by a classical and medieval theory of natural law in Edmund Burke's political thought and have pointed to its foundation in a realist doctrine of metaphysics. But no one, so far as I am aware, has until now undertaken a book-length study of the metaphysical suppositions of Burke's political philosophy. In the present book Joseph Pappin III supplies that need.

He is at odds with many, if not most, writers on Burke among the statesman's latter-day British compatriots. Steeped in an empiricist tradition, they find it difficult to see in Burke's thought anything more than an elevated utilitarianism, embellished with theological and natural law trimmings, to be sure, but antirationalist and antimetaphysical in its substance. As Pappin points out, Burke was indeed vehemently opposed to the rationalism of his day, which derived a political ideology by logical deduction from abstract ideas. But to conclude from this that Burke rejected metaphysics is to misunderstand him badly.

The question is not whether Burke's political philosophy rests on a metaphysic, but rather on what metaphysic it is based. Pappin's aim in this work, as he says in his Conclusion, is "to make explicit the implicit metaphysical core of Burke's political thought." Such explication is admittedly a risky undertaking because of the danger that one will end up fitting Burke into a framework of one's own choosing rather than explaining what is really implicit in his writings. The risk, however, is one that must be run.

It cannot be avoided, in fact, for it is a risk incurred by any interpreter of Burke, whether one makes him out to be a pragmatist, a utilitarian, a historicist, or a metaphysical realist. Burke was not a systematic writer on philosophy, or even on political theory, but a practicing politician—albeit one of unusual depth of mind—whose almost every writing was addressed to an immediate political issue. His philosophy furnished him with the premises of political argument, but was not itself presented in an organized or fully developed fashion. His premises therefore cry out for explication and interpretation. Risks are involved, as they are in all interpretation, but they are ones that any serious writer on Burke must take.

Burke's writings, however, are rich enough and his statements of or allusions to his basic philosophical principles are numerous enough to furnish a standard by which a reader may measure and judge varying interpretations of those principles. Pappin's main goal in this study is, as he says, "to demonstrate that Burke's political philosophy is grounded in a realist metaphysics, one that is basically consonant with the Aristotelian-Thomistic tradition" (pp. 170–71). Perhaps more importantly, he uses metaphysics as an explanatory key to what Burke actually wrote. It is a key that fits the lock better than any other that scholars have offered. The only proof of this statement, of course, is to read Burke in the light of Pappin's exegesis and to ask oneself if it does not reveal the unity, the coherence, and the meaning of Burke's words with greater clarity and depth than any competing interpretation.

I believe that it does do this by offering us a more thorough analysis of Burke's understanding of God, creation, nature, man, and society than has previously appeared. Those who disagree with Pappin's analysis—and surely there will be some—must at least admit that they have met a worthy antagonist. Scholars on both sides of the issue will, I am confident, find the growing "literature" on Burke enriched by this book.

FRANCIS CANAVAN, S.J.
Fordham University

Introduction

AN UNSOLVED PROBLEM in the literature on Edmund Burke's political philosophy is whether Burke's thought is avowedly anti-metaphysical, as some of his pronouncements indicate, or whether he rejects only a type of metaphysics and its misapplication to politics. Furthermore, if Burke has a metaphysics, as I shall maintain, what are the sustaining principles of that metaphysics? In the present work I will attempt to answer these questions in the light of Burke's political thought.

The controversy surrounding the question of a Burkean metaphysics has led to two basically opposed interpretations. On the one hand, many scholars consider Burke as belonging to the utilitarian tradition in morality and politics; on the other, some place him in the classical natural law tradition. The exponents of the former view see him as anti-metaphysical, dismissing the efficacy of speculative reason. Representatives of the latter see the evidence for natural law as a cornerstone of a metaphysics within Burke's political theory, with Burke affirming the efficacy of human reason and the inherent order of the physical and moral universe.[1]

To define the nature of the problem and to contribute to its solution, I have envisioned the following goals for this study, listed in the order of their importance, not according to the sequence of their development within the body itself.

First, I aim to demonstrate that Burke's political philosophy has a metaphysical basis as does his philosophy of God and human nature. His metaphysics provides, therefore, the philosophical scaffolding and thematic guidelines for his political philosophy. This demonstration involves negative and positive elements.

Negatively, it is important that I make two qualifications: (1) Burke is not a professional metaphysician. He is not to be regarded as another of the systematic metaphysicians belonging to a tradition from Aristotle through the modern idealists; he shares many of their conclusions but little of their methodology. In fact, his metaphysical views are more matters of assumption than argued conclusions. (2) The metaphysical elements of Burke's thought are recognized by him to differ from the popular metaphysics of his day. Burke is no rationalist. As a political activist, he is sensitive first and foremost to claiming nothing politically substantial unless it be manifested in political experience. In other words, his metaphysical beliefs are not precepts brought *a priori* to the political arena, but truths which are revealed in, and give intelligibility to, experience.

Positively, I will initially show that Burke's metaphysics features the principles of change and stability, and reflects a universe of order. To regard either principle at the expense of the other is to distort his conception of nature and, hence, of politics. These apparently discordant principles disclose a reality in which, through the struggling interplay of opposed forces, a reasonable and purposeful harmony in nature and society emerges. Therefore, Burke's metaphysics reflects the reality and constancy of change within the context of a stable, hierarchically structured universe as created and sustained by God.

Next, I consider the evidence for arguing that Burke has an anti-metaphysical position. I hope to refute any such conclusion by showing that, although he is through choice not a speculative philosopher, his invective is aimed against a false metaphysics, especially the metaphysics of the French Enlightenment philosophers, whose metaphysics Burke took to be rationalistic, deductive, oblivious to concrete facts, and imposing its utopian abstract scheme upon society. There are many general philosophic descriptions of Burke, such as utilitarian, pragmatist, empiricist, historicist, and organicist. I shall examine utilitarianism, the most noted and comprehensive of these descriptions, and show that it is an inadequate interpretation of Burke's position.

Finally, I locate Burke's metaphysics on a philosophic spectrum. In other words, I intend to identify in a general way the philosophical movement with which Burke's thought is most compatible, without damaging the complexity of his thought.

The realist quality of his metaphysics is difficult to ignore, and I shall argue, in particular, that there are parallels with the realism of the Aristotelian-Thomistic tradition. Yet this aim is secondary to the demonstration of Burke's metaphysics and its principles.

In Chapter 1 I simply explore the significance and problems raised by relating metaphysics and politics. At first blush, the passion for certainty rooted in the metaphysical quest contrasts sharply with the contingent realm of politics. Some, if not most, today, would deny altogether the possibility of obtaining certainty in metaphysics, much less applying these truths in any manner to the political sphere. Nonetheless, to take a political concept such as "justice" as an example, the question is raised as to whether or not any adequate understanding of such a concept can be obtained, independent of its various usages, without metaphysical insight into human nature? In raising the question of the interrelation between metaphysics and politics the question does not presuppose the reality of human nature, or ignore the historicity of human existence. But it does require an inquiry into the nature of things in order to consider the relation between human beings and society and the consequent implications for justice. Nor does this inquiry ignore the Burkean counsel against imposing abstract universals on politics regardless of circumstances.

But at this point, the stage is simply being set for the examination and presentation of Burke's metaphysics. This chapter also anticipates problems inherent in such a presentation.

In Chapter 2, I shall discuss "The Problem of a Burkean Metaphysics," setting forth the evidence in Burke which is often taken as reflecting an anti-metaphysical attitude. This evidence does indeed, at least, reflect Burke's suspicion about rationalist metaphysics. Herein, I shall turn to certain utilitarian interpretations of Burke's thought, especially attending to the claimed rejection of any metaphysical foundation of his thought.

It is important to understand that I have something specific and limited in mind for this chapter. I do not want to anticipate in this chapter the main argument of the study. I want only to establish that Burke's thought is not anti-metaphysical. I do not intend to argue here that he has a particular metaphysics; that will come later.

In Chapter 3 the presentation of "The Case for Burke's Metaphysics" begins. This will entail first a consideration of what metaphysics is, and an understanding of the task of the metaphysician. The nature and task of metaphysics in this context will be traced within the bounds of the Aristotelian-Thomistic *philosophia perennis*. It is within this realist framework that Burke's metaphysics will be shown to rest. I will present the case for a Burkean metaphysics, concentrating on those elements that seem most pivotal, and serve best to integrate the whole substance of his thought.

In this chapter I shall focus in particular on the elements of change and stability and on their relationship to Burke's notion of substance, essence, and nature. These elements sustain the thesis of an ordered, intelligible, hierarchical, developmental, and teleological reality. My interpretation will gain further clarification in this chapter by way of a concise comparison and contrast with certain French Enlightenment thinkers and with John Locke in regard to certain of their ideas concerning these elements. Finally, after Burke's metaphysics are separated from a metaphysics of radical existentialism and extreme essentialism (with their inordinate emphasis upon change or stability respectively), his philosophy will be shown to reflect a favorable comparison with Aristotelian-Thomistic metaphysics.

In Chapter 4 these elements of Burke's metaphysics will be more specifically traced through his philosophy of God and human nature. Links between his metaphysics and political philosophy will be sought throughout this study, but they will especially come to light when the discussion of human nature is extended to a consideration of Burke's theories of liberty and equality. The philosophical principles of order as revealed in the treatment of change and stability will receive further amplification in this chapter, revealing themselves as the thematic threads that connect the various parts of Burke's metaphysics.

His view of human nature shows how the elements of his metaphysics come together. For Burke, human nature is structured yet dynamic. The essence of man remains constant amid historical and social change. Human nature is both rational and social, although sentiment and feeling often predominate. Man exists for the perfecting of his nature in society. The will and designs of God, especially as known to man through the natural law, reveal in part the universal moral laws for the perfecting of human nature.

In Chapter 5 I will consider the teleological and natural law elements of Burke's metaphysics. This will underscore yet again the principles of order and the parts that change and stability play throughout his philosophy. The element of teleology evolves from the discussion of change, God, and human nature, and points to the purposefulness of all reality for Burke. At this point, the chaotic disturbance of evil will be contrasted with the telic character of reality.

An integral element of the argument for Burke's metaphysics is the concept of natural law. Although this specific link in Burke's philosophy has been the subject of recent secondary literature, it cannot be ignored if my interpretation is to be sustained. More importantly, I will apply the previously outlined metaphysical principles to an assessment of the natural law foundation of Burke's politics. This law has a universal and timeless application to all mankind, sustaining the orderly yet developmental vitality of reality.

The final chapter raises the specter of a metaphysical nihilism and inquires into implications of the same for a radical individualism. These final reflections are the natural culmination of the preceding deliberations. For some, a metaphysical nihilism grounded in atheism leads to the liberation of human beings. The upshot tends towards a radical egalitarianism and democratization that too easily slides into an irrationalism unleashing a new tyranny. This pursuit of radical freedom is boldly contrasted with Burke's metaphysical realism, which grounds human freedom and equality in an ordered reality, universe and society that structures human action providing a bulwark against political extremism and absolutism.

It is my hope that the relationship marked between Burke's metaphysics and political thought will not only contribute to an increased understanding of a rich and fertile mind, but also prove timely for those who search for a political vision with a foundation in the order of reality, not simply in ideology. The only viable setting for politics is one that seeks its support beyond the aspirations of the oppressed or the designs of utopian visionaries. Politics must reflect reality as it is, not just as we wish it to be. And to know what reality is, we need to seek a basis for political thought in a metaphysics which discloses being. This I believe Edmund Burke has done.

NOTE

1. For clarification of Burke's own use or meaning of reason, see pp. 19-21.

1
Metaphysics and Politics

FEW CONCEPTS seem more opposed to one another than the terms "metaphysics" and "politics." Metaphysics aims at exactitude, striving to find certain knowledge of the nature of reality itself. Politics appears so remote from exactitude that any attempt to include it within the range of philosophy seems forced and contrived. Inexactitude bedevils political philosophy because of the extreme contingency of its subject matter, which is the actions of men in governing society and the structure of government and its great multitude of functions. In order to relate metaphysics to politics, it is necessary to inquire into the nature of metaphysics and our desire for metaphysical knowledge.

The scholastics qualify metaphysics as the science of being as being. Metaphysicians vary drastically among themselves, yet all work to provide mankind with the deepest and most profound insights into reality. Nothing short of reality in its most basic structure will suffice for the honest metaphysician. Still, having noted this similarity among metaphysicians, we also must note the dissimilarity in results. Being is presented in ranges from pure materiality to pure immateriality. In case this range does not exhaust the alternatives, then metaphysical nihilism denies completely the reality of being. One, of course, must overlook the status of the denial itself to see this as even being an alternative, and yet, as the sophist Gorgias reminds us, nihilism is not simply a recent philosophical position. Still, metaphysicians rarely hedge their bets. From Pythagoras' doctrine of the One to Sartre's treatment of consciousness as nothingness, all philosophers who consider the ultimate nature or character of reality approach the subject with apparent equal solemnity, if not always piety, as Heidegger might wish it. Metaphysics is serious business and requires a discipline of mind and speculative curiosity that escapes all but the most philosophically inclined.

What stimulates our desire for metaphysical knowledge? Why are we impelled beyond the pure data of our senses in the direction of obtaining the supra-sensible, not knowing if that is even possible? What is the driving force of thought that requires of us that we come to know reality in its deepest sense?

I would suppose that the dominant mode of Anglo-American philosophy, analytic philosophy, would find a certain disease of the intellect at the basis of the metaphysical impulse. We are told that we are bewitched by language. How are we bewitched? We are bewitched into thinking that for every concept there must be a reality for which it stands—if you will, a Platonic Form or Idea. Every concept, therefore, as a universal that transcends the particular to which it is related, is ultimately timeless, eternal, and so requires that there be a transcendent, timeless, eternal reality as its metaphysical ground. To deny this would be, according to this metaphysical straw man depicted by analysts, to assert the absurdity and meaningless character of reality. It would be to permit reality to disintegrate into an amorphous, jelly-like substance, with no structure, oozing forth in random directions, having no sense. No one should attempt to match Roquentin's depiction of the absurdity of existence in Sartre's *Nausea*.

What then is the peculiar disease that bewitches the intellect according to this characterization? It appears that it is man's inability to face the truth of reality, namely, that reality bears no truth or value save the truth or value we impart to it. As concepts are actually only fragments of a web that reflect a peculiar life-form, we should recognize that their ground is not a transcendent Form of which they are only a reflection, but simply the current social state by which our thoughts are fused and conditioned. What concepts tell us, then, is not about a transcendent metaphysical reality, but about how culture and human beings as bearers of culture happen to think about particulars, or how we have come to structure our own culture at the present moment. Rather than telling us about the reality we seek to know, concepts tell us about a social life-world of which we are a part. We come to know the ways in which we know and those elements that condition knowing rather than about any known. Metaphysics is impossible. The social sciences, though, rush forth to supplant the realm of being vacated by metaphysics. This attitude has been assumed to a large extent both by analytic philosophers and by the movement of critical theory.

In the approach which turns to social structures as the condition of all knowing, one still can see that the desire to know more deeply than surface appearances remains an impelling force in our quest for knowledge. What seems lost is the quest for being as being, for the being of all beings. This quest has been relegated to the dustbin of the history of philosophy where all previous attempts to answer this question are heaped. And yet, to answer that all knowledge reflects a life-form or social structure will not suffice. It becomes a bad infinite in the sense that it arbitrarily attempts to answer our desire to know being as being by saying this far and no further. It is infinite in that all our knowing appears grounded in social structures, and bad in that there is no adequate reason offered for claiming that our concepts are simply woven out of the social matter of our own historical epoch. This is not to deny the influence of one's own age on thought and perhaps the outright source of much of our knowledge in our social structures and institutions. But this is a limited response to the question of being. It does not serve to fill the potentially infinite horizon from Plato onward. It relativizes the metaphysical quest for the being of beings and fails the criterion of exactitude and necessity that is the felt need of the intellect in metaphysical knowing.

In fact, few philosophers recognized so clearly the tremendous impact of social structure on the thought of man as Plato. The formation of society and the state was crucial in the education of man and hence in his capacity as one who knows. So scrupulous was Plato's design of the state in the *Republic*, so cautious was he in providing the proper education and social setting of those who were to lead, that he has incurred the criticism and sometimes outrage of countless philosophers, from his own student, Aristotle, to Sir Karl Popper in our own century. And yet his utopian designs were a reflection of his assent to the proposition that knowing is conditioned in large part by the structures of society and the state. Never did he, though, succumb to the relativism of his own age. *Our* own age witnesses a relativism that finds all knowledge conditioned by other factors which militate against the acquisition of any absolute truth—that is, all knowledge save the knowledge of these same all-pervasive relativizing conditions. Plato's entire life was spent responding to such extreme skepticism, knowing all the while the profound effect social structures have upon the individual.

Those who reflect the relativism of our own times are confounded by one inescapable element in the metaphysical impulse—the desire to know absolutely. Answers to the question of the nature of reality that fall short of absolute certainty haunt those who wish to know with absolute certainty. This might be discounted by some as a remnant of rationalism, by which thinkers turned from the radical plurality and diversity of sense experience to certain innate truths of the mind. According to the rationalists, the mind is the bearer of a few simple truths which, if adhered to, will give absolute certainty about the wildly fluctuating world of experience itself. Again, what accounts for such an intractable desire, to know with absolute certainty, and how to quiet this desire? Of course we know the rebuke, "don't ask, look and see." This injunction throws us back into the arms of experience, but in order to comprehend what one sees, one is forced beyond sheer experience. Inherent in thought seems to be an oscillation between the pre-reflective world of experience and reflection. And yet what is it that reflection discloses? Does it disclose a metaphysical ground of experience? We are back to our point of departure. But a different answer might be offered, with a similar goal to that initially examined: to explain the impulse to know in a way that rids us of the question of being. Perhaps the question of being finds its ground not within any metaphysical structure of reality, nor in any reduction to social structures, but in an anthropological reduction. Perhaps the mind is so structured as to think experience in certain patterned ways that trick us into thinking that there is a reality lying beyond the world of appearance. If one digs deeply enough, what one discovers is not a metaphysical structure or essence, but the mind itself as necessarily structured and ordered by its own categories of thought. And now the impulse to know stems from the structure of the mind itself. Due to this structure I necessarily think beyond the data of experience, I necessarily think essentially, and such thinking requires the use of concepts. The ground of these concepts lies not in the structure of the social life-world, but in the structures of the mind.

Our own age has tried to remove metaphysics as the cornerstone of all philosophy, regarding all metaphysical constructions as meaningless. If metaphysics is to be removed, or at best reduced to a descriptive endeavor, then it hardly makes sense to relate what has no meaning to politics. One would not want to find a ground for politics in that which is without meaning. If exactitude is a condition of metaphysical knowledge, and yet is not to be found, then we are all the more certain of not finding it in knowledge of political things. Further, if politics finds no ground in metaphysics because metaphysics has been surpassed by the social sciences or linguistic analysis, then politics must seek its ground in that by which metaphysics has been surpassed. So, if we ask the politically significant question "What is Justice?" we must not look to a metaphysics in which that question might derive its significance. Instead, we might look to the various usages of the term "justice" within society. It is likely to be used differently in our own society from how it was used in the ancient world. Our own culture would find the concept "justice" used in a society which permits and even justifies slavery to be a total contradiction. But why? Because we see man as meant to be free, untrammeled by social structures that prevent basic freedoms. It is not right to enslave, to prohibit arbitrarily the exercise of our proper freedoms. But again, why is it not fair to consider certain types of men as unfit to assume the privileges of the free citizen? Is it due to the nature of man as transcending any cultural barrier or historical epoch? Is it due to man's rationality and his free will as the constitutive elements of his nature? Hardly could this be the case according to the analyst or critical theorist. Perhaps the meaning of justice lies simply in the factual arrangement of political things that presently declares slavery as unjust, that declares all improper restrictions of freedoms as against the present order of things.

Such a justification for the rejection of slavery seems arbitrary and easily subject to change. Perhaps the time will come when all those who reject the secular values upon which our modern state increasingly depends in the name of spiritual and religious values will need to be incarcerated. But then justice will be seen as requiring the enslavement of those whose free speech undermines the secular values of the state and it will then be just and fair to remove freedoms from such threats to the modern state. In that case in what does the concept of "justice" find its support? If it finds its support or ground simply in usage, or as a reflection of the current social-welfare structures of the state, then the concept "justice" lacks any fixity. It is a convenience, essentially fluctuating to adapt in a useful manner to the positive structure of the state of society.

Certainly, any concept of "justice" that does not reflect the law of nature (which law for Burke included both permanence and change) and that does not reflect the nuanced circumstances and conditions of the age, or the moment, will be restrictive. But if justice has no moorings, no ground in the nature of things, then it will be merely a name, subject to the caprice of power. It will serve to sanction whatever actions a ruler will choose to engage in; it will be subject to the caprice of the strongest. But if there is no nature of things, no fixed ground around which the flux of time and changes of circumstance might move, then we are indeed reduced to a fluid concept of justice, one that is in fact vacuous, being only what the will, caprice, and strength of man as socially contextualized might wish.

Here is an instance, a fundamental and profound instance, in which metaphysics and politics come to bear. What is justice? How are we to determine what is just? In what is the meaning of the term grounded? Does justice reflect being, the order of being, the nature of things, of which nature is a metaphysical question? Or if natures and essences are simply putative and tell us more about the structures of society than about the way things are, then to find the meaning of justice as reflecting the way things are is useless.

What does metaphysics have to say to questions of justice, of liberty, of equality, and of the state? If metaphysics is simply a symptom of the diseased intellect which continually asks questions for which there are no answers, then man's attempts to answer such questions are purely reflective of the wishes of the individual who speculates. They are entertaining, but they are only mental vapors. But if metaphysics truly gains insight into what things are, then its significance for politics is paramount. If it is the nature of human beings to think and to act freely, then to wantonly and unreasonably restrict them from the exercise of thought and action is a violation of human nature. Thus, to know what things are is of vital significance to politics.

If man is naturally free and unnaturally a member of society and yet if society is necessary to his survival, then the questions of justice become increasingly complex but no less dependent upon the metaphysical question "What is man?" If we determine that all men are to be treated equally then we must ask, "Are all men by nature equal, or are they equal in some respects and not others?" Or, "are men bound together naturally into society and can society survive without some sense of structure and subordination of parts and hence of certain natural forms of inequality?" How can these questions be ignored? Yet how can they be answered without inquiring into the nature of things, without thinking metaphysically?

But we return to our initial concern with the disparity between the exactitude of metaphysics and the inexactitude of politics.

Is metaphysics capable of exactitude? Can we know the nature of things exactly as they are? Can we know the true being of beings, or is metaphysics capable of only approximate knowledge? Among the sciences, metaphysics is the first concern of St. Thomas Aquinas:

> Particular sciences are posterior in nature to universal sciences, because their subjects add to the subject matter of the universal sciences, as is clear in the case of natural philosophy which adds to being as such, the subject of metaphysics, and to quantified being, the subject of mathematics. Therefore the science which treats simply of being and the most universal things is most certain.[1]

Not only does metaphysics achieve certainty for Aquinas, it is the most certain of sciences. It achieves certain knowledge, not provisional knowledge, about its subject matter, being, and the character of being in itself as infinite. How can I make this claim in light of the relativist critique of metaphysics?

If I question the very possibility of metaphysics, then I question the possibility of being itself and its knowability. And if I extend the entire range of the question to its implied extent, then I am asking, "Is there anything at all?" But the question of being is in fact something. It is an act, the act of the questioner who inquires. Being is affirmed in the question of being. I have certainty of this; this knowledge is exact. It is meaningless to assert otherwise.

More than that, the question reveals the limited nature of the questioner. In asking the question of being, in searching for the answer, the questioner necessarily reveals his own finite nature. To inquire is a form of not-knowing. If I knew, I would not inquire. But, as Socrates revealed in the *Meno*, to question, to inquire, is a knowing not-knowing. I cannot be absolutely ignorant of being or else how am I to ask the question of being? There is a pre-apprehension of being given in the very question of being. Reflection reveals that this pre-apprehension contains within it the pre-grasp of infinite being, implicitly, but not explicitly. For how am I to come to know my own finitude as the one who questions, save for my pre-apprehension of being as unlimited, as infinite? Reflection upon the question of being reveals, therefore, not only that being is, and that the being of the questioner is finite, but also the necessity of being in itself as infinite. The question of being discloses certain knowledge of being.

While achieving certain knowledge, though, it is like certainty amid considerable uncertainty. We know from the principle of identity "Whatever is, is." But what does it mean to be identical to oneself? Or we can know that action follows nature. But what precisely is the relationship between one's acts and one's nature? And in what sense is our nature further realized through our acts? Likewise, to know something according to what is is to apprehend its essence. We know that the essence of a tiger is different from that of a human being. But precisely what is the essence of a tiger, or how penetrating is our knowledge of human nature? Can I know the essence of a being and yet acquire further insight into that selfsame essence? While obtaining certain knowledge, we appear in the midst of considerable uncertainty. The difficulty in knowing the essences of things is attested to by Aquinas himself. Still, metaphysics is nothing if it is not exact.

It is precisely the character of metaphysics as an exact science that leads many to conclude the inapplicability of metaphysics. This is Burke's conclusion and he cites Aristotle's authority (SCA II 170). To follow a rationalist metaphysics with a mathematical fervor, disregarding the circumstances in which one's conclusions about politics is to be realized, is to reduce politics to metaphysics. The formality of such reductionism may be intellectually gratifying, but it defies the contingent-fraught nature of the realm of politics. A wedding such as that between metaphysics and politics is bound to fail, or bound to play havoc with society. But the insights gained through metaphysical reflection into, for example, human nature, law, justice, community, and the state, insights that clarify the nature of these political things, are necessary to the practicalities of politics. How does one implement positive law to protect the proper freedoms of man if one has no knowledge of what man is? Yet, if man's nature is rational and social then that same nature is not realized in a vacuum but in concrete interaction with others. And the result of that interaction is the ontological realization of both self and other in a community which achieves man's second nature, his social nature. We realize an increase in being and a permanent alteration of our nature in the context of social interaction. One cannot abstractly consider what that context will be which will, in concert with our free choices, lead to an ontological realization of the human person. Metaphysics cannot, in abstraction, anticipate and legislate all the circumstances of the human condition in terms of sheer speculation. Yet, as metaphysics reflects on human nature in society, it can serve to disclose the fundamental nature of man, the community, the state, without forcing in *a priori* fashion conditions upon the polity. The adjustment of man's nature to his distinct historical, social, environmental circumstances requires the prudence of the legislator and the wisdom of the ages as vested in custom and tradition.

The misapplication of metaphysical conclusions to the political sphere obtains when abstract designs are imposed upon the state without any care given to the concrete circumstances in which they are to be realized. It is to move from the speculative realm to the practical affairs of state without benefit of a medium or guide. That guide, which views the necessary verities of metaphysics and the contingent complexities of the state and society with an eye to what can be done, is the guide of prudence. Burke's own often-repeated assessment of the relationship between philosophy and politics best marks the synthesis required: "It is the business of the speculative philosopher to mark the proper ends of government. It is the business of the politician, who is the philosopher in action, to find out proper means towards those ends, and to employ them with effect" (TPD I 530). Certainly, the politician cannot proceed without the "proper ends of government" in mind. But just as certainly the politician cannot have recourse to the speculative philosopher for detailed application of speculative conclusions to the complexity of circumstances in which those ends are to be realized.

A metaphysics ignorant of the need of prudent politic wisdom in the pursuit of its ends gives over easily to fanaticism. To mindlessly blow asunder the fabric of society so slowly knit together, preserved, and amended for generations is to seek to enact speculative perfection in the imperfect, inexact region of politics. But to ignore the determination of ends, the signaling of bounds, and the governance of means that metaphysics so splendidly provides is to submit the sphere of politics to the self-serving ends of tyranny and anarchy.

Note

1. St. Thomas Aquinas, *Commentary on the Metaphysics of Aristotle*, trans. John P. Rowan (Chicago: Regnery, 1961), I, lesson 2, no. 47.

2
The Problem of a Burkean Metaphysics

MY CONCERN is to support the position that Edmund Burke's political philosophy has a metaphysical foundation and to indicate what that foundation is. In this chapter I will show some of the complexities involved in discovering and securing this position.

These complexities in Burke's thought are in large part due to the following elements. First, almost all his writings, speeches, and letters deal with the occurrence of a political event or crisis. Second, since he writes in response to specific events, such as the Catholic problem in Ireland, or the American or French revolutions, he generally engages in urging action or response to these crises. Consequently, the purpose of his writing is not that of composing a systematic political philosophy. His writing, although eloquent, is born of haste. James T. Boulton, in a work of literary criticism, discovers method in Burke's apparent haste: "Perhaps the dominant impression given by the *Reflections* is of a relentless pace in writing: the imperative tone, the cumulative effect of image and illustration, the apparently inexhaustible fertility of Burke's mind, all combine to forbid effective reply except from the most incisive minds."[1] Third, much of Burke's thought is couched in the philosophical and political parlance in vogue in the eighteenth century. In a letter, dated July 22, 1791, responding to a criticism of his writing style in the *Reflections on the Revolution in France* (1790), he provides a reply that applies nearly to all his works: "But surely you forget, that I was throwing out reflexions upon a political event, and not reading a lecture upon theorism and principles of Government. How I should treat such a subject is not for me to say, for I never had that intention" (C VI 304). As Dreyer notes, Burke "talked to his contemporaries in language that they understood and claimed their support on principles that they could hardly disavow."[2] Yet, while using the political language of his age, he infuses it with his own meaning that places his thought often at variance with the meanings given these terms by his contemporaries. He uses such terms as "utility," "expediency," and "natural rights" in a manner that neither eighteenth-century natural right theorists nor utilitarians and empiricists would employ. This lends to the apparent ambiguity of some of Burke's language. Fourth, the complexities surrounding the foundations of his philosophy are heightened by the varying interpretations of his thought in the secondary literature. Those most prominent in denying a metaphysical base to Burke's politics most commonly mark him a utilitarian. We will consider representative utilitarian assessments of Burke's philosophy later in this chapter.

Since Burke does not write in a systematic manner, one must read him very carefully in order to uncover the fundamentals of his philosophy.[3] Even in his most profound political treatise, the *Reflections*, he purposely avoided, by his own account, a systematic mode. In a letter to Philip Francis he writes: "I had no Idea of digesting it in a Systematik order. The Style is open to correction, and wants it. My natural Style of writing is somewhat careless . . ." (C VI 89). Still a careful reading of Burke will disclose a consistent political philosophy[4] that, far from disparaging reason, and far from being anti-metaphysical, in fact reveals a firm metaphysical grounding that is orderly and contingent upon God's creative, conserving power.

It is necessary that any false expectations *à propos* of Burke's metaphysics be laid to rest before we proceed with our inquiry. There is no systematic treatment of metaphysical principles in Burke. Nonetheless, evidence for a metaphysical basis of his political philosophy not only exists throughout his works, but such metaphysics is a necessary condition for a correct comprehension of his political thought.

To seek a foundation for Burke's political philosophy in a metaphysical position is not to suggest that Burke philosophizes in a rationalistic, deductive fashion. Far from it. The philosophical underpinnings found in Burke are generally dogmatically stated, as if the force, clarity, and impact of the truth itself should be self-evident. There are, though, some few occasions when Burke engages in philosophical arguments in support of certain first principles of being. Certainly there are arguments for causality, sufficient reason, and God's existence, as well as a refutation of skepticism and relativism in the *Inquiry*. Nevertheless, as a politician by profession, Burke speaks of himself as the "philosopher in action" (TPD I 530). His actions are predicated on principles primarily bequeathed to him through the wisdom of generations past, principles that are checked against the testimony of circumstances. So, although Burke typically avoids speculative thought, he does not always do so, having written one speculative treatise. Still, he does present a position which, far from being anti-metaphysical, is consonant with a kind of metaphysics which is most compatible with the traditional, classical realism of the Aristotelian-Thomistic school.

Evidence for Burke's "Anti-Metaphysical" Position

Remarks abound by Burke which appear to disclose an unswerving animus toward metaphysics. A sampling of these remarks may help highlight the wrath of Burke toward abstract theorizing, especially when it occurs in the realm of politics.

Instances of this distrust of metaphysical speculations occur early in Burke's thought. We have only to turn to the *Notebook* containing various entries by both Burke and his kinsman William Burke in the 1750s:

> They [men] naturally measure their Duties to the Divinity by their own wants and their feelings, and not by abstract Speculations.
>
> In the one they cannot be deceived, in the other they may. . . .
>
> Metaphysical or Physical Speculations neither are, or ought to be, the Grounds of our Duties; because we can arrive at no certainty in them. They have a weight when they concur with our own natural feelings; very little when against them [NB 71].

This suspicion of abstract reasoning is reflected elsewhere in the *Notebook*: "Great subtleties and refinements of reasoning are like spirits which disorder the brain and are much less useful than ordinary liquors of a grosser nature. . . ." Burke's skeptical remarks continue:

> Most of our Enquiries, when carried beyond the very Superficies of things, lead us into the greatest Difficulties and we find qualities repugnant to each other whenever we attempt to dive into the Manner of Existence. . . . Perhaps the bottom of most things is unintelligible; and our surest reasoning, when we come to a certain point, is involved not only in obscurity but contradiction [NB 90, 92–93].

This concern for the remoteness of abstract thought from the concreteness of existence is carried over into Burke's more mature thought. In his *Appeal from the New to the Old Whigs* (1791), Burke denounces the application of universals to the province of politics and morals, universals being the very stuff of speculative thought, whereas the realm of politics and morals reflects a world of contingency. Burke bluntly states that "pure metaphysical abstraction does not belong to these matters" (ANW IV 80–81). Unlike mathematics, itself a most fertile field for abstract thought, morality lacks exactitude. Instead, morality admits of exceptions and modifications, and these exceptions are introduced through prudence, not logic. Furthermore, "Metaphysics cannot live without definition; but Prudence is cautious how she defines" (ANW IV 81).

The incongruency between metaphysical speculation and politics and morals is echoed again by Burke in his *Report on the Lords' Journals* (1794): "But as human affairs and human actions are not a metaphysical nature, but the subject is concrete, complex, and moral, they cannot be subjected (without exceptions which reduce it almost to nothing) to any certain rule."[5] Burke's apparent opposition of rules to human affairs appears to be amended, or even rescinded, in the *Reflections* when he argues that "It is far from impossible to reconcile, if we do not suffer ourselves to be entangled in the mazes of metaphysic sophistry, the use of a fixed rule and an occasional deviation,— the sacredness of an hereditary principle of succession in our government with a power of change in its application in cases of extreme emergency" (RF III 258). Apart from the status in Burke's mind of general moral rules, metaphysics is used in a disparaging fashion, implying a type of metaphysics rendered inflexible before the complexity of human affairs.

Elsewhere Burke appears to assail metaphysics as being nothing short of a pollutant of virtue itself. In his *Letter to a Member of the National Assembly* (1791), he rebukes the French for the demoralization of their own young. He bemoans the loss of gallantry and refinement, where love is grafted to the virtues, and instead finds lewdness, bitterness, and all manner of corrupted dispositions, in part a result "of metaphysical speculation blended with the coarsest sensuality" (LNA IV 31). Again, abstract metaphysical speculation seems to lead man far from his concrete nature as historically revealed and as blended with his situation. This flight from the concrete which Burke finds in the metaphysical speculator is echoed in the same *Letter* when he admonishes statesmen to attend the circumstances, and search out the fortunate moment "not in the conjunctions and opposition of men and things" (LNA IV 44).

A general metaphysical impulse is at the bottom of all theorizing which ignores the concrete reality of politics while attempting to dictate, by blueprint, the behavior of government and peoples. This theme becomes most pointed in Burke's *Speech on Conciliation with America* (1775). Here he attacks "refined policy," that is, detached, removed analysis of what government should be doing without actual attention to the circumstances involved. In this instance, it fit the Parliament's conception of the colonies completely that they were under the suzerainty of the British Empire. And, as subjects, they were bound to contribute to the fiscal needs of the empire; Parliament, as the rightful representative of said empire, was well within its prerogative to tax the colonies. Burke acknowledged this prerogative, the "right to tax," but he renounced the prudential application of this right when the result could be the revolt of the colonists. Burke concludes that "refined policy" is ever "the parent of confusion" (SCA II 106). Here he urges his fellow members of Parliament to rule according to the circumstances, not by abstract ideas of right, or by general theories of government (SCA II 109).

As for himself, Burke prefers politics to be shaped consonant with tradition, not speculation. In this spirit he determines to distrust his own abilities and to denounce every speculation (SCA II 145). By doing so, he is simply affirming the wisdom of generations over that of the single individual, however endowed with genius any individual may be. Tradition reveals the historical interests of man, and man, Burke notes, acts on interest, "and not on metaphysical speculations" (SCA II 170).

In his *Speech on the Petition of the Unitarians* (1792), Burke declares that "no rational man ever did govern himself by abstractions and universals" (W VII 41). The same can be said of governments. This conclusion is upheld in The *Letter to the Sheriffs of Bristol* (1777): "Nothing universal *can be rationally affirmed* on any moral or political subject" (LSB II 227).

The metaphysical realm of universals flies in the face of the factual sphere. The actions of both men and governments are practical matters; they affect the lives of individuals. Burke claims that "the doctrine of free government [is not] an abstract question concerning metaphysical liberty and necessity" (LSB II 228). In fact, "The extreme of liberty (which is its abstract perfection, but its real fault) obtains nowhere, nor ought to obtain anywhere; because extremes, as we all know, in every point which relates to either our duties or satisfactions in life, are destructive both to virtue and enjoyment" (LSB II 229). Burke appears to focus on the act of theorizing as a flight from reality, a symptom of an unhappy populace. While people are happy, they are unconcerned with theory (LSB II 230).

The scathing criticism Burke invokes against theorists and metaphysicians continues in his *Reflections on the Revolution in France* (1790). He is particularly scornful of those who, in a dream-like fashion, from their unleashed imaginations, speculate upon a science of government in *a priori* fashion. Instead, the science of government is not a deductive science but an experimental science (RF III 311). By experimental science Burke continues to call us back to the circumstances that color and distinguish every system of government, rendering them all unique. Those who disregard the circumstances surrounding politics, and devise a list of rights for individuals which governments are bound to honor, have ignored Burke's admonition. As Burke explains in the *Reflections*, "These metaphysic rights entering into common life, like rays of light which pierce into a dense medium, are by the laws of Nature, refracted from their straight line. Indeed, in the gross and complicated mass of human passions and concerns, the primitive rights of men undergo such a variety of refractions and reflections that it becomes absurd to talk of them as if they continued in the simplicity of their original direction" (RF III 312). The "rights" extolled by theorists, Burke maintains, insofar "as they are metaphysically true, . . . are morally and politically false" (RF III 313). We are not urged to ignore reason, but to attend to a special kind of reason called "political reason." Burke denies that this is a metaphysical sort of reasoning; rather, "political reason is a computing principle: adding, subtracting, multiplying, and dividing, morally, and not metaphysically or mathematically, true moral denominations" (RF III 313).

Metaphysical distinctions appear to evoke a brooding, loathing reaction from Burke, a sentiment which is also reflected in his *Speech on American Taxation* (1774). Burke writes that "I am not here going into the distinctions of rights, nor attempting to mark their boundaries; I do not enter into these metaphysical distinctions; I hate the very sound of them" (W II 72–73).

By now the very term "metaphysics" appears to have an opprobrious ring for Burke. The thesis that Burke's political philosophy has its basis in a metaphysical position seems severely tested by the weight of evidence presented thus far.

Evidence for Burke's Metaphysical Position

What Burke vilifies is not so much theory or metaphysics per se as its application to the highly contingent realm of morals and politics, especially when this entails ignoring the circumstances of a nation.[6] A view of false theory begins to emerge when it is contrasted with a view of what should be required of theory. Burke warns that there is no theory apart from circumstances, "without a concurrence and adaptation of these to the design, the very best speculative projects might become not only useless, but mischievous. Plans must be made for men" (LNA IV 43). Burke further notes that considering theories divorced from circumstance has led to much havoc, and that without tending to circumstance, "the medicine of today becomes the poison of tomorrow" (LNA IV 46). So it is not theory as such which is misguided, but an incomplete theory, untouched by the concrete, practical, less refined air of the mundane world.

Earlier, Burke's *Speech on the Petition of the Unitarians* (1792) was cited to the effect that rational man acts without regard to abstractions and universals. Burke goes on to say: "I do not put abstract ideas wholly out of any question; because I well know that under that name I should dismiss principles, and that without the guide and light of sound, well-understood principles, all reasonings in politics, as in everything else, would be only a confused jumble of particular facts and details, without the means of drawing out any sort of theoretical or practical conclusion" (W VII 41). By implication, Burke here suggests a distinction between abstractions and universals, and principles. Obviously, the universal realm lacks all contact with the realm of practice, whereas Burke's use of the word "principle" suggests a fusing of the two, and the fusion, for Burke, takes place in prudence. In Aristotelian language, the realm of universals concerns sheer speculative wisdom, whereas the notion of principles concerns practical wisdom. The distinction is better brought forward by Burke when he speaks about political problems in the *Appeal from the New Whigs to the Old* (1791). The resolution of political problems does not concern truth or falsehood, but good or evil.[7] Burke remarks that "what in the result is likely to produce evil is politically false; that which is productive of good, politically true" (ANW IV 169).

Burke's position on theory now invites qualification. It is not so much theory or metaphysics per se as their false application, regardless of the infinite array of particulars brought to bear in the realm of morals and politics by the concrete world. In this world, that which is true politically is that which is good. The good is not pronounced *ex cathedra*, as it were, and embraced without a view towards the extant political, social, economic, and historical circumstances. These and other details the statesman must consider as he shapes the laws and policies of a nation. As Burke states in his *Speech on the Petition of the Unitarians* (1792):

Circumstances are infinite, are infinitely combined, are variable and transient: he who does not take them into consideration is not erroneous, but stark mad; *dat operam ut cum ratione insaniat*; he is metaphysically mad. A statesman, never losing sight of principles, is to be guided by circumstances; and judging contrary to the exigencies of the moment, he may ruin his country forever [W VII 41].

Burke recoils from a blueprint for society that fails to account for the peculiarities, the differences in customs and traditions in which each nation is steeped. Utopian designs are best left in the thin air of speculation. They are, quite literally, "nowhere." No ideally conceived plan of government or society could in any way account for the infinite diversity which obtains in concrete reality.

Burke the politician is suspicious of theory that fails to account for the circumstances in which a people find themselves.[8] Yet he does not relegate theory to some remote area where it can harmlessly spin its solitary thought as an Aristotelian "absconded God." Burke clarifies his position on theory: "I do not vilify theory and speculation: no, because that would be to vilify reason itself. . . . No,—whenever I speak against theory, I mean always a weak, erroneous, fallacious, unfounded, or imperfect theory; and one of the ways of discovering that it is a false theory is by comparing it with practice" (SC VII 97).

Burke serves warning that speculative theory, when it comes into the practical, contingent sphere of morals and politics, is inadequate to guide man.[9] It must be tempered by political reason, a prudential guide to man's practical endeavors. The metaphysicians—Burke generally has in mind the French philosophers of the Enlightenment—can scheme and theorize to their hearts' content, but it is the circumstances that, as Burke claims, "render every civil and political scheme beneficial or noxious to mankind" (RF III 240).

It does not appear that Burke is any more extreme in his limitation of the scope of reason than Aristotle or Aquinas. They qualify the use of speculative reason and urge its guarded application in the field of politics. They recognize a practical reason, separate in its application or function, not in the very unity of reason itself. According to Aquinas, "The speculative intellect by extension becomes practical. But one power is not changed into another. Therefore the speculative and practical intellect are not distinct powers."[10] Aquinas refers to Aristotle, who differentiates the speculative and the practical intellects according to their ends. Aquinas summarizes the distinction thusly:

> Now, to a thing apprehended by the intellect, it is accidental whether it be directed to operation or not, and it is according to this the speculative and practical intellect differ. For it is the speculative intellect which directs what it apprehends, not to operation, but to consideration of truth, while the practical intellect is that which directs what it apprehends to operation.[11]

At the outset it may be helpful to note that Burke disparages logical, abstract, discursive, private reason as applied to politics regardless of circumstances. He is opposed to both the empirical inductive method, and the rationalist deductive method, or a combination of the two methods. (It was, of course, the combination of the two methods which gained prominence in Locke's *Essay Concerning Human Understanding* and characterized the method and meaning of reason as used by Enlightenment philosophers.[12]) Burke's own use of reason more nearly accords with what is typically referred to as practical, normative, or right reason. Burke himself, as cited previously, uses the term "political reason" in referring to the practical application of reason (RF III 313). In effect, "political reason" is a prudential use of reason, reflecting on the moral law, as applied to the particular and contingent circumstances of social and political reality.[13]

Nonetheless, while skeptical of abstract, speculative reason, and scornful of its application to politics, Burke acknowledges the worth of speculation in its proper realm, yet demands that "political reason," guided by principles, be applied instead of speculative reason in the realm of politics.

It cannot be denied that even though Burke acknowledges the capacity of speculative reason to make use of certain principles, such as the principle of causality, in the affirmation of speculative conclusions such as the existence of God, he nevertheless believes that the reliance upon the speculative use of reason is difficult.[14] He concludes that "It is by a long deduction and much study, that we discover the adorable wisdom of God in his works . . ." (ISB I 185). Consequently, the progress of speculative reason requires the strictest attention to the principles governing its movement, and those who rely exclusively on speculative reason as applied to politics will necessarily perish in the contingencies of particular circumstances.

The conclusion of Francis Canavan that in Burke's "concern for the practical, he tended at times to assimilate all reason to practical reason"[15] serves to underscore the fact that as the philosopher in action Burke was most concerned with reason in its practical or political use. He did not aim to achieve a speculative, theoretical foundation for politics independent of the prudential, practical use of reason in trying to comprehend the appropriate means to attain what limited political good was possible in an imperfect world. Thus, in this work, when reference is made to Burke's use of reason it will be assumed that practical reason, or better, "political reason," is meant, unless otherwise stated or implied by the context in which the term occurs.

Burke, therefore, does not attempt to deny that characteristic or quality that distinguishes man in his very essence, namely, his rationality. Burke's fear is an errant reasoning, a reasoning that attempts, for example, mathematical exactitude in the area of morality. It is, in short, to ask the unreasonable. But, again, this is not to foreclose a principled assessment of moral or political behavior. Rather, the principles fail to spell out in a precise way and for every occasion what is right and what is wrong. For this, man has to develop and practice his practical reason. Is all this so far removed from Aristotle or Aquinas?

Burke does not indulge flights of utopianism. He does not have to learn his lesson as did Plato, a lesson the former incorporates in the *Tract on the Popery Laws* (1765). As the *Republic* extols a state in which the virtues of man attain perfection, and as the *Laws* take into account man's fallible nature, so Burke refuses the fetching cry of utopia, the perfectibility of man. In a personal letter to his son, Richard Burke, Jr., in 1791, he writes: "we must not struggle with the order of Providence; nor contrive our matters so ill, that, as Cicero says, whilst we are struggling to be in the Republick of Plato, we may find ourselves in no republick at all" (C VI 358).[16]

Man possesses both an incomplete perception of the good—a limitation of his intellect—and an inadequate desire to pursue the good—an imperfection of the will. No reorganization of government, no radicalization of society can succeed in overcoming this internal battle, which occurs in the very hearts of individuals. At best, in this fallible world, one can hope to minimize the evil, and increase the good somewhat.

So, for Burke, metaphysics practiced in a deductive, *a priori* manner expresses utopian thought and a neglect of man's concrete nature. Utopianism assumes the impossible—the perfectibility of man.[17] And in doing so, it attempts the absurd: an overthrow of existing society with all its positive blessings and admitted failings, in hopes of a heaven on earth. This repudiates all that history reveals about this passionate creature who is man.

Burke, as our thesis maintains, does not decry the legitimate function of metaphysics. His own philosophy, it will be shown, is spawned from Aristotelian-Thomistic metaphysical roots.[18] This is clear from our reconsideration of even a superficial reading of Burke. Nonetheless, a sizeable secondary literature places Burke within an anti-metaphysical, utilitarian framework of philosophy, steeped in English empiricism. This requires our attention and response.

THE UTILITARIAN INTERPRETATION OF BURKE'S POLITICAL PHILOSOPHY: A LOOK AT SELECTED SECONDARY LITERATURE

As noted earlier, Burke gives us neither a convenient summary nor a systematic presentation of the fundamental tenets of his thought. His works are strewn throughout with words that have a unique meaning and usage sometimes peculiar to Burke alone. For example, he speaks of "prejudice" and "habit" as social virtues leading to the cohesiveness of society, where today "prejudice" is a form of opprobrium and "habit" may be thought to stymie social progress. These are some of the difficulties impeding a correct understanding of Burke's political philosophy. And these difficulties primarily emerge from the incorrect assigning of premises to Burke's thought which easily lead the interpreter far afield. This is the case with those who mistakenly lump Burke with the utilitarian school of writers such as Hume, Bentham, and Mill. This is not to say this lumping process has not taken place without some discrimination. Yet notable errors remain. A review of certain select utilitarian interpretations of Burke's thought should help highlight misunderstandings and misgivings about a metaphysical basis for Burke's political philosophy.

John Morley set the early standard for Burkean interpretation. In his first work on Edmund Burke, Morley confused Burke's attack on natural rights with an assumed advocacy of what Morley terms the "utilitarian truth, that the statesman is concerned, not at all with the rights of government, but altogether with the interests and happiness of the governed. . . ."[19] Morley concludes that for Burke the guiding principle of public policy is "expediency." "The baneful superstition that there is in morals, some supernaturally illumined lamp, still survives to make men neglect the intelligible and available tests of public convenience and practical justice, which is no more than expediency in its widest shape."[20]

In a second work on Burke, Morley credits Burke's study of literature for providing him with a political method of great "flexibility." Literature emancipated him "from the mechanical formulae of practical politics . . . partly in drawing him, even when resting his case on prudence and expedience, to appeal to the widest and highest sympathies; partly, and more than all, in opening his thoughts to the many conditions, possibilities, and varieties of untried being in human character and situation, and so giving an incomparable flexibility to his methods of political approach."[21]

Morley qualifies Burke's thought as "utilitarian liberalism" in the context of "historic conservatism."[22] This interpretation, though, does not wholly categorize Burke's political theory, forcing Morley to concede that "In spite of the predominance of practical sagacity . . . at the bottom of all his thoughts . . . there lay a certain mysticism."[23]

In *The History of Civilization in England*, Henry Buckle acknowledges Burke to be among the greatest intellects England ever produced, and certainly her most eminent political philosopher. In any number of subjects of study Burke demonstrated not only learning, but the ability to show "their connexion with general principles, and the part they have to play in the great scheme of human affairs."[24] But when Burke's attention turns to politics, political principles are "far from being speculative," and instead are "altogether practical."[25] Further, Burke saw clearly that the purpose of politics "was purely empirical" and that "the aim of the legislator should be, not truth, but expediency."[26] Thus, the object of government is "not the preservation of particular institutions . . . but the happiness of the people at large. . . ."[27] Politics as purely practical and empirical; expediency as the norm of legislative action; happiness as the end of government of the people—Buckle unhesitantly, although without naming it as such, puts Burke in the utilitarian camp. The result for politics is that the people and their will are the measure and norm of all political action. There is no hint in Buckle of any transcendent standard existing for Burke outside the contingent and variable will of the people by which to judge political acts. His view is that of a radical democrat without any higher court of appeal who believes that he has found in Burke a champion for his political views. It is only when the French Revolution emerges and Burke opposes the will of the people that Buckle despairs of Burke. Such is his despair with Burke that he in no manner is forced to rethink his interpretation of the latter, to see if a broader more comprehensive view of politics incorporates his apparent use of utilitarian discourse. Instead, he concludes that concerning the French Revolution and Burke's response to it, certainly Burke "fell into a complete hallucination."[28]

Charles E. Vaughan in his short study of Burke struggles courageously to grasp the underpinnings of the political philosophy of the Irish-born English orator and statesman. In the end those underpinnings, those props for action, escape Vaughan but the result, while flawed, is illuminating and worthwhile for the reader to follow through.

According to Vaughan, the test of politics for Burke is expedience, not speculation, not notions of "Right." Expediency is not to be taken in the narrow sense of self-interest but in the wider sense of the "good of the whole community."[29] In order to determine what that good is, Burke relies upon the historical method and upon "the experience of the past and the lessons which it offers to the guidance of the present."[30] Therefore, any claim to rights must be subordinated to expediency, and that which is expedient is determined by what has been proven over time to be beneficial to society. It is inescapable, Vaughan declares; Burke is a conservative, although, in the end, not one who is averse to progress. Vaughan holds that both Burke's temperament, which was conservative, and his principles, which entailed primarily expediency and experience, blended well together.[31]

But Vaughan proceeds to wrestle with the meaning of expediency for Burke, its relationship to other components of his thought, and, under the press of unfolding world events, not least of which was the French Revolution, the evolution of the principle itself. Further reflection reveals a shift in meaning in this principle which Vaughan seeks to clarify. Its earliest meaning for Burke places expediency in direct opposition to any claim of rights. Expediency includes the idea of "reason, justice and humanity," so Vaughan quotes Burke. As expediency entails an appeal to the past and seeks "not the interest of the moment," but "the permanent welfare of the whole nation"; and as the notion of "right" is an abstraction, from some timeless sense of the idealized past, rooted in the radical individualism of the social contract theory, it is clear the two must be in opposition.[32] In his attack on right Burke was aligned with Hume and Bentham.[33] Vaughan is quick to add that Burke's reliance upon expedience and experience was not to be construed as a blind reliance; rather Burke interpreted it "in the light of humanity and discretion," or "humanity and justice."[34] But even in so doing, Vaughan regards this as a reliance upon principles actually foreign to expediency. Vaughan seems almost equivocal on this point. The early Burke holds to a principle of expediency that is so broad in scope as to provide little guidance, to be practically a "mere blank," to simply sanction the wisdom and institutions of the past.[35] Yet, then we find the principle is not completely unrelated, but is to be interpreted by the dictates of reason, humanity, discretion, and justice. How does Vaughan mean to have it here? Has not Burke, even in the narrow way in which Vaughan has read him, at least signaled to Vaughan something more than pure expediency, something more than pure utility? Vaughan's assessment vacillates on this point and leaves standing an obvious contradiction in his interpretation of Burke—a contradiction, that is, in Vaughan's interpretation.

But then Vaughan moves us to the emergence of a revised principle of expediency, one that comes to be supported by duty, with duty buttressed by the moral law and by religion. The link between the two versions of the principle remains the Irishman's "strongly conservative bias."[36] Now the principle of expediency "comes charged with the strongest sanctions of duty and religion."[37] Further, the past and tradition become vested with the cloak of mystery and reverence, and breaking with them becomes not only inexpedient but even immoral.

For Vaughan, this buttressing of expediency with the sanctions of duty, the moral law and religion is both a tacit admission of the inadequacy of the naked principle of expediency by Burke, and, with revision of the principle, a clear break from "Hume and the utilitarians."[38] Under the revised principle the "whole object of Society . . . is to secure the welfare of its members; the whole function of Government, as the directing organ of Society, to provide for the advantage of the governed." Elaborating on this point, Vaughan concludes that "The most essential element in man's welfare is not his material comfort, but his moral good; not the assertion of his supposed rights, but the enforcement of his plain duties."[39] Thus, if rights are limited by expediency, then expediency is limited by a more profound principle, that being the end of society as the moral perfection of man.[40]

At this point one can only be amazed that Vaughan did not make the connection among the moral end of society, the qualifying of expediency by the moral law and duty, and Aristotle's and Aquinas' political philosophy. Why did Vaughan not follow up on the clue given by the moral law; why did he not see that in the use of notions such as rights, social contract, and state of nature, Burke appropriated them and yet gave them his own distinct meanings, apart from the French *philosophes*, apart from Hobbes, Locke and Rousseau? Instead of acknowledging or realizing his own failure in interpretation, Vaughan could only pass the blame on to Burke himself, claiming "that Burke was guilty of inconsistency." Astonishingly enough, Vaughan all but stumbles onto the truth when he notes, almost in perplexed exasperation, that there were those times when Burke, by the sheer force of his own native strength, reverts back "to the surer ground marked out by Aristotle and by Cicero." Here, "Burke asserted that the real parentage of society was to be sought not in contract, but in instinct; that man was essentially a social creature; that the real state of nature for man was not isolation but communion."[41] Vaughan struggles mightily, but flounders on what he perceives to be irreconcilable principles in Burke's political thought, principles which find their uncertain unity in the Irishman's conservative and religious instincts.

Sir Leslie Stephen's account of Burke's political thought is much inferior to Vaughan's, although the results are fairly similar. Like Vaughan, Stephen holds Burke in high regard, maintaining that "no English writer has received, or has deserved, more splendid panegyrics than Burke." As a "master of English prose," Burke is unsurpassed, Stephen finds. Commenting on Burke's gift of oratory, Stephens claims that the Irishman's "magnificent speeches stand alone in the language."[42]

Turning to Burke's political thought, he is seen to rely upon experience and expediency. Stephen compares Burke to the "cruder empiricists," claiming that he "admires the 'rule of thumb' as the ultimate rule, and consecrates mere prejudice under the name of prescription."[43] So it is that prejudice and presumption undergird recourse to experience and expediency in political matters. Even so, Burke failed to reconcile "expediency with morality," depending, instead, upon the wisdom of generations to express itself historically in the affairs of the nation. Against the incipient radical individualism surfacing across the English channel, Burke countered with the organic conception of society, and its continuity with the past.[44] Burke himself stands with "All English theorists" who believe "that political truth must be based upon experience."[45] Still, while finding common ground, Stephen does not confuse Burke with the English utilitarians. Whereas Burke prized social institutions as venerable and deserving of respect for having stood the test of time, the utilitarians, claims Stephen, demanded that all institutions can justify their existence only in terms of practical results. Further, they sought to advance a utilitarian calculus, deductive in method, by which to hold the utilitarian standard against the institutions of society.

John MacCunn offers a more balanced appraisal of Burke's political philosophy than most of the nineteenth-century commentators on Burke. While asserting that Burke's interests are mainly practical,[46] he denies that his method is "purely empirical."[47] In fact, Burke's thought is based on convictions that he assumes, unproved, some of which are "psychological, and some are metaphysical."[48] Of the metaphysical ones, MacCunn includes "That God willed the state, that He willed likewise the nation of man, and that the whole course of a nation's life is 'the known march of the ordinary providence of God.' "[49] MacCunn refers to these as "theological principles," taken on faith.[50]

Burke's convictions about the nature of man and his relation to God conditions his politics, which are, of course, conservative. MacCunn finds that, like Bentham, Burke opposes the theorists of rights, but that, unlike him, Burke does not deny rights completely. What he does deny is their abstract character when they are thrust into the contingent realm of politics oblivious to circumstances.[51] With Bentham Burke opposes the dogmatism of the theorists of rights, particularly when applied in disregard of human nature. For Burke, "Utility comes in: it comes inasmuch as the happiness of the people is recognized as the supreme end."[52]

Here, MacCunn establishes the framework for comprehending rights in Burke's politics. The framework is practical: rights exist, but they exist in the practical realm of political affairs only as they contribute to the public good. So, rights are not ultimate, not original; rather they are derivative. They are justified "because they can be shown to be conducive to the happiness of a people as this is construed in the light of the facts and laws of human nature and social existence."[53]

MacCunn concludes that, like the utilitarians, Burke fixes on the public good, claiming that the happiness of the people is foremost in politics. Consequently, rights must be proved useful, and they must be supported by the "concrete realities and expediencies of practical politics."[54] One must not forget that "there are duties and utilities towards the public good, by which the exercise of all rights . . . must always be qualified and controlled."[55]

Like certain other commentators on Burke, MacCunn does not neglect altogether the influence of the metaphysical, which he reads as "theological principles," in Burke's political thought. Nor does he align Burke with the calculating utilitarianism of Bentham, or deny a place to rights in Burke's thought. Nonetheless, happiness and the public good appear to provide the framework within which all the rest is drawn together.

Alfred Cobban is moved by Burke's rejection of natural rights, which are replaced by civil rights governed by the "realm of expediency," to conclude that "Burke is, in the broad sense and with far more consistency than Locke, a utilitarian."[56] Comparing Locke and Burke, Cobban finds that the former framed his political theory within "the system of natural rights," which framework is "practically discarded by Burke, who lets a conscious and noble utilitarianism provide its own justification."[57] The end of government, therefore, is not the realization of some abstract system of rights, but the concrete happiness of "actual individuals." "The lesson of expediency," concludes Cobban of Burke, "is to be learnt from him in full measure."[58] Burke's utilitarianism leads him necessarily to disparage "the poor 'Bill of Rights people,' " basing everything as they do on "abstract rights." Burke, on the other hand, holds as the standard of government "the happiness of the people."[59]

What for Cobban characterizes Burke's utilitarianism beyond the "happiness principle"? "His utilitarianism . . . turns out to be in the main an acceptance of that which has been proved useful, or at any rate workable, that is, of things as they are. Reason and utility both abdicate before the achievements of the past. . . . [R]eason is displaced by utility, and for utility Burke reads history."[60] Thus said, Cobban breaks no new ground on Burke.

In his *A History of Political Theory*, George Sabine combines his consideration of Burke with that of David Hume. This is not unusual for historians of political thought. Two reasons help to explain why this is the case. First, Burke, as presented by Sabine, "accepted Hume's negations of reason and the law of nature."[61] Of course, all are familiar with Hume's scrutiny of reason; reason reveals no certainty concerning matters of fact. At best, it is useful in comparisons of ideas, yet inadequate for the confirmation of any necessary truths about reality, or of eternal verities concerning the law of nature or of morality. So fruitless, for Hume, is reason in the comportment of man that it is to be subservient to the dictates of the passions.[62] In truth, this is the positivist element in Hume, and Sabine sees this same mode of thought as prevalent in Burke. For Burke, Sabine holds, society is not structured on reason, but it is a product of convention. It is artificial and contrived, not natural. Further, Burke's politics form the natural sequel to Hume's in that Burke showed "the reaction that was to follow upon Hume's destruction of the eternal verities of reason and natural law. Sentiment, tradition and idealized history stepped in to fill the vacancy left by the removal of self-evident rights. . . ."[63] This interpretation of Burke indicates that Hume's skepticism of the ability of human reason to know eternal truths is acceptable to Burke. With the removal of rational insight into such truths, man is forced to consult sentiment and tradition in order to acquire direction for life. Truths come to be revealed not through abstract reason, but through man's natural instincts and passions. Of course as Aquinas demonstrates, truths may be obtained through inclination or instinct and be compatible with reason. We have, for instance, a natural or pre-philosophical knowledge of certain speculative and moral first principles.[64] This is a knowledge by "inclination" according to Aquinas, not through discursive reason: "there is present in man an inclination toward knowing the truth about God, and toward living in society."[65] In fact, the latter presupposes the former. Aquinas is an example, therefore, of a thinker who affirms both a knowledge by instinct or inclination and the ability to obtain truth through speculation.[66]

For Sabine, though, to affirm the role of convention, tradition or instinct in the structure of human society appears to exclude the role of human reason. Sabine maintains that not only does Burke accept "Hume's negations of reason and the law of nature," but that in the place of reason Burke considers society to rest upon "obscure instincts and propensities—even on prejudices," and furthermore, "that its standards are conventions."[67]

Burke's apparent rejection of reason, as depicted by Sabine—an interpretation this study hopes to refute—of itself does not render Burke a utilitarian. Nor do other apparent convergencies between the thought of Burke and that of Hume result in such a categorization of Burke's thought. This is in part because Hume's own relationship to utilitarianism is somewhat ambiguous. This ambiguity may be resolved, along with Burke's relationship to utilitarianism, through a clarification of the meaning of utilitarianism.

As there is much diversity within the utilitarian tradition, it is not as easily characterized as one might think. All are familiar with Bentham's famous definition of "the principle of utility" by which "is meant that principle which approves or disapproves of every action whatsoever according to the tendency which it appears to have to augment or diminish the happiness of the party whose interest is in question"; and with John Stuart Mill's definition of the "Greatest Happiness Principle" which "holds that actions are right in proportion as they tend to promote happiness, wrong as they tend to produce the reverse of happiness. By happiness is intended pleasure, and the absence of pain."[68] Antedating both Bentham and Mill "as the proper founder of utilitarianism is David Hume."[69] Hume provides the later utilitarians with the word "utility" and, more importantly, with the pleasure and pain principles.[70] Concerning these principles Hume writes "that virtue is distinguished by the pleasure, and vice by the pain, that any action, sentiment, or character, gives us by the mere view and contemplation."[71]

With an emphasis upon pleasure as virtuous and pain as vice it is easy to mistake utilitarianism for egoistic hedonism. To desire only one's individual pleasure without deference to the greatest happiness principle is to end with an incomplete utilitarianism. The greatest happiness principle requires that the pleasure sought be the happiness of the greatest number possible.

Anthony Quinton remarks that "utilitarians have generally taken it for granted . . . that happiness is a sum of pleasures." Implementing the greatest happiness principle Quinton constructs the following definition, claiming that "the rightness of an action is determined by its contribution to the happiness of everyone affected by it."[72] It is the aim of the state to ensure that the greatest happiness principle is achieved and that selfish interests are reconciled. Consequently, the purpose of the state for the utilitarians is not to protect any putative natural rights, "but to give men more abundantly the happiness they always seek."[73]

Interestingly, Burke also rejects the claims of the "rights of man" protagonists, but for different reasons. It is not the purpose of the state to reconcile conflicting selfish interests between men in order to better pave the way toward happiness that Burke considers basic. Rather, it is the state which should assist man where possible in the perfecting of his nature throughout the development of his reason and the development of the virtues; in short, the state helps to civilize man.[74]

In considering the province of reason in utilitarian thought, the results vary. For Hume, reason is to be subordinate to the passions, for "it is impossible that the distinction betwixt moral good and evil can be made by reason."[75] Hume is indicating that our passions determine the proper ends we are to choose, not our reason, although reason can aid the passions in the means of obtaining pleasure. Reason, for Bentham, provides a calculating function which can be used to determine where man's happiness lies. It functions to aid man in obtaining happiness; that is, reason serves a function of utility.

For the utilitarians, experience reveals to us what is pleasurable and what is painful. They underplay the role of reason in the sense of an *a priori* deductive determination of what is good or bad for man. This is not to discount the valuable assistance reason renders mankind in securing pleasure. Yet, as Plamenatz records, "It is experience that teaches us which actions usually have pleasant consequences and which have painful ones; and learning from experience involves the use of reason."[76]

From this consideration of utilitarianism it is apparent that, as J. R. Dinwiddy writes, "Utility . . . means conduciveness to happiness or pleasure."[77] Consequently, when we take note of such terms as "utility," "prejudice," "expedience," and "convenience," all used frequently by Burke, we might hastily conclude that Burke is a utilitarian of some type. Nonetheless, as Wilkins notes, such terms are often contrasted "by concepts such as *justice, equity, law of nature, and natural right*."[78]

Before making a determination on the matter of Burke's supposed utilitarianism, and the lack of a metaphysical basis for his politics, I will consider further select utilitarian interpretations of his thought.

Other alleged bases for Burke's utilitarianism are found by John Plamenatz and Elie Halévy. In *The English Utilitarians*, Plamenatz cites Halévy for providing the criteria for Burke's utilitarian philosophy.[79] Those criteria stem from the latter's theories of prescription and prejudice. These theories all note that the fact that social institutions, constitutions, customs, and traditions "hav[e] lasted a long time is itself proof of [their] utility, of [their] conduciveness to human happiness."[80] Their duration proves their utility in outlasting decay and disintegration. There is a presumption favoring what has served well in meeting the needs of man throughout the years. That presumption supposes that the durable in terms of institutions, customs, and traditions has a utility for men in society, and is therefore beneficial for man.

Plamenatz draws back from putting Burke squarely within the utilitarian tradition. In fact, he seems undecided as to how to locate Burke on the utilitarian continuum, indicating in one place that Burke comes close to being a genuine utilitarian; in another he speaks of Burke's utilitarian bias; and, in yet another, he writes that "Burke was not primarily a utilitarian; but in so far as he was one, he was closer to Hume than to any other representative of the school."[81]

Halévy considers Burke a "conservative utilitarian." He writes of Burke as "making use of the principle of utility," as "adopting the point of view of utility," as deducing "an antidemocratic political theory . . . from a Utilitarian philosophy," and as being a forerunner to theological empiricism.[82] Rather than asking the question of right, notes Halévy, Burke asks the one of "political expediency." For Halévy, it is Burke's utilitarian stance that underscores his refutation of the "rights of man" theorists.[83] Men receive their rights not from any abstract theory of rights or hypothesized state of nature, but from such theories as that of *prejudice*. For Burke, "it is prejudice, preconceived opinion and ready-made ideas which give unity and continuity to the life of the honest man, and make of virtue a habit."[84]

The theory of prescription for Halévy and Plamenatz provides the other pillar supporting Burke's utilitarianism. Prescription sanctifies an ancient right because it has endured for many ages. When such a right is contested by claims for rights based on rational principles, then "the presumption is in favor of the ancient right which claims its origin from prescription, that is to say from experience."[85] Halévy summarizes Burke's political philosophy with the following statement: "Burke's political philosophy is an empiricism, a philosophy of experience: the duration whether of an idea or of an institution, its mere persistence through time, is a presumption in favor of the idea or of that institution."[86] So in Burke Halévy finds a thinker of utilitarian stripe, who offers an empirically grounded philosophy, emphasizing the theories of prescription and prejudice.

Harold Laski is yet another writer who positions Burke's thought in the utilitarian tradition of Hume. Writes Laski, "The metaphysics of Burke, so far as one may use a term he would himself have repudiated, are largely those of Hume."[87] Laski writes of the emphasis Burke places on habit, social instinct, the inadequacy of reason, resistance as a measure of last resort, the disavowal of the social contract notion, and respect for order as being staples of his political thought.[88] Further, "Burke was a utilitarian who was convinced that what was old was valuable by the mere fact of its arrival at maturity."[89] The various elements of Burke's philosophy such as prescription and prejudice are bound together by this underlying sentiment, conjoined with a deep religious presentiment on Burke's part, religion itself having utility. For Laski, that Burke sees religion as foundational to the state amounts to the grounding of social facts mystically, and to a depreciation of reason.[90]

A more recent author, Frank O'Gorman, speaks of Burke as a practical politician and propagandist, but not a philosopher.[91] O'Gorman cites Burke's "constant pragmatism and undogmatic realism which informs so much of his political philosophy."[92] So unprincipled is his pragmatism evidently that when Burke makes obvious use of the natural law as he does in his *Tracts on the Popery Laws* (1765), O'Gorman reduces this use of the natural law to a "polemical technique."[93] O'Gorman forthrightly underscores Burke's anti-metaphysical bias, going so far as to speak of "Burke's anti-rationalism."[94] For O'Gorman, Burke's "philosophy—even its most basic assumptions—amounted to little more than an unthinking acceptance and reiteration of some of the traditional themes of political and intellectual life...."[95]

C. B. Macpherson prefers to advance the problem of coherence in Burke's political thought beyond the natural law versus utilitarian interpretation. Both the liberal utilitarian and the natural law readings of Burke are incomplete. "Both fail to resolve, indeed largely fail to see, the seeming incoherence between Burke the traditionalist and Burke the bourgeois liberal."[96] Macpherson's Marxist orientation is apparent in his interpretation of Burke's notion of natural law in terms of an economic reductionism. For Macpherson, Burke's traditionalism served to affirm a society that had already moved decisively in the direction of a free market economy. Burke makes use of the "Christian Natural Law," Macpherson maintains, but he does so by changing its content. The form of the natural law is retained through Burke's use of it to uphold "a traditional social order against any threats."[97] Yet its content is altered in order to justify a new social order, bourgeois and free market in content, yet wedded to the old social framework. In short, Burke utilizes the natural law in order to validate a hierarchical status-bound society fused with a free market, capitalistic economy. Macpherson concludes that for Burke, "Utility and Natural Law were the same because capitalism and the traditional order were the same, because capitalism needed the sanction of tradition and habit."[98] In short, according to Macpherson, Burke achieves greater coherence when seen as a bourgeois political economist who makes the economy dependent not on contract, but on status. His use of the natural law is subordinated to the utilitarian purpose of economy. With O'Gorman, whom he praises and recommends as a corrective to other writers on Burke,[99] Macpherson regards Burke's "recourse to Natural Law on some other *a priori* principle" as so much rhetoric.[100] While claiming to resolve the utilitarian Natural Law debate on Burke by transcending it to a higher level, in the end he simply resolves it by placing Burke back into a utilitarian category, albeit on the order of a bourgeois political economist.

George Fasel finds Burke's political thought both consistent and conservative. His conservatism is reflected in that "the future lay in the past." This required Burke to "guard against its erosion, labor incessantly to renew it, meet all attempts to 'interpret' or 'modernize' it with the coldest suspicion."[101] But what is the ground for this conclusion? Fasel replies that "Like so many men in the eighteenth century, his highest criterion for public acts was social utility, which for all intents and purposes he equated with preservation of the English constitution."[102] Why social utility, why not the classical natural law as the ground of his conservatism? Fasel claims it is not due to the "implausibility" of such a ground, but to "extremely sparse and scattered evidence in his writings. The most that can be said is that if Burke was indeed a part of that ancient intellectual tradition, then he employed its conceptual apparatus and its vocabulary far less than any of his predecessors."[103] We are not informed by Fasel how often evidence must appear in order to count as a fundamental principle of politics. It would seem that if one's thought basically reflected a particular principle it is possible that the principle need not be mentioned at all, or perhaps only once, and only if the context of the work, or, as often is the case for Burke, speech required enunciation of principles.

Christopher Reid offers a literary study of Burke's political writings in which he examines the "relationship between literary form and political practice."[104] Reid investigates the "ways in which a political discourse such as [Burke's] was constituted and put into effect."[105] Reid's study reveals the empirical and experimental method of Burke. This method is foreshadowed by the *Philosophical Inquiry*, itself governed by a "sensuous materialism." Burke's "empirical approach" serves to support his "noted pragmatism."[106] Reid finds agreement with Macpherson in describing Burke's "style" as one of "empirical generalization."[107]

The author notes Burke's "conservatism," and without elaboration states that it is grounded in "an appeal to metaphysical principles."[108] It is not clear what is meant by "metaphysical principles" save to assume that the religious nature of the "framework of ideas and images" that envelop the *Reflections*, coupled with "Burke's reverence for tradition" and its expression at times in the "language of Natural Law," does not become central to Reid's understanding and interpretation of the Irishman.[109] If they did, why would he insist on the term "ideology" to characterize Burke's fundamental thought? Why would he refer to Burke as an "ideologist,"[110] cite the "ideological"[111] in Burke, or note "Burke's ideological role,"[112] or Burke's "empirical method . . . in the realm of ideology"?[113] What does Reid mean by the use of this term which is fraught with such difficulties in the history of more recent political thought? And how could Reid, so concerned as he is with literary forms and styles, not seek to detail for us what is meant by this term? Does he mean to go as far as Conor Cruise O'Brien in referring to Burke as "a conscious and deliberate propagandist," one who "had long been aware of the value of verbal violence" and who was committed to the "method of tactical overstatement which distinguishes the true propagandist from the mere believer in a cause"?[114] Would Reid agree with O'Brien in conceding that "Burke . . . never sets out to deceive, but he does—quite often—aim at seducing, or at intimidating."[115]

It is strange indeed when Reid, who at first finds Burke's empirical approach supporting his pragmatism, then affirms his conservatism as based on an appeal to metaphysical principles, finally acknowledges that Burke is not now recognized as a philosopher with a coherent theory. Instead, the picture Reid paints is one of a skillful rhetorician, whose aim is to evoke "feeling" within his listener or reader, sufficient for them to "experience as 'true', the values and beliefs of the dominant culture of his time."[116] More than expediency, temporized and refined by rhetoric, Burke aims to communicate "a complex experience of history,"[117] according to Reid.

F. P. Lock renews the debate over the utilitarian–natural law interpretation of Burke's political thought.[118] His own interpretation reflects views of previously mentioned authors in various respects. Lock contends that "Burke was certainly a utilitarian in the sense that he believed that government should be for the benefit of the governed."[119] He argues further that Burke "would even have agreed with the Benthamite formulation of 'the greatest happiness of the greatest number', provided that the judgment of what would conduce to their greatest happiness was not left to the greatest number to decide."[120] Yet Lock is ultimately as uncomfortable in categorizing Burke on the spectrum of political theory as Plamenatz is, although Lock, unlike Plamenatz, does not discover a consistency in Burke's thought sufficient to give rise to a political philosophy.[121] "Many of Burke's modern critics," according to Lock, ". . . have detected a political philosophy in and behind his writings. My own view is that the search is essentially misconceived." And on the question of consistency, Lock concludes: "It would hardly be reasonable to expect a practical politician, speaking and writing on a wide range of issues over a period of thirty years, to achieve the systematic consistency that is not always reached in the works of professed political philosophers."[122] Concerning Burke, Lock proclaims that "the search for his political 'philosophy' is illusory."[123] So, it is no surprise that at one time Burke makes use of the natural law and at another he writes like a utilitarian. "If Burke is not a consistent exponent of the 'natural law', neither is he an exclusive utilitarian."[124] In fact, "Burke uses utility, as he uses the law of nature, how and when it suits his purpose."[125] Thus, for Lock, "Burke was not a philosopher, but a politician and a rhetorician."[126] So it is that the *Reflections* "is a work of persuasion, not of philosophy."[127]

Iain Hampsher-Monk's assessment of the place of natural law in Burke's political philosophy is similar to that of Reid and Lock in that Hampsher-Monk appears to grant a grudging acknowledgment of Burke's use of natural law, yet concludes that its use is mainly rhetorical, aiming to move the reader to affirm tradition, custom and prejudice already historically formed, and eschew radical change. In making use of natural law, Burke is making use of "the language of English and European politics."[128] In addition to drawing from the language of natural law, Burke also drew from the language of "utilitarianism, from the English adaptation of classical republicanism, and from an emergent romanticism." While doing so, "Burke never wholly identifies himself with these arguments, for he never accepts the authority of the metaphysics behind them." Rather, Burke is using these languages for rhetorical purposes, recognizing "their power to move an audience."[129] And what is the aim of these rhetorical devices? For what purpose does Burke seek to sway his auditors? The aim is a functional or utilitarian one. Burke aims for the "preservation of political institutions, the customs and beliefs on which they depend, and the transmission of the whole through time. . . ."[130] It is for this reason, as viewed by Hampsher-Monk, that Burke defends prejudice, "without regard to the content because it renders human behavior within society more predictable and manageable."[131] The conclusion is obvious: "What holds a political community together is its shared susceptibility to certain kinds of rhetorical appeal, and the appeal to the past holds a peculiar susceptibility for the English. . . ."

On the one hand it is true that "there is an ultimate standard of metaphysical right,—Natural Law . . . ," and yet Burke's political theory is not one of natural law since it does not make up "the irreducible moral reality of political life." Instead, natural law's relationship to political society "is tenuous and mitigated by the historical experience of the community."[132] One wonders if Hampsher-Monk means to imply that natural law is incongruous with historical development, something neither Aquinas nor Burke believed, both holding that custom in effect constituted a second nature in man.[133]

In sum, Hampsher-Monk's construction of Burke reveals a political thinker who holds to tradition, regardless of content, because it is functional—it works. And in working it possesses a presumed utility, that of more or less satisfying individuals within the political community. To remove the historical apparatus that is the substance of society is to venture something perilous, for while history may have built up certain onerous patterns for social interaction, to undo what history has done is a risk not worth taking. It is not functional to do so, for men function best in the context of the customs, institutions and habit of mind bequeathed to them by the historical evolution of society.

Most paradoxical in Hampsher-Monk's account is his claim that Burke "never accepts the authority of the metaphysics" supporting natural law, or that of any other political philosophical position, conjoined with his other claim that "there is an ultimate standard of metaphysical right,—Natural Law . . . ," clearly implying that Burke held to such a standard. Failure to explain this apparent inconsistency undermines Hampsher-Monk's presentation of Burke's political philosophy.

Summary and Reply to the Utilitarian Interpretation

In what follows I wish to point out some of the basic themes that emerge from the foregoing assessments of Burke. First, the inability of political reason to ascertain the first principles of politics is readily cited. Rather than exploring by the light of political reason the foundations of society, Burke is seen by these writers as recoiling from such an inspection, the only effect of which would be to diminish the veneration and awe that hallow the ground of morality and society.[134] Again, the emphasis imputed to Burke is that the old is good because it has endured, and this endurance is an indication that it has served, and is serving, a worthwhile purpose for man.

As I have urged earlier, Burke does not reject political reason. What he rejects is a certain vainglory that so readily elevates the *a priori* conjectures of the single individual, or small group of intellectuals, above the demonstrated wisdom of the ages. He writes, "We are afraid to put men to live and trade each on his own private stock of reason . . ." (RF III 346), and "The individual is foolish . . . but the species is wise, and, when time is given to it, as a species, it almost always acts right" (SC VII 95). Burke is not discounting the single individual or a prudent use of one's reason. What he objects to are those individuals who discount the wisdom of the past as outdated and irrelevant, and who attempt to utilize an abstract, individual, geometrical reason in the realm of politics. I will attempt to show in the next chapter that both the universe and man's social existence give evidence, for Burke, of order and intelligibility. It is no mere expedience, or a simple, indiscriminate prejudice for what *is* that forms the substance of Burke's thought.

A second theme in the literature just presented is that the ideas of prescription, prejudice, and expediency are the main principles supporting Burke's political philosophy. Indeed, these theories do carry great weight, but they do so only insofar as they are grounded in Burke's metaphysics of a God-created universe, divinely ordered, purposefully moved, and grounded in the natural law. Burke clearly favors that which is sanctified because it reflects a continuity required by the universe and the social order. Burke writes that prescription is not "formed upon blind, unmeaning prejudices" (SC VII 95). That which has stood the test of time is more likely to be hallowed in the eyes of mankind since ". . . it is in the nature of man . . . to defer to the wisdom of times past, whose weakness is not before his eyes, than to the present, of whose imbecility he has daily experience. Veneration of antiquity is congenial to the human mind" (TPL VI 339). Prescription and prejudice are valuable not simply for rendering a majority happy, but also as reflective of the created universe of order; they are valuable, for Burke, because they reflect the continuity and permanency that obtain in reality.

An institution may be useful because it brings pleasure. But, as John Stuart Mill came to recognize, the useful must be consonant with man's nature, a nature which Burke recognizes as rational. For Burke, the standard for expedience lies outside that which simply and at present is; or that which brings the greatest amount of happiness to the greatest number of people. Rather, the standard for these principles lies within the reasonable and ordered nature of both the physical and the moral universe. As Burke notes in his consideration of the taxation of America by Britain, it is not what "I *may* do, but what humanity, reason, and justice tell me I ought to do" (SCA II 140–141).

Third, the utilitarian critics write of Burke's empiricism and of his philosophy of experience. These features indeed play a pivotal part in Burke's philosophy. Hume and Burke both sought to supplant pure abstractions with concrete experience. But to make this claim does not warrant placing Burke in the tradition of Hume, especially as embodying British empiricist epistemological premises. All that restrains certain of Burke's interpreters from doing as much is Burke's religious orientation—hence the rubric, "theological empiricism or utilitarianism." Burke's emphasis on experience is in part to counter the deductionistic theorists of the rights of man, such theorists who hypothesize a state of nature and a list of abstracted natural rights to fit this state. As in certain other matters, Burke and Hume alike reject the natural rights thesis. In addition, experience and empirical observation and the effects of nature reveal the crucial principle of causality, which principle for Burke leads the human mind to assent to God himself (ISB I 142–43). And here Burke and Hume part company.[135] Consequently, Burke's concern with experience is crucial to his thought, but not sufficient to render him a utilitarian with no metaphysical grounding.

Fourth, even when acknowledging Burke's reference to and use of natural law, Burke's utilitarian critics frequently explain such references away as nothing more than rhetorical devices to achieve a desired effect on his reader or auditor. Even if one were to grant these critics that Burke's speeches and writings were purely for rhetorical purpose (which I do not believe and which would strike me as a defenseless display of Sartrean *mauvaise foi* on Burke's part), even then it would be hard to account for his obvious references in his *Correspondence* to the natural law as an expression of God's divine reason in the nature of man, society, and the universe.

Yet it is in his *Correspondence* that we find Burke referring to the "Law of Nature" (C III 374), to the "rights of humanity and Laws of Nature" (C IV 416), to "the God of Law and order" (C IX 48), to the "instinctive principles of self deffence and . . . executive powers under the legislation of nature, enforcing its first law" (C VI 266), to the "establishd Laws of Nature" (C IX 84), and to the "immutable Laws of Nature, and the principles of Essential Justice" (C X 40). It is hard to escape Burke's appeal to a higher law than the laws of Parliament as being an appeal to natural law when he is moved to reply by letter to certain merchants among his constituents in Bristol who had written Burke to protest his support of legislation favoring Irish trade. Without impugning "the Right of the Parliament of Great Britain to make Laws for the Trade of Ireland," Burke nevertheless speaks "of what Laws it is right for Parliament to make." In an eloquent appeal to the natural law and God as its source, Burke writes to the Bristol merchants:

> The Author of our Nature has written it strongly in that Nature, and has promulgated the same Law in his written Word, that Man shall eat his Bread by his Labour; and I am persuaded, that no man, and no combination of Men, for their own Ideas of their particular profit, can, without great impiety, undertake to say, that he shall not do so; that they have no sort of right, either to prevent the Labour, or to withhold the Bread [C III 442].

Finally, the role of religion is seen by some of Burke's interpreters as crucial to an understanding of him. Though they are correct in this assessment, I believe they are mistaken in the part they assign to religion in Burke's thought. For example, in Laski's interpretation, religion for Burke serves the function of both obscuring the ultimate ground of social facts and supplying the ultimate foundation for society. Implying the sacred and the reverent as religion does, it too easily serves to dissuade adequate inquiry into the ultimate, humanly knowable principles of society and the universe, so Laski suggests. Religion serves to further secure that which has already been deemed venerable throughout time. Two thoughts emerge here: first, religion feeds Burke's anti-rationalism and second, it is useful in maintaining the conventions, customs, and traditions of society.

Religion is more than this for Burke. It is true that religion, especially the state religion of the Anglican Church, does secure order, and order is willed by God. The church should not simply secure any order, but a just order, one that comports with original justice. This is indeed of utilitarian value. But it is neither simply the utility of the status quo nor the utility of justice as set forth by the original archetype of both justice and man's nature: God.

The role of utility and religion in the thought of Burke does not justify the label of "theological utilitarian." While God certainly wills happiness for us, he also wills the acquisition of virtues and the preservation of order—not simply as these serve to enhance human happiness. God calls us to fulfill our station in life and the duties that come with our position in society.

These duties and the virtues necessary to their fulfillment engage Burke's attention more than does the question of happiness. He remarks:

> that the awful Author of our being is the Author of our place in the order of existence—and that, having disposed and marshalled us by a divine tactic, not according to our will, but according to His, He has in and by that disposition virtually subjected us to act the part which belongs to the place assigned us. We have obligations to mankind at large, which are not in consequence of any special voluntary pact [ANW IV 165-166].

There is a "positivist" presumption in the utilitarian interpretation, revealing the empiricist epistemological basis of its claim. This echoes the Humean empiricism which grounds our ability to know exclusively in the empirically observable world. It undercuts and disavows any inductive move from this world of observation to the recognition of eternal verities. For this reason Hume wishes to side with man's natural feelings and passions which find a warm responsiveness to custom, habit, and tradition, bringing an ordered, happy populace. Burke himself is also responsive to "ancestral wisdom," and to experience. Although he wishes the great bulk of men to rest content with what the generations before have bequeathed to them, he likewise affirms change as the great law of nature, which he holds should be orderly and deliberate, not destructive. Contentment with their heritage permits human beings to maintain their invaluable links with the stabilizing ties of tradition, eschewing the "spirit of innovation."[136] Yet, Burke does believe that one can, through reason, come to know those ultimate principles and standards which serve as judge over this tradition. And these principles and standards are found in Burke's implicit metaphysics, to which I now turn.

Notes

1. *The Language of Politics in the Age of Wilkes and Burke* (London: Routledge & Kegan Paul, 1963), p. 104.
2. Frederick Dreyer, *Burke's Politics: A Study in Whig Orthodoxy* (Waterloo, Ontario: Wilfrid Laurier University Press, 1979), p. 83.

Steven Blakemore, "Burke and the Fall of Language," *Eighteenth-Century Studies*, 17, No. 3 (Spring 1984), 288–89n8.

3. Cf. Frederick Dreyer, "Edmund Burke: The Philosopher in Action," *Studies in Burke and His Time*, 15, No. 2 (1973–1974), 121.

4. Cf. John Plamenatz, *Man and Society: Political and Social Theory*. I. *Machiavelli through Rousseau* (New York: McGraw-Hill, 1963), p. 333, and Dreyer, *Burke's Politics*, p. 87.

5. W XI 69.

6. Cf. R. R. Fennessy, *Burke, Paine, and the Rights of Man: A Difference of Political Opinion* (The Hague: Nijhoff, 1963), p. 136.

7. Cf. John MacCunn, *The Political Philosophy of Burke* (London: Longmans, 1913), pp. 38–39.

8. Cf. Michael Freeman, *Edmund Burke and the Critique of Political Radicalism* (Oxford: Blackwell, 1980), p. 237 and J. R. Lucas, *The Principles of Politics* (Oxford: Clarendon, 1966), p. 363.

9. Cf. C. P. Courtney, *Montesquieu and Burke* (Oxford: Blackwell, 1963), p. 154.

10. *Summa theologica* (New York: Benzinger Brothers, 1947), Ia, 79, 11.

11. Ibid.

12. Cf. Peter J. Stanlis, "Edmund Burke and the Scientific Rationalism of the Enlightenment," in *Edmund Burke, the Enlightenment, and the Modern World*, ed. Peter J. Stanlis (Detroit: University of Detroit Press, 1967), p. 111n11.

13. For the meanings and usages of "reason" by Burke, see Peter J. Stanlis, *Edmund Burke and the Natural Law* (Ann Arbor: University of Michigan Press, 1958), p. 162, and Stanlis, "Edmund Burke and the Scientific Rationalism of the Enlightenment," p. 103.

14. Cf. Leo Strauss, *Natural Right and History* (Chicago: The University of Chicago Press, 1953), p. 305.

15. Francis P. Canavan, S.J., *The Political Reason of Edmund Burke* (Durham: Duke University Press, 1960), p. 51.

16. The editors of the *Correspondence* relate that no such quote from Cicero can be found.

17. Michael Freeman argues that "Burke was a quasi-perfectionist," this being "the dominant ideology of the Western World today" although not quite as confidently held as sometime before. What is a "quasi-perfectionist"? One who believes "that in the fairly recent past progress reached its highest point, so that present-day society is nearly perfect, requiring only minor reforms and adaptations to changing circumstances." Freeman, *Edmund Burke*, p. 99. While arguing forcefully for this conclusion, Freeman does not locate for us textual

support for the claim of the near-perfection of late-eighteenth-century English society in Burke's *Works*. Furthermore, there is no argumentation offered by Freeman for his sweeping generalization concerning quasi-perfectionism as the dominant ideology of the West. In fact, Freeman's analysis on this point reflects a fundamental misinterpretation of Burke. Burke's "traditionalism" does not lie in a belief that society, which exists for the moral perfection of the person, is somehow nearly perfect. Freeman's analysis represents a misunderstanding of Burke's view of human nature—a nature that Burke regards as flawed by original sin and a will that too often is swollen by pride and unbounded self-preference. How could Burke, who holds that in political society we can obtain at best a balance between good and evil, never a utopian state—how could Burke at the same time be a "quasi-perfectionist" who held that society has become nearly perfect? The opposite is true. Burke cherished the achievements of society as having prevented even greater evils than an uncivilized state could possibly achieve. There is no false sentimentalism concerning these achievements just as there is no secular eschatology aiming to realize a utopia in the future.

18. It is Leo Strauss's conclusion that Burke integrates his political thought "into a classical or Thomistic framework." Strauss, *Natural Right and History*, p. 296.

19. John Morley, *Edmund Burke: A Historical Study* (New York: Knopf, 1924), p. 122. This a reprint of the original 1867 first edition.

20. Ibid., p. 123.

21. John Morley, *Burke* (New York: Harper & Brothers, 1879), p. 209.

22. Ibid., p. 213.

23. Ibid., pp. 162–63. Such vague, imprecise conclusions about Burke's "mysticism" provoke a sharp rejoinder by Russell Kirk: "To describe as 'mysticism' this vivid and sagacious piety of Burke's is a gross abuse of philosophical terms, illustrating the semantic Dark Age into which the twentieth century has been slipping. . . . A man who believes that a just God rules the world; that the course of history has been determined, though commonly in ways inscrutable, by His Providence; that individual station in life is assigned by 'a divine tactic'; that original sin and aspiration toward the good both are part of God's design; that the reformer first should endeavor to discern the lineaments of a Providential order, and then endeavor to conform political arrangements to the dictates of a natural justice—skeptics may believe a man who declares those convictions to be mistaken, but skeptics are muddled if they call him a 'mystic.' " *The Conservative Mind: From Burke to Eliot* (Chicago: Regnery, 1960), p. 37.

24. Henry Buckle, *The History of Civilization in England* (New York: Appleton, 1882), p. 328.
25. Ibid.
26. Ibid., p. 330.
27. Ibid.
28. Ibid., p. 334.
29. Charles E. Vaughan, *Studies in the History of Political Philosophy Before and After Rousseau*, ed. A. G. Little, 2 vols. (Manchester: Manchester University Press, 1925), II p. 10.
30. Ibid., p. 4.
31. Ibid., p. 13. Other references to Burke's conservative "instinct" or bias occur on pages 22 and 29.
32. Ibid., pp. 16 and 14.
33. Ibid., p. 19.
34. Ibid., pp. 20 and 36.
35. Ibid., p. 37.
36. Ibid., p. 29.
37. Ibid., p. 37.
38. Ibid.
39. Ibid., p. 45.
40. Ibid., p. 47.
41. Ibid., p. 61.
42. Sir Leslie Stephen, *History of English Thought in the Eighteenth Century*, 2 vols. (London: Smith, Elder, 1881) II, 219.
43. Ibid., p. 280.
44. Ibid., p. 253.
45. Ibid., p. 280.
46. MacCunn, *Political Philosophy of Burke*, p. 195.
47. Ibid., p. 13.
48. Ibid.
49. Ibid., p. 14.
50. Ibid.
51. Ibid., pp. 192–93.
52. Ibid., p. 204.
53. Ibid., p. 208.
54. Ibid., p. 211.
55. Ibid., p. 215.
56. *Edmund Burke and the Revolt Against the Eighteenth Century* (New York: Barnes & Noble, 1960), p. 46.
57. Ibid., p. 49.
58. Ibid., p. 47.
59. Ibid., p. 59.

60. Ibid., pp. 84–85.
61. 3rd ed. (New York: Holt, Rinehart and Winston, 1961), p. 607.
62. All of these points are ratified by Sabine, ibid., pp. 599–600.
63. Ibid., p. 607.
64. Aquinas, *Summa theologica*, I–II, 94, 6, c.
65. Ibid., I–II, 94, 2, c.
66. Cf. Jacques Maritain, "The 'Natural' Knowledge of Moral Values," in *Challenges and Renewals*, edd. Joseph W. Evans and Leo R. Ward (Cleveland: Meridian, 1968), p. 231.
67. Sabine, *History of Political Theory*, p. 607.
68. Jeremy Bentham, *An Introduction to the Principles of Morals and Legislation* (New York: Hafner, 1948), p. 2, and John Stuart Mill, *Utilitarianism, Liberty and Representative Government* (New York: Dutton Everyman's Library, 1951), p. 8.
69. John Plamenatz, *The English Utilitarians* (Oxford: Blackwell, 1958), p. 22.
70. Ibid., p. 28.
71. David Hume, *A Treatise of Human Nature*, 2 vols. (London: Dent and Sons, 1911), II, 183.
72. Anthony Quinton, *Utilitarian Ethics* (New York: St. Martin's, 1973), p. 1.
73. Plamenatz, *English Utilitarians*, p. 12.
74. Burke writes, "They conceive that He who gave our nature to be perfected by our virtue willed also the necessary means of its perfection: He willed therefore the state: He willed its connection with the source and original archetype of all perfection." RF III 361.
75. Hume, *Treatise of Human Nature*, II 171.
76. Plamenatz, *English Utilitarians*, p. 29.
77. J. R. Dinwiddy, "Utility and Natural Law in Burke's Thought: A Reconsideration," *Studies in Burke and His Time*, 16, No. 2 (1974–1975), 105.
78. Burleigh T. Wilkins, *The Problem of Burke's Political Philosophy* (Oxford: Clarendon, 1967), p. 11.
79. Plamenatz, *English Utilitarians*, p. 56, and Elie Halévy, *The Growth of Philosophic Radicalism*, trans. Mary Morris (London: Faber & Faber, 1928).
80. Plamenatz, *English Utilitarians*, p. 56.
81. Ibid., pp. 56–58.
82. Halévy, *Growth of Philosophic Radicalism*, pp. 157–64.
83. Ibid., p. 157.
84. Ibid., p. 159.
85. Ibid., pp. 163–64. Also Plamenatz, *English Utilitarians*, p. 57.

It is from Halévy that Plamenatz lifts all but verbatim his arguments for Burke's utilitarianism.

86. Halévy, *Growth of Philosophic Radicalism*, p. 163.

87. Harold Laski, *Political Thought in England* (London: Butterworth, 1932), p. 122. To say that Burke's metaphysics "are largely those of Hume" seems an odd statement. Surely Hume is noted for his rejection of metaphysics and, as Laski acknowledges, Burke's language appears to repudiate metaphysics. How is it that one adopts the metaphysics of one whose thought constitutes a sustained rejection of such philosophizing as does Hume's? I can find a solution for such a statement by Laski only in assuming that both Burke and Hume, as Laski sees it, reject the province of reason in discovering timeless, eternal truths of thought or being, so their common metaphysics must be, instead, a common epistemology. But, even here Laski is in error.

88. Ibid., p. 123.

89. Ibid., p. 182.

90. Ibid., p. 183.

91. Frank O'Gorman, *Edmund Burke: His Political Philosophy* (Bloomington: Indiana University Press, 1973), p. 11.

92. Ibid., p. 92.

93. Ibid., p. 19.

94. Ibid., p. 108.

95. Ibid., p. 143–144.

96. Macpherson, *Burke* (Oxford: Oxford University Press, 1980), p. 4.

97. Ibid., p. 69.

98. Ibid., p. 71.

99. Ibid., p. 77.

100. Ibid., p. 36.

101. George Fasel, *Edmund Burke* (Boston: Twayne, 1983), p. 129.

102. Ibid.

103. Ibid. Rather than "sparse and scattered evidence" of a natural law position perhaps the problem is scant attention to where the evidence actually lies in the Burkean corpus. According to David Cameron "references to natural law appear throughout his writings, although it should also be noted that the passages in which the matter is most fully discussed are located in relatively minor works which until recently have not come in for a great deal of scholarly attention." *The Social Thought of Rousseau and Burke: A Comparative Study* (Toronto: University of Toronto Press, 1973), p. 78. B. W. Hill holds that "Burke's references to natural law are at least as numerous as his appeals to natural rights. . . ." "Introduction," *Edmund Burke on*

Government, Politics and Society, ed. B. W. Hill (Glasgow: Fontana/ The Harvester 1975), p. 51.

104. Christopher Reid, *Edmund Burke and the Practice of Political Writing* (Dublin: Gill and Macmillan, 1985).
105. Ibid., p. 14.
106. Ibid., p. 192.
107. Ibid., p. 194.
108. Ibid., p. 219.
109. Ibid., pp. 218 and 221.
110. Ibid., p. 1.
111. Ibid., p. 215.
112. Ibid., p. 220.
113. Ibid., p. 191.
114. Conor Cruise O'Brien, "Introduction," *Edmund Burke, Reflections on the Revolution in France*, ed. Conor Cruise O'Brien (Baltimore: Penguin, 1969), pp. 51, 53 and 54.
115. O'Brien, *Edmund Burke, Master of English*, The English Association Presidential Address 1981 (Mitcham, Surrey: Hartfield, 1981), p. 3.
116. Reid, *Edmund Burke and . . . Political Writing*, p. 219.
117. Ibid., p. 223.
118. F. P. Lock, *Burke's Reflections on the Revolution in France* (London: Allen & Unwin, 1985).
119. Ibid., p. 95.
120. Ibid.
121. Ibid., pp. 89–99.
122. Ibid., p. 90.
123. Ibid.
124. Ibid., p. 94.
125. Ibid., p. 96.
126. Ibid., p. 98.
127. Ibid., p. 99.
128. Iain Hampsher-Monk, "Introduction," *The Political Philosophy of Edmund Burke*, ed. Iain Hampsher-Monk (London and New York: Longmans, 1987), p. 37.
129. Ibid.
130. Ibid., p. 36.
131. Ibid., pp. 35–36.
132. Ibid., p. 40.
133. Cf. pp. 114–15.
134. Cf. Peter J. Stanlis, "Reflections on Dinwiddy on Mill on Burke on Prescription," *Studies in Burke and His Time*, 18, No. 3 (Autumn 1977), 194.

135. Their parting company occurs not only in philosophical matters, but in personal terms as well. Hume's religious scepticism led Burke to conclude " 'that keeping company with David Hume, in a strict sense, is hardly defensible.' " *Boswell Papers,* X1, 268, quoted by Thomas W. Copeland, *Our Eminent Friend, Edmund Burke* (New Haven: Yale University Press, 1949), p. 167. Burke also refers in a book review of James Beattie's *An Essay on the Nature and Immutability of Truth* in the *Annual Register* for the year 1771 to "the sceptical systems of Bishop Berkley [sic] and Mr. Hume; the one made with good intentions but with bad effect; the other with intentions to produce that infidelity to which it leads so evidently." (*Annual Register* XIV [1771], 255). Both of these references were discovered in Canavan's *Political Reason of Edmund Burke*, p. 43.

136. Burke, writing on the abuses of the revolution in France, states, "A spirit of innovation is generally the result of a selfish temper and confined views. People will not look forward to posterity, who never look backward to their ancestors" (RF III 274).

3
The Case for Burke's Metaphysics

IN THE SECOND CHAPTER, primary and secondary sources were utilized to confront squarely the evidence against a Burkean metaphysics. In each instance arguments were advanced to refute the anti-metaphysical interpretation of Burke's thought, and to lay the groundwork whereby the task of presenting his metaphysics might proceed. It is to this latter work I now turn.

Before searching out the elements of a Burkean metaphysics it is necessary to ask, What is metaphysics? What is the province of metaphysics and the role of the metaphysician? And, what is Burke's position on these issues?

In answering these questions I will refer primarily to the Aristotelian-Thomistic tradition with its common-sense, moderate realism, for it is with this tradition that Burke's philosophy finds its most basic agreement. At the same time, there is an aspect of Burke's philosophy that relates to the modern movement of existentialism. Still, even here his metaphysics demonstrates a compatibility with the existential Thomism which has been cited by modern Thomists such as Jacques Maritain as the authentic interpretation of Aquinas' metaphysics. Consequently, in responding to the question "What is metaphysics?" as a backdrop against which to develop the case for Burke's metaphysics, it will be instructive to outline the Thomistic position with special reference to Maritain's understanding of the same. To do as much is not for me to argue that Maritain's position is, in fact, the authentic interpretation of Aquinas. That is a matter for more competent authorities than I to determine. My sketch is simply an outline of a realist metaphysics with the purpose of obtaining a comparison with Burke. Finally, the sketch is not developed in order to support an extreme and untenable thesis that Burke, *mirabile dictu*, is an existential Thomist. The outline is intended to permit my development of the thesis that Burke has a metaphysics and that this metaphysics is compatible with the realist tradition of Aristotle and Aquinas, and that it reveals an existential theme that is comparable to aspects of modern existentialism and Maritain's existential Thomism.

Such a thesis does not aim to deny compatibility of Burke with empiricism, or utilitarianism, or pragmatism. Instead, my thesis simply argues that Burke does have a metaphysics, one that is most compatible with an Aristotelian-Thomistic realism, while not exclusive of all other comparisons. This, obviously, is a limited thesis.

The Realist Tradition in Metaphysics

Metaphysics is concerned to know being as being, to know the real insofar as it exists, and to know the first causes of being.[1] It is not concerned with knowing being in order to obtain power, or live the good life, or certify one as a savant. Rather it seeks simply to know being insofar as it is. This comports with the opening passage of Aristotle's *Metaphysics* that "All men by nature desire to know." The human person, through the power of reason, possesses a natural inclination toward gaining knowledge; he desires wisdom. What is the wisdom sought for and what is the relationship between wisdom and metaphysics? Writing on Aristotle, Copleston states: "Metaphysics is . . . Wisdom par excellence, and the philosopher or lover of Wisdom is he who desires knowledge about the ultimate cause and nature of Reality, and desires that knowledge for its own sake."[2] Wisdom is knowing reality as it most essentially is, which, as this quote suggests, means knowing the causes of reality. This implies that wisdom ultimately is knowledge for its own sake. Does this further suggest, for Aristotle, that pure, undefiled wisdom is to be put to no further use? It does not. Knowledge of one's nature should provide some guide to life. But the knowledge or insight wisdom brings is not initially knowledge for human conduct. Instead, it is knowledge fulfilling one's desire to know for the sake of knowing. This allows knowledge to reveal reality for no other purpose than that of the disclosure of being. Surely the kind of knowledge thereby obtained would more nearly approach the truth of reality, that is, as reality is in itself, than the knowledge of reality obtained for an end beyond itself. Therefore, wisdom for Aristotle and Aquinas is initially to be sought for its own sake. Burke likewise declares the prevention "of the means of improving our rational nature to be the worst species of tyranny that the insolence and perverseness of mankind ever dared to exercise."[3] To obstruct reason and its natural bent toward wisdom is thus to deform man. And yet the search for ultimate principles when done from a motive lacking in piety or reverence toward the mystery and awesomeness of being, can prove subversive to the very wisdom that is our heritage.

In distinguishing the types of philosophical traditions in the history of philosophy, W. H. Greenleaf includes transcendental realism, empirical nominalism, and philosophical idealism.[4] To consider realism as transcendental realism is a distinction which pertains most nearly to Platonism. As Greenleaf defined "transcendental realism": "It stressed the deceptiveness of what we learn through our senses and asserted the need to transcend this changing world of Becoming (to use the Platonic terms), to get beyond it to the realm of stable Being."[5] For Plato, being is identified with the Ideas or Forms of things, what might be termed their nature or essence. These Forms are not present substantially within the things themselves, but, somehow, transcend the temporal flux of the material, empirical world. Thus, the reality of things, what they really are, cannot be found at all within the shadow realm of time and space. Instead, this shadow realm is but a copy of the really real, the Forms of things. The Forms are not spatial, temporal, or quantifiable, but are transcendent and immutable, hence eternal. There is a gap which ontologically cannot be bridged between the two realms, although things are drawn towards their Forms and seek to imitate them.

The true nature of the Forms are shrouded in mystery for Plato, and are not open to the analytic mind. As mysterious they are not in themselves irrational and do not fall below reason. Rather, they transcend the grasp of a reason whose daily orientation is towards the realm of the mutable. The Forms are suprarational in that they escape the mundane use of reason. Through the use of dialectic, human reason can be prepared for gaining insight into the Forms. But the dialectic gives way to a vision that most of us cannot receive or acquire.

But transcendental realism does not exhaust the types of realism. The Aristotelian-Thomistic philosophical position may be termed a moderate, or common-sense realism; both Aristotle and Aquinas locate the forms substantially within material being. So, the form of the apple is actually present to the apple, as is the human form, or the form of tree. This is common sense. Things, in a sense, are what they appear to be. Apples are really apples; trees are really trees; humans are human.

Plato's realism on the other hand is both transcendental and radical. It is radical in supposing that the forms have only a transcendental reality,[6] and denying any reality to the material realm. But Aristotle and Aquinas attribute a reality to that which appears as such to common sense. Our senses do not deceive but assist us in gaining metaphysical knowledge. For Aquinas, an empirical element vitalizes his metaphysics and epistemology, as he holds that nothing is in the mind that is not first in the senses. And this brings us to Aristotle's and Aquinas' moderate realism.

Again, the forms are real and substantially present to the things themselves. But as opposed to Plato, the forms for Aristotle and Aquinas are subject to another mode of existence, that mode obtained through mental abstraction. The experience of sensation carries within it the germ of true knowledge. For Aquinas, true knowledge can only be obtained when the knower becomes one with the known. Thus, the datum of experience as sensorially grasped carries *in potentia* the form of the thing sensed. Sense experience is transformed immediately by the interior senses. These help synthesize the data provided by the various external senses, resulting in the image of the thing, a product of the imagination working on the datum of sensation. The result is the phantasm or image which is not the picture or representation of the thing as it is for the empiricism of Locke. The image for Aquinas is that through which the thing presents itself to the speculative power of the intellect.

As both Aristotle and Aquinas divide the realm of being into act and potency, finite reality reveals an active and passive mode of being. The human intellect, in its active mode, and operating upon the image, is able to separate out of the image by an act of abstraction the universal element of the thing which has manifested itself to the knower; hence, the form becomes really present to the human intellect. The form becomes present to the extent that, again, the knower becomes one with the thing known. This unity, of course, is not substantial, but accidental, as the knower retains his own unity. And yet, the reality of the thing known as disclosed by the form reveals the second mode of existence which the form obtains.

But here Aquinas adds a third mode of existence for the form, not apparently held by Aristotle. For Aquinas the form pre-exists its substantial presence in the knowing mind. It pre-exists these other two modes of existence in the divine mind of God, which eternally conceives the form of every existent thing. In this regard, there is a crucial difference between the metaphysics of Aristotle and that of Aquinas.

Transcendental and moderate realism may not exhaust the genres of realism, but they obviously are quite distinct from one another. Moderate realism has a keen appreciation for the worldliness of things, for their existential condition. Moderate realism does not seek to abrogate the reality of the material realm, while it clearly subordinates it to the immaterial. Instead, it presents an authentic existentialism as opposed to the radical essentialism of Plato and the radical existentialism of Heraclitus or Sartre.

Further, it treats as natural the phenomenal manifestation of things. In fact, it refuses to radically bifurcate what later "transcendental" metaphysics of the idealist stripe term the phenomenal-noumenal realms. A certain type of being naturally instantiates itself within the spatial-temporal realm. More than that, it finds its authentic mode of being not in a temporal flight from matter, but by seeking its perfection materially, historically, and spiritually. Thus, it is natural, hence right, for human beings to exist materially and to realize themselves in this state. But, as opposed to material forms, such as the forms of vegetative and animal existence, for Aquinas human beings are not exclusively material. They have an immaterial mode of being, a soul which, while naturally drawn to matter, transcends its own material conditions through knowledge. When the knower is one with the thing known, he realizes a spiritual mode of existence which signifies his ultimate destiny, apart from matter.

The Existential Nature of Thomism

This brings us to the existential element of Thomism, the emphasis upon *esse*, or the act of existence. Each human person has its own unique act of existence, which existentializes, or "realifies"[7] its substantial being. For Aristotle, the realm of being is divided exclusively into act and potency, and all of reality can be subsumed under the ten categories which he enumerates. Moreover, in the human, composite act refers to the essence or substantial form of a thing. But for Aquinas, more is required. What is necessary for an existent to come into being is the act of existence which gives being to the whole. Hence, the form of the existent itself is dependent for its being on the act of existence, the *esse*. Thus, while the form is in one sense an act, actuating and perfecting matter, in another sense it is in potency itself to a further act, the *esse* or act of existence.

In turn, the *esse* of each existent is causally dependent upon the conserving creative act of the one, pure act, which is unlimited being. For Aquinas, this is God. While Aristotle himself acknowledges the existence of God as the unmoved mover, he does not offer an authentic existential metaphysics, but a metaphysics of being as substance. Aristotle failed to grasp the creative role of *esse* in the human composite, and the Creator as creating.[8] Aristotle's God is a producing and sustaining God, but he does not create *ex nihilo*. While Aristotle does not fall prey to the Platonic illusion of chaotic matter existing independently of form, he does hold to the eternality of matter as informed and existing in the world. For Aquinas, God brings being out of nothing, with his own being as the divine exemplar for all subsequent being.

The distinction between transcendental realism and moderate, common sense realism is important in this consideration of the nature of metaphysics not only for the distinction itself within realism, but also to call attention to a significant feature that often escapes general discussion on metaphysics. Too often, assault on the very possibility of metaphysics is really an assault on Platonism. It is an assault that focuses on a single presumed feature of realist metaphysics, its so-called other-worldliness, its reputed emphasis upon the metempirical as if disconnected from and antagonistic towards the material. When A. J. Ayer in *Language, Truth, and Logic* fulminates against metaphysical claims to knowledge of a transcendent reality devoid of any possibility of empirical verification, he is tilting at a Platonic metaphysical windmill, not an Aristotelian-Thomistic conception.[9] In fact, Michael J. Loux in his essay on "The Problem of Universals" explicitly equates "metaphysical realists" with "Platonists."[10] There is, as I have outlined, a conception of metaphysics which does not turn its back upon the empirical in affirming the metempirical. There is, in a moderate realism, an affirmation of the existential reality of the concrete material world, one that in its existential condition is suffused with the immaterial, bringing actuality to the otherwise purely potential. There is a concreteness, a robustness about a moderate realism that does not seek an escape from the material world, but seeks to understand it and explain it as it is, and as sustained by the act of being.

It is the act of conceptualization and subsequent focus on the concept that leads metaphysicians too easily to treat as real the concept rather than actual existence. And the concept, after all, grasps the essence of the thing, which essence is confused by Plato as the ultimate reality. But the act of the intellect involves more than conceptualization; it also involves judgment, a judgment termed by Maritain in *Existence and the Existent* as the existential judgment.[11] It is the judgment that in its act of affirmation does more than conjoin an essence with its proper subject; it affirms the existential character of the act of existence as it realifies the subject, and permeates it with existence.

For Maritain, the authentic metaphysician makes good use of his senses and has an indepth awareness of the objects of sensation. Furthermore, the metaphysician "should be plunged into existence, steeped ever more deeply in it by a sensuous and aesthetic perception as acute as possible, and by experiencing the suffering and struggles of real life, so that aloft in the third heaven of natural understanding he may feed upon the intelligible substance of things." For Maritain, while the Thomist "is dubbed scholastic . . . scholastic pedantry is his peculiar foe." Maritain concludes that "The Thomist philosophy, therefore, is, in the sense just explained, an *existential* philosophy."[12]

While this presentation of moderate realism has proceeded thus far on the speculative level, Thomism, as an *existential* philosophy, does not extinguish mystery. Maritain draws an important distinction between mystery and problem in terms of philosophical inquiry. For Maritain, a problem is something for the intellect to solve, such as finding the solution to a mathematical problem. This is the attitude of modern philosophy, Maritain maintains, an attitude which reveals a loss of reverence for the ultimate mystery of being. For Maritain, so overwhelming is the object of our metaphysical inquiry that it must be a science in which mystery predominates.[13] For Maritain, a "philosophy unaware of mystery would not be a philosophy."[14]

The speculative enterprise springs from the acknowledgement of the character of the mystery of being. Being cannot be grasped in a concept or exhausted in a judgement by speculative reason. When turning to our natural knowledge of God, Aquinas holds we know *that* God is, not *what* God is in himself. God's pure knowledge of himself and his creation bears no mystery, since he is translucent to himself.

But the existential nature of Thomist philosophy does not culminate on the level of pure speculation. It is also "applicable to . . . *practical philosophy*. . . ."[15] According to Maritain, "This tends to concrete acts which must be posited into existence. This time directly and in the distinctive sphere for its practicality . . . the intellect, the practical intellect (*voluntate conjuncta*), tends to existence and lays hold of existence to regulate and determine it."[16]

There is a third way in which Thomist philosophy is existential, according to Maritain. This third way moves from the "domain of the intellect but to that of the will." In this domain, the thinker attempts to live the truth his mind has yielded to and acknowledged. The thinker thereby "draws and assimilates it into his subjective being."[17] It is in this domain that modern existential philosophy typically applies.

When turning to concrete existents themselves we recognize a metaphysical composite of existence and essence, act and potency, form and matter. It is the nature of existents to be actual, fully real, and yet in a state of development. There is a metaphysical structure that does not impede but governs change. The existent is a subject, which is actualized by the act of existence, and defined and limited by its essence.[18]

Now that the relationship of the act of existence to the subject, the distinguishing feature of an existential Thomism, has been developed, as has the existential character of Thomism, the place of substance in Thomism and its pivotal position in realist metaphysics in explaining permanence and change require elaboration.

Although Aristotle in his metaphysics presents more than one sense of substance, its central sense concerns that which exists in itself, not in another. For Aristotle, a substance is "not predicated of a subject, but everything else is predicated of [it]."[19] The meaning given to substance by Aquinas is "an essence to which it pertains to exist by itself."[20]

Aristotle makes a further distinction holding that "substance is of two kinds, the concrete thing and the formula (I mean that one kind of substance is the formula taken with the matter, while another kind is the formula in its generality). . . ."[21] For formula, one could more easily read nature or essence, for the essence defines the substance.

Here, three things can be said of substance. First, it has the sense of independence and being fundamental to other attributes of the thing. Second, it has the sense of standing under and supporting accidental modifications of the thing and yet permeating them. Third, it exists as a source of activity.[22] This Thomistic conception of substance does not succumb to the Lockean notion of a "supposed, but unknown support of those Qualities, we find existing, which we imagine cannot subsist *sine re substante*, without something to support them; we call that Support *Substantia*; which . . . is in plain *English, standing under*, or *upholding*."[23]

Rather than standing under, the Thomist conception of substance entails existing in and being present to every part of the thing in its entirety. The substance is not somehow cordoned off from the knower by its accidents or qualities. Locke's representational or picture model of knowledge forces him into this mistaken interpretation. The substance suffuses itself throughout the thing, and as such is a cause and "support" for all accidental modes of being.

While substance has the sense of independence, in the order of finite substance there is the necessity of further perfections. These perfections, or accidents, inhere in the substance they modify; thus in the order of modification the accidents are to acts as substance is to potency. Finite substance is in potency to accidental modifications, modifications which fall under the various Aristotelian categories of predication save that of substance itself. Thus, while substance has the sense of existing in itself, but not in another, accident has the sense of existing in another, but not in itself. Consequently, in the Thomist tradition, an accident is referred to as an *ens entis*, a being of a being. Further, rather than masking or concealing the substance in which they inhere, accidents disclose or manifest the substance.

Obviously, as Maritain remarks, Thomism is an intellectual existentialism, in that it distinguishes various aspects and interrelations within reality in order to discover the unity that transcends distinction. Reality possesses an order, hence is intelligible. Yet, it is concealed while being unconcealed before the penetrating gaze of the intellect. At bottom, as stated, a mystery surrounds the depths of being, but one that invites speculative reason to look more deeply, at the same time acknowledging the paradox of reason's limitations before the boundless vastness of being.

This mystery is apparent in the consideration of substance. For Aquinas there is no direct intuition of substance, and yet substance is disclosed through its accidental modifications. The same is true of the human soul. There is no direct apprehension of the human soul, and yet the soul is known through its activities. This confirms a basic principle of Thomist philosophy, that action follows nature. That is, things act according to what they are. We do not see the intellect as such, but we do see the activities resulting from the intellect. The substance is different from any of its accidental modifications in that they may change, or, for certain accidents, be removed entirely, and the substance remains. Still, the substance does undergo a change in being as the subject of accidental change, without becoming something substantially different since the substance does exist in every aspect of the thing. Thus, an increase in knowledge occasioned through years of study permanently alters my substance, while I retain the unalterable structure I possess as a rational creature. In fact, dementia, or brain disease may permanently impede the use of my rational faculty. My substance is forever altered, yet I retain the metaphysical structure of rationality. There is, at bottom, for Thomism, a dynamic, not static view of being, which, at the same time, does not succumb to a Heraclitean metaphysical view in which "all is flux." Thomism maintains an active, dynamic view of substance, with the very act of existence itself actuating the realm of substance. But that action follows a law of its own nature, determined by the essence of the thing, and this law governs and structures the action which perfects the existent. As John Wild notes, "Action and existence are never found without structure and essence."[24]

As act and potency divide the realm of being, there is an active and passive principle present to every finite being. Substance is a composite of form received in matter, all actuated and sustained in being by the act of existence. As a substance, we have seen, it is capable of accidental change while remaining what it is. In every accidental change something is acquired and something is lost and something remains the same, yet modified. That is, while the tree loses its leaves during the fall and is thereby changed from being a leafy tree, it is nonetheless still a tree. Yet it lacks the rich color of green provided by the leaves and the bounteous quantity of leaves that grace the yard with shade. Instead, it is a somber, barren tree awaiting the icy breath of winter that blows against its limbs.

In addition to accidental change, there are substantial changes. The apple of the tree is eaten by man, and changes into nourishment and energy, assimilated by the person. The apple is substantially changed. It has lost its form, and its matter is absorbed by the person and is changed with the new form of humanity.

Change is essential to nature. It is required for growth and development, and, as change ensures the greater perfection of the thing, it realizes the thing's potencies. Here, Aquinas' metaphysics discloses its teleological character. Wisdom perfects the human person at the level of the intellect; virtue perfects the person at the level of the will. These are accidental perfections in that while they are being acquired the individual remains, in one sense, substantially the same; the person is human. In another sense, his substance is further perfected through the actuality of accidental modifications, such as an increase in knowledge.

Again, action and dynamism are central to a Thomist metaphysics. And this is no surprise as *esse*, the very act of existence, is foundational to the ontological reality of the thing. And *esse* finds its ontological ground in the pure actuality of God. The Thomist metaphysics is an act-centered metaphysics, one that is structured by an intelligible order, revealed through the essence as grasped and affirmed by the intellect. The notion that Thomistic philosophy is not a static Platonic essentialism is crucial to a comparison with Burke's metaphysics.

Change, therefore, has a metaphysical ground. Within the substance itself, changes occur through accidental modifications. This is explained by both Aristotle and Aquinas who recognize that being does not have one, univocal sense—an understanding which led Parmenides to conclude that since only being is, no change is possible. For Aquinas, an accidental perfection requires of the substance being in act and being in potency. The substance of a thing, the result of the reception of form in matter, is actual. Yet substance is in potency to the reception of further acts. Thus change requires the composite of act and potency. As Andrew Reck puts the issue, "Change goes on within substances; it is in the process of translating their potentialities into actualities. . . . While changing, substances endure. . . ."[25]

Underscoring the existential nature of Thomism is the distinction between existence and essence. Neither of these principles of being may exist on its own, as an existent thing would. Yet no existent thing can exist without these complimentary principles of being. Why is this so, and what relationship do these metaphysical principles bear to one another?

The essence of the thing determines what the thing is, the *quiddity*, as the medieval philosophers stated it. The essence defines the substance. It determines the substance to be this kind of being rather than another. Yet in itself it is insufficient to complete the thing in the order of reality. What is further required is *existence*, the act of existence. Existence gives reality to the composite whole, or, realifies. Existence is to essence as act is to potency.

As principles of being without which no thing can exist, they are real and really distinct. One can conceive of the essence of a phoenix independent of its existence. One cannot conceive of existence as such, but one can recognize that existence is required to actualize in the order of reality what otherwise resides only at the level of conceptualization. The potency for existence requires the influx of existence.

Existence is primary, for even the essence, which provides a formal finality within the existent thing, requires the actual finalizing of the act of existence in order to be.

From this a better grasp of the relationship between permanence and change should emerge. As accidents actualize the potency of the substance, the substance continues to endure throughout change. Stated in the paradoxical manner of modern existentialism, I am and I am not yet. I am someone definite. There is a permanent, continuing, abiding reality sealed by my essence as a constituent principle of my substance. But as this essence is received in a substance capable of further determinations, this permanent, abiding reality that I am continues constantly to change, to develop and, ultimately, to corrupt. Permanence and change are both principles of my being, hence laws of nature. Neither can exist without the other.

This discussion on permanence and change reflects our ordinary experience of living. This is common sense. What is not common sense is to accept either permanence or change as elements of reality without the other. But Parmenides and Heraclitus attempted just that. For Parmenides, only being is real and for it to change is for it to become what it is not, that is, nothing. As nothing is unreal, only being is. Hence permanence exists without change.

On the other hand there is the Heraclitean world in which all is flux, nothing abides. In such a view of things there is no basis for knowledge since nothing remains constant; the food of the intellect requires something permanent. Otherwise, knowledge is reduced to a mental construct or, as Nietzsche correctly saw, becomes a fiction imposed upon the constant flux of reality. In short, nothing can be known with certainty, not even the flux.

In contrast, as Copleston remarks, is Aquinas' metaphysics which "presents an abstract theoretical picture of a developing universe which has at the same time sufficient permanence and intelligibility to make knowledge possible."[26]

The universe or world for Aquinas of course is not a self-contained absolute. The world does not entail a certain consciousness of being. Rather, the world or universe is composed of the sum total of substances and their interrelationships. Still, as signified by the existence–essence relation, there is an existential instability present to each thing that is, in that nothing is the cause of its own being, and yet every thing is dependent on another for its existence. No finite essence contains in itself its reason for being. But for everything to be in a state of dependency on either dependent beings like themselves or nothing is impossible. Consequently a being that is independent, uncaused and whose essence it is to exist must be. And that being for Aquinas is God.

The principle of causality governs the intelligibility of the world. To know something metaphysically in the moderate realist tradition is to know its causes. Those various causes are fourfold, namely, formal, material, efficient, and final causality. The form is the formal cause of any thing. The thing's material is that from which it is composed. The efficient cause is that by which it is made. The final cause refers to the purpose or end of its being, that for which it exists. To understand something metaphysically is to understand it causally. Causality responds to the human desire to know or to grasp the intelligible structure of things.

A final tenet of Thomist metaphysics to call to mind in this brief summary is the analogy of being. This is a more complex doctrine than appears at first glance, but it is crucial to the distinction between the orders of beings.

The human person, the apple tree, the boulder on the cliff, and the divine being all possess being. They are similar insofar as they exist. Yet their respective beings also possess radical differences: The boulder is inanimate; the apple tree possesses life, but no intelligence; the human person is living and capable of acts of reason. But divinity surpasses all in that it suffers no restrictions due to finitude. The divine being exists, but is not mutable; his reason comprehends everything, suffering no limitations. There are, thus, analogous modes of beings scaling the hierarchy of being. They all are; in this they are similar. Yet they exist according to different modes, the most radical difference being between finite being and the infinity of God's own being.

What are the central elements of Thomist metaphysics, especially as they permit a comparison with Burkean metaphysics?

First, it is out of the experience of the fact-world that all metaphysical reflection emerges. Metaphysics for Thomism is not an *a priori*, rationalistic, deductive enterprise. For that fact, though, it is a false dichotomy to therefore reduce Thomism to empiricism, requiring thought to be a process of inference and empirical generalization. Metaphysics is rooted in experience. Copleston admirably summarizes the procedure of metaphysics and its relationship to experience: "The metaphysician first considers the intelligible structure of things . . . and the fundamental relationships between them." He considers the "categorical structure of empirical reality." The metaphysician seeks to "isolate and analyze abstractly the most general principles and categories" which inform our practical life, whether or not we are aware of them. This is not due to the determination of "purely subjective forms or categories"; rather, Copleston maintains, these categories are apprehended implicitly in experience.[27]

Several points are noteworthy in Copleston's depiction of the metaphysician's task. Restated, the task of the metaphysician is to abstract from the data of experience the intelligible, categorical structure of empirical reality; to analyze these resultant principles and categories of reality as revealed through experience; and to note their interrelationships with one another and with the realm of reality, seeking an adequate explanation of the latter consonant with the metaphysical principles already revealed.

The first element, that experience of the fact-world grounds metaphysical reflection, entails the second: namely, that not only does experience reveal the flux, but it also discloses through reflection upon experience, a stability, a core or substance which grounds and orders the flux. Thus, the real, common-sense world in which we are plunged reveals an intelligible order, which reason can grasp and articulate. There is an order to things, to the world—one that, furthermore, points to an orderer.

Third, while reflection upon experience discloses an orderly world, the ultimate ground of that order, the depths of the permanent things themselves, though affirmed by reason as real, is shrouded in mystery. It is one thing to know that the world is real, extra-mental, and intelligible; it is another thing to know the source of that order and the ultimate causes of things is a mystery that poses a limit to reason. This limit does not point to an irrational ground, but one that surpasses the power of finite reason. The mysterious ground of things points to an infinite that reason cannot comprehend, except to know that it is, not what it is.

Fourth, Thomist metaphysics is act-centered and dynamic, not static. It is existential in that its central point is not the radical essentialism or transcendental realism of Plato, or substance-centered metaphysics of Aristotle. Rather it affirms the act of existence as present to and realifying all beings.

Fifth, emerging out of the dynamic center of metaphysics is the reciprocal relation of permanence and change. Existents change, develop, perfect. They are capable of realizing their natures through change and development. Still, while changing, they retain their gravity of being, their substantial center, which orders the developmental process. Change should be according to the nature of things, thus reasonable, not according to caprice or the whim of the will. Change develops the permanent things, and yet preserves them when the change is according to the design of things.

Having sketched the metaphysical elements of Thomism, and drawn out of that sketch points for comparison with Burke, I shall turn to the presentation of Burke's metaphysics. But first I wish to consider the youthful Burke's initial encounter with philosophy.

The Young Burke and Philosophy

Before considering Burke's metaphysics it may be instructive to review what evidence there is for the influence of philosophy on the formation of Burke's thought. Indeed, this ground has been tilled before, and with considerable thoroughness by others. The "Thomist connection" in Burke's thought received articulation early on by Sir Ernest Barker who held that "Burke was always an Aristotelian, perhaps because he was also, even if unconsciously, a Thomist."[28] Even before Barker, Ewart Lewis discovered a connection between Aquinas and Burke on the theme of expediency in relationship to natural law, human laws and the importance of customs in obedience to laws.[29] Leo Strauss argued that Burke integrated the ideas of "the state of nature, of the rights of nature or of the rights of man, and of the social compact . . . into a classical or Thomistic framework."[30] Peter Stanlis went further and asserted that "a careful reading of the *Reflections* will reveal that Burke took his stand on the ground of Aristotle, Cicero, St. Thomas Aquinas, and the traditional conception of the Natural Law."[31] Like Stanlis, Canavan willingly acknowledged the influence of the Common Doctor on Burke, but he also admits that this influence is not directly cited by Burke. "But although there are strong reasons for believing," Canavan surmises, "that Burke had studied the Thomistic theory of natural law, and while the distinction between conditioned and unconditioned moral principles seems to be implicit in his writings, it is nowhere clearly explicated."[32]

The problem of a lack of evidence that Burke had direct acquaintance with Aquinas is taken on squarely by Wilkins. "Where the Thomistic reading of Burke is concerned," states Wilkins, "it must, however, be frankly acknowledged that there is no evidence either from the works of Burke or from the list of books in Burke's library of any firsthand acquaintance on his part with the writings of Aquinas."[33] This does not prevent Wilkins from concluding that "Textual and/or biographical evidence supports the thesis that save for Aquinas Burke had read the most important formulations of natural law doctrines, classical, Christian, and modern. . . ."[34] Moreover, it is clear to Wilkins from Burke's undergraduate readings of such works as "Franco Burgersdicii's *Institutionum Logicarum libro duo*, Eustachius's *Ethica, sive summa moralis disciplinae*, Martin Smiglecki's *Logica*, and Robert Sanderson's *De juramenti promissori obligatione* and *De obligatione conscientiae* . . . all in the Aristotelian-Thomistic tradition . . . that Burke, while he may never have read Aquinas, was nevertheless exposed to a warmed-over scholasticism."[35] Wilkins proceeds to the conclusion that "Burke's philosophy seems consonant with and, in some respects, perhaps ultimately derived from Thomism." Still, this conclusion is qualified by Wilkins: "But there is no concealing that despite significant resemblances there are significant differences as well, in doctrine or in emphasis."[36]

There is, though, direct evidence of both Burke's reading and appreciation of Aristotle. Arthur L. Woehl, in his study of "Burke's Readings," states that "Direct evidence of a wide reading in Aristotle . . . are frequent."[37] Burke refers to Aristotle in the *Speech on Conciliation with America* (1775) as "the great master of reasoning" (SCA II 170). Elsewhere he cites "an author who is more spoken of than read, I mean Aristotle."[38]

What of Burke's encounter with philosophy from his time as a student at Trinity College, Dublin? His first reference to the study of philosophy is to the work of Burgersdijck made in a letter to Richard Shackleton, his friend from his school days in Ballitore, whose father was the School Master, Abraham Shackleton. Richard was three years Burke's senior and, being of the Quaker faith, he was unable to continue Trinity College with Burke. The work by Burgersdijck is a textbook that is the only work in philosophy mentioned by Burke in his *Correspondence* while in College.[39] Thomas Copeland, general editor of Burke's *Correspondence*, identifies Franco Burgersdijck (1590–1635), as "a Dutch philosopher of the Rhamist school." His textbook "was first published in Leyden in 1626 and became an influential textbook . . ." (C I 4*n*2). Canavan elaborates on Burgersdijck's relationship to Peter Ramus: "According to Arthur Samuels and Canon Murray, Burgersdijck was a Ramist, that is a follower of Peter Ramus, who led a partial revolt against Aristotelian logic and is considered a forerunner of Bacon and Descartes."[40] As for Ramus, Copleston, in his *A History of Philosophy*, notes: "The artificial character of the Aristotelian-Scholastic logic was . . . insisted on by the famous French humanist Petrus Ramus or Pierre de la Ramee (1515–1572). . . . Men like . . . Petrus Ramus were strongly influenced by their reading of the classics, especially Cicero's writings. In comparison with Cicero's orations the logical works of Aristotle and the Scholastics seemed to them dry, abstruse and artificial."[41] Returning to Burgersdijck, Canavan, citing the authority of R. B. McDowell and D. A. Webb, contends that he "was in general an Aristotelian, although the school of the *Systematici* to which he belonged had been influenced by both sides in the Ramist controversy." Canavan claims that his own "examination of the text bears out their contention, because it shows that Burgersdijck quotes Aristotle too consistently to be hostile to him."[42]

The initial encounter with Burgersdijck's textbook was far from pleasing to Burke, as he writes to Richard Shackleton on May 24, 1774: "I am now . . . sitting at my own Bureau with Oh! hideous, Burgerdiscius"—Burke's latinized version of the author's name. Later in the letter, Burke continues: "Never Look Burgy in the face! By Jove th'thoughts divine, The Blackguard stuff, the hoard of exploded nonsense, the Scum of Pedantry, and the refuse of the Boghouse school-Philosophy, I assure you I stink of that Crabbed stuff as much as any vile fresh in the Uni. and I believe it will ruin me in my next Examination . . ." (C I 9). But some few weeks later Burke's study of Burgersdijck appears to have resulted in a profitable discipline of the mind, sufficient for him to speak now with approval in a letter to Richard Shackleton written on July 10, 1744: "but if you had read a little more of that Sprightly Dutch author Burgersdyck he would have taught you to have thrown your Syllogisms into a more concise method" (C I 28).

In an apparently subsequent letter to Shackleton, Burke claims "There is implanted in man (Doubtless for a good end) an insatiable Desire of truth we spare no pains in search of it . . ." (C I 44). Granted, this brings to mind Aristotle's famous opening lines of the *Metaphysics*, "All men by nature desire to know." Still, Aristotle receives from the young Burke a harsh rebuke. In the same letter he writes of "how justly do we admire at the Credulity and Sottishness of mankind who for many ages without further Examination swallowed down all the Errors and absurdities of Aristotle, and those not the mean and vulgar but even the greatest and Wisest men" (C I 45).

Despite the disparaging aside to Aristotle, Burke makes fervent use of syllogistic reasoning in a letter dated March 19, 1744/45, to refute a position of Shackleton's over a theological question, "whether God can sin. . . ." Shackleton had apparently, according to Burke, reasoned as follows: "God cannot Lye, to Lye is to sin therefore God cannot sin. The Sophistry," Burke argues, "is apparent, for Lying is not every Sin, tho all lies may be Sins, and tho a man may be a murtherer" (C I 49). Burke reasons further, but it is sufficient to show that, presumably, the study of the "Sprightly Dutch author Burgersdyck" has taken hold of Burke's reasoning powers. So, it should be no surprise to hear Burke write to Shackleton on July 12, 1746, that he is "deep in Metaphysics and poetry" (C I 68).

We must realize that the youthful Burke is brimming with curiosity and full of new knowledge, although with, as he himself allows, little depth. Again to Richard Shackleton on October 15, 1744 Burke offers this self-assessment:

> knowledge is Doubtless the greatest acquisition we can make because it is what Denominates us men and as you remark'd is the most essential difference between us and the brute-Beasts. I shall say no more about it, for fear I should be ask'd the question why I don't follow what I so much approve and be more Studious? Perhaps bona videoque proboque deteriora sequor [which the editors translate from Ovid: "I see and approve the good; I follow the worse"] is applicable to me. I know what is Good like the Athenians, but Don't practise like the Lacaedemonians. What would not I give to have my spirits a little more settled? I am too giddy, this is the bane of my life, it hurries me from my Studies to triffles and I am afraid it will hinder me from knowing any thing thoroughly. I have a Superficial knowledge of many things but Scarce the bottom of any [C I 32].

We do not have to take Burke's self-assessment at face value, for as a student of merely fifteen years of age he is certainly far from destitute of learning.

Although Burke considered his own knowledge superficial he did see himself as having a passion for learning. Taking a retrospective look at a period of two years at Trinity, he reviews his own development in the following terms in a letter to Richard Shackleton dated March 21, 1746/1747:

> I have often thought it a humorous consideration, to observe and sum up all the madnesses of this Kind I have fallen into this two years past—First I was greatly taken with natural philosophy which while I should have given my mind to Logic, employed me incessantly this I call my furor Mathematicus, but this worked off as soon as I begun to read it in the College, as men by repletion cast all off their Stomachs all they have eat then I turned back to logic and Metaphysics here I remained a good while and with much pleasure. And this was my furor logicus. A disease very common in the days of ignorance, and very uncommon in these enlightened times [C I 89].

It takes no great interpretive skill to recognize that while Burke's first encounter with textbook philosophy evoked considerable fulminations about "the hoard of exploded nonsense, the Scum of Pedantry, and the refuse of the Boghouse school-Philosophy," it was not long before he was commending what earlier he exclaimed to be "hideous, Burgerdiscius," to his logically erring friend, Richard Shackleton, and that some years later he writes of having studied logic and metaphysics "with much pleasure."

We have cited Wilkins' summation of Burke's study of philosophy as an undergraduate, and reviewed Burke's own correspondence, but Francis Canavan has engaged in the most in-depth study of the subject. Canavan reached the following conclusions:

> Burke may be taken to have studied while at Trinity College, the textbooks of seven writers on philosophy. Two of these, Puffendorf and Le Clerc, represent a rather early stage of the sensism and rationalism which came to full flower in France during Burke's own lifetime. The other authors, Burgersdijck, Smiglecki, Baron, Eustache de St. Paul, and Sanderson, represent in

varying degrees the scholastic tradition of medieval Christian Aristotelianism.[43]

Canavan holds that such a background provides grounds for identifying sources of Burke's purported " 'Thomism' in his college education." Choosing to err on the side of caution, Canavan takes a temperate stance: "Yet it would be rash to suggest that Edmund Burke graduated from Trinity College a scholastic philosopher," or embraced an explicit form of scholasticism, viz., Thomism.[44] Still Burke without doubt was exposed to textbooks in philosophy that reflected scholastic and Aristotelian influences, and such works were consciously incorporated into, and helped shape, Burke's thought. And, further, Burke acknowledged the benefit of his studies in philosophy, including metaphysics.

Burke's Metaphysics

In remarking that the metaphysical tradition with which Burke's philosophy is most compatible is that of the perennial philosophy of the Aristotelian-Thomistic tradition with its moderate realism,[45] it is appropriate to underscore the word "compatible." Burke is not a systematic philosopher, and certainly not a speculative philosopher. Yet he recognizes the legitimate role of the metaphysician and relies upon and makes use of fundamental metaphysical principles throughout his works. He writes that "it is the business of the speculative philosopher to mark the proper ends of government. It is the business of the politician, who is the philosopher in action, to find out proper means towards those ends, and to employ them with effect" (TPD I 530).[46] Despite his objections to certain kinds of metaphysics, this statement affirms Burke's appreciation of the legitimate province of the metaphysician.

There is no prescribed definition of metaphysics in Burke's writings. There is, though, a warning against too much inquiry into the ultimate foundations of reality, and of society in particular. "The foundations on which obedience to governments is founded," Burke records, "are not to be constantly discussed. That we are and here, supposes the discussion already made and the dispute settled."[47] Those who constantly set about to inquire into ultimate principles too often serve to undermine what those principles help to secure. Our allegiance to our domicile, to our community, and to our nation are not to be obtained by a rational assent to a philosophically extolled principle, but through our natural feelings and sentiments. But this is not to denigrate wisdom, or man's love of the same. For Burke there was never a "jar or discord between genuine sentiment and sound policy. Never, no never, did Nature say one thing and Wisdom say another" (3LRP V 407). Instead, Burke is incensed by the prying intellect that seeks to elevate an individual's reason against the ancestral wisdom of generations, especially if that individual prides himself in discovering previously undiscovered principles. The assumption here is not that knowledge fails to develop and deepen its grasp upon reality, but that the principles which guide reason have already been discovered and defended. "We know that *we* have made no discoveries," Burke concludes in the *Reflections*, "and we think that no discoveries are to be made, in morality,—nor many in the great principles of government, nor in the ideas of liberty, which were understood long before we were born altogether as well as they will be after the grave has heaped its mould upon our presumption, and the silent tomb shall have imposed its law on our pert loquacity" (RF III 345). Later, in the same work, Burke reasons: "Those whose principle it is to despise the ancient, permanent sense of mankind, and to set up a scheme of society on new principles must naturally expect that such of us who think better of the judgment of the human race than of theirs should consider both them and their devices as men and schemes upon their trial" (RF III 450). Therefore, to presume the discovery of new principles governing reason is to presume ignorance over the basic principles upon which all reason and societies rest.

Man's humility is increased through the recognition wisdom brings to him, namely, that reality in its infinity transcends the limits of the human mind. This recognition is not to terminate the increase of knowledge; rather, it is to evoke a fundamental awe and a sense of piety over the limitless range of reality. "We fear God; we look up with awe to kings, with affection to Parliaments, with duty to magistrates, with reverence to priests, and with respect to nobility. Why? Because, when such ideas are brought before our minds, it is *natural* to be so affected" (RF III 345–46). It is this reason, not an anti-intellectualism on Burke's part, that leads him to warn against searching for new foundations or principles of government. The search for wisdom should inspire a reverential awe.

Burke's love for wisdom is obvious. Many saw in him one of the oustanding intellects of England for his time. Samuel Johnson remarks: "Yes; Burke *is* an extraordinary man. His stream of mind is perpetual."[48] Yet Burke resents an investigative type of search for knowledge, as one who seeks to solve a problem. There is a sense of mystery that surrounds Burke's own inquiry concerning the ultimate principles of reality disclosed to reason, a sense that tells him that as he searches for knowledge, he draws most near not only to the sustaining principles of society but to the Deity himself (ANW IV 166). Concerning human society, Burke calls attention in the *Reflections* to "the disposition of a stupendous wisdom, moulding together the great mysterious incorporation of the human race" (RF III 275). Writing of Providence in the *Inquiry* he claims that God's "wisdom is not our wisdom, nor our ways his ways" (ISB I 115). He also refers to "the dispensations of a mysterious wisdom" (RF III 338). Obviously, God's Providence exceeds our comprehension, and is shrouded in mystery, hence evoking faith and "faith is not contrary to reason, but above it," Burke remarks (C VI 228).

This appreciation of the ultimate mystery surrounding one's inquiry is certainly part of the Thomistic tradition. Earlier we noted Maritain's distinction between mystery and problem. Evidently for Burke and for Maritain metaphysical inquiry does not eliminate the central aspect of mystery. This gives a good insight into what to many appears to be Burke's anti-rationalism.

Although he is highly skeptical of the fruits of speculative inquiry, especially those which bear on the existing social conditions of man, he gives little doubt concerning the steady and august principles that sustain reality, however cloaked they may be in the depths of God's being. Burke even links physical causes with moral duties: "The instincts which give rise to this mysterious process of Nature are not of our making. But out of physical causes, unknown to us, perhaps unknowable, arise moral duties, which, as we are able perfectly to comprehend, we are bound indispensably to perform" (ANW IV 166). Burke would find agreement with Maritain's statement that a "philosophy unaware of mystery would not be a philosophy."[49]

Burke, as is clear in the *Inquiry*, does not lack a concern for the first causes and fundamental nature of reality. Aristotle sees metaphysics as dealing with the first principles of all reality, and Burke's thought consistently embraces and reflects the use and knowledge of certain of these principles. These principles or causes for the realist philosopher are obtained, Copleston notes, through an interpretation and understanding of the data of experience.[50] "The Metaphysician," continues Copleston, "first considers the intelligible structure of things . . . and the fundamental relationships between them."[51] He considers the "categorical structure of empirical reality." The metaphysician seeks to "isolate and analyze abstractly the most general principles and categories" which inform our practical lives, whether or not we are aware of them. This is not due to the determination of "purely subjective forms or categories;" rather, these categories are apprehended implicitly in experience.[52]

Several points are noteworthy in Copleston's depiction of the metaphysician's task. Restated, the task of the metaphysician is to abstract from the data of experience the intelligible, categorical structure of empirical reality; to analyze these resultant principles and categories of reality as revealed through experience; and to note their interrelationships with one another and with the realm of reality, seeking an adequate explanation of the latter consonant with the metaphysical principles already revealed.

What are these intelligible structures of reality for Burke? If any intelligible aspect of reality reveals itself to Burke it is that of change and stability, so interwoven as to display an invariable order in reality. That there is a structure to reality, a structure which accommodates change (in itself a metaphysical principle) allows the intelligibility and the reasonableness of things manifesting themselves to the human intellect. The unfolding or development of reality within the structures of the universe demonstrates a constancy of design and purpose. Change and development are not the result of caprice or chance. This would be unreasonable, as reason reveals itself for Burke through order. Consequently, he can say that "whatever has its origin in caprice is sure not to improve in its progress, nor to end in reason" (3LRP V 459).[53] This statement has ready application to the order and structure of all reality, although it occurs within the context of what he sees to be the mindlessness of the French Revolution. Order does not imply a static order, but *structured* change, in which certain principles and realities retain their essential sameness, yet accommodate and order the necessary changes of reality. This structure discloses a divine order, prompting Burke to claim: "I know there is an order that keeps things fast in their place: it is made to us, and we are made to it."[54] This order is not without purpose or design, a notion to be taken up later when we come to Burke's teleology.

This Burkean emphasis upon order is not the refuge of an antiquarian conservative. The old is not to be preserved simply for its own sake. The appellation "pure conservative" as Whitehead applies it when he writes, "The pure conservative is fighting against what is the essence of the universe," cannot be assigned to Burke.[55] If Whitehead means that the essence of the universe is process, the conclusion follows that the conservative is one who resists change and who resists process. This is clearly not the case with Burke, who affirms change without embracing it as coterminous with reality. Burke writes, "We must all obey the great law of change. It is the most powerful law of Nature, and the means perhaps of its conservation."[56] Burke accentuates change, yet grounds it in the enduring essence of things. The concepts of essence and substance refer to the abiding, stable features of the universe.

Burke's philosophy both in its application to the universe in general and politics specifically demonstrates a balanced view of change moderated by stability. In referring to the theories of Parliament, he lauds the principle of renovation that attends to the "union of permanence and change," declaring "that in all our changes we are never wholly new." Yet there is to be "enough of the new to invigorate us," that we "may have the advantage of change without the imputation of inconstancy."[57]

Most of Burke's utilization of the concepts of change and

stability is to be drawn from his political concerns. Yet he makes it clear that political reality "is placed in a just correspondence and symmetry with the order of the world, and with the mode of existence decreed to a permanent body composed of transitory parts." In this vein he writes of "a condition of unchangeable constancy," which, "by preserving the method of nature in the conduct of the state, in what we improve, we are never wholly new; in what we retain, we are never wholly obsolete" (RF III 275). Thus, the metaphysical elements of change and stability or permanence are to be found in both the physical and the political realm of the universe for Burke. The interplay of change and stability results in an orderly universe.

Change, with the aid of human wisdom, must be orderly and almost imperceptible. Slow change avoids what Burke considers the inconveniences of mutation. Yet this governance of change, this attempt to moderate its speed and impact, is not to bridle an otherwise fast flow of nature; rather, it is to temper change according to nature's way. This position is confirmed by Burke in the following statement: "It would be wise to attend upon the order of things, and not to attempt to outrun the slow, but smooth and even course of Nature."[58]

Change is not to be radical, or nihilating. It is to be ordered. The term "development" helps clarify the use of the word "change" in this instance. Development implies that there is or should be an orderliness to change, not a random or dissociated series of events succeeding one another in a chaotic or annihilating fashion. Burke's "law of change" suggests the development of possibilities through expansion and growth. Change should improve and preserve. That which exists, whether it be man, society, the nation, or social institution should be altered and developed if a static, atrophied world is to be avoided, yet without violence to essential structures. For example, each man should seek to improve through knowledge and virtue, but without violence to his rational human nature. Yet, throughout these changes, something remains abiding, substantially and essentially unchanged.

Burke's thought is replete with many concepts utilized in traditional metaphysics. He often speaks of "essences" and "substances" and "natures."[59] He writes of categories, quantity, change, habit, and alteration, in addition to his use of Aristotelian-Thomistic concepts used in ethical works, such as cardinal virtues, moderation, temperance, etc. But more than that, he gives these terms the same sense as that given in a realist metaphysics. He recoils from any theory of evolution, process, or historicism which might suggest the inevitability of progress. If such theories also call for the rejection of essences or natures as something static and recalcitrant to change, Burke refuses this point as well. It is this emphasis upon change analogously applied to the social realm that the revolutionary *philosophes* see as written into the very nature of things, a law born to bear fruit, fruit generated from the corruptible ruins of monarchy. It is, as Burke interprets the thought of the radical French ideologues, as if the active principle of reality is to assert itself in society and politics through force, enterprise, and talent without the tempering restraint of a passive principle. This is change incarnate without restraint; for Burke such change spells chaos rather than order.

Burke's sensitivity to the proper use of a conceptual framework is apparent. In formulating a principle of change, or, as applied to the political realm, a principle of reformation, he writes, "I would not exclude alteration neither; but even when I changed, it should be to preserve" (RF III 561–62). The use of the term "alteration" suggests a qualitative change, whereby the substance of a thing is modified, perfected, or further determined. Burke continues, "I would make the reparation as nearly as possible in the style of the building" (RF III 562). That is, the abiding essence is to be sustained, but not without the qualitative improvement thereof.

The problem of change and stability relates to the notion of substances, essences, and natures. It is necessary to deepen our understanding of the metaphysics of change and stability through a review of Burke's use of these terms which suggest an intelligible structure of reality. This review will better be served by a contrast with the empiricist tradition which informed the intellectual milieu of Burke's time and impressed the *philosophes* of the French Enlightenment, such as Voltaire, Condillac, Diderot, d'Holbach, and d'Alembert.

In light of the growth of empiricist philosophy, especially in

England after Locke, one might expect Locke's meaning of substance to infuse that of Burke. This is not the case. When Locke uses the term "substance," it carries with it the idea of a substratum, foundation or support for qualities. This use of the term brings to mind the idea of substance as pincushion.[60] The idea of substance as a support for accidents or qualities is not that of Aristotle, Aquinas, or Burke. Rather than standing under, evoking the spatial imagery that it does, substance in the realist tradition is more of a permeation of the entire entity. Substance for Aquinas "means the ultimate subject which is not predicated of any other thing," but which is capable of being modified through individual, accidental perfections. The subject referred to here "is the particular individual in the genus of substance. In another usage," Aquinas continues, "substance means the form or nature of the subject."[61] Whereas for Locke, the substance lies beyond experience as an unknown substratum, for Aquinas substance is a distinction made within the total data of experience.[62] It is unnecessary to observe a thing called a "substance" or an "essence"; rather, it is possible to discover aspects of metaphysical import within the data of experience itself. Hume says "the idea of a substance . . . is nothing but a collection of simple ideas that are united by the imagination and have a particular name assigned them."[63] How does this compare with Burke?

For philosophers in the empiricist tradition the language of metaphysical substances becomes superfluous and lacking in the kind of empirical evidence their epistemology demands. Burke, on the other hand, while constantly and everywhere asking us to consult our experience, and wary of an *a priori*, deductionistic metaphysics, does not discount as unreal essences or substances due to their abstract metaphysical character. It is not simply the abstract character of speculative thought which Burke discounts, for, as the following statement on abstract ideas indicates, taken from his *Speech on the Petition of the Unitarians* (1792), to ignore in *a priori* fashion abstract thought is to remove the light of reason.

> I do not put abstract ideas wholly out of any question; because I well know that under that name I should dismiss principles, and

that without the guide and light of sound, well-understood principles, all reasonings in politics, as in everything else, would be only a confused jumble of particular facts and details, without the means of drawing out any sort of theoretical or practical conclusion [W VII 41].

Burke's use of substance, essence, and nature, along with the realist school of metaphysics, shows that something may be altered or modified without being essentially changed. Regarding the state, Burke discovers its basic moral purpose: "The state, in its essence, must be moral and just. . . ." Innumerable aspects concerning the state may change or vary according to time, circumstance and place, but a state must embody in its essence morality and justice or it is simply usurpation and tyranny (1LRP V 325). Commenting in his *Speech on the Plan for Economical Reform* (1780) on the essence of a nation, he notes the substantial and enduring presence of a commonwealth amid the passage of generations: "Individuals pass like shadows; but the commonwealth is fixed and stable. The difference, therefore, of today and tomorrow, which to private people is immense, to the state is nothing" (W II 330). The essence of a commonwealth includes the people yet it is more. It includes the people as morally linked to one another through various associations, groupings, and incorporations. In a passage from his *First Letter on a Regicide Peace* (1796), Burke seeks to identify the essence of the French nation. It is not mere locality. It includes the "majesty of [the] throne . . . [the] dignity of [the] nobility . . . the sanctity of [the] clergy" and various other associations and "the respect due to [the] movable substance represented by the corporations of the kingdom. All these particular *moleculae* united form the great mass of what is truly the body politic in all countries" (1LRP V 326). The essence of a nation is more than the several identifiable parts separately open for inspection. There is a unity that permeates and grafts the parts together, that remains intact beyond the separate existence of the several parts themselves. For Burke, the "nation is a moral essence, not a geographical arrangement, or a denomination of the nomenclator" (1LRP V 326). France, for instance, transcends simple space and time. He declares that "France is out of her bounds, but the kingdom is the same" (1LRP V 326). Still, the essence of a nation is not different from but includes all the duties, stations, property, social classes, and beliefs that comprise it.

Burke's use of the concept essence brings forth the following conclusions: first, essence is that which identifies and renders distinct an entity; second, essence endures specifically unchanged throughout time; third, it is not separate from, or identifiable with, any of its particular parts, yet it permeates and unifies these parts into a substantial whole. This places Burke's notion of essence firmly within the realist tradition.

As we have seen, Burke's metaphysics indicates the inclusion of two fundamental principles: change and stability. In the tradition of realism the principles accounting for change and stability, according to whether the change is partial or substantial, include the following: partial change entails the principles or components of substance and accidents, and substantial change entails those of substantial form and prime matter. No such combination of principles is developed by Burke. Yet Burke's recognition and respect for the lawfulness of reality, its ordered dimensions, and the principles that fix our nature and guide our actions indicate his concern with principles of change and stability. And his recommendation of the Aristotelian list of categories to the *philosophes* would suggest some familiarity with the metaphysics of the Stagyrite (RF III 478). Burke's recognition that there are principles permeating the very substance of our being is evident when, in the context of writing about the principles of morality and politics, in a letter to Dr. William Markham, November 9, 1771, he states: "The principles that guide us in public and private, as they are not of our devising, but moulded into the nature and essence of things, will endure with the sun and the moon" (C II 282). The principles of change and stability, substance, essence, and nature vitalize Burke's political philosophy, even though he generally does not attempt to develop a metaphysical analysis of these principles, typically accepting them as premises of his thought. There are some few exceptions to this generality, such as those occurring in the *Inquiry* as discussed previously. What he does do is to show the result of incorrectly held principles, especially for society.

The points made thus far about Burke's metaphysics and the conceptual framework employed are not simply noteworthy but pivotal to an understanding of his philosophy. Burke's universe is not a static, ossified universe of sheer permanence. It is a changing, yet orderly universe and the metaphysical elements of his thought reflect this order and change. His metaphysics is developmental, assimilating change, and allowing for the actualization or realization of the essential structures of reality, be they such as the improvement of man's essential rationality through increased wisdom, or the directing of the commonwealth toward increased good or virtue, hence further realizing its moral essence. Burke's framework of order is not meant to inhibit change, but rather to found it upon the timeless principles that govern nature and, when applied to nations, to the political system.

This is important for an understanding of his metaphysics and also for seeing its value in Burke's critique of the *philosophes*. The *philosophes*, advocating the natural rights of the people, were often opposed to both the religious and the political institutions of their times, and their thought is seen to be at least partly responsible for the turning from monarchy to bourgeois democracy. Burke believed that their atheistic principles destroyed the morality of, especially, the young: "But I have observed that the philosophers in order to insinuate their polluted Atheism into young minds, systematically flatter all their passions natural and unnatural" (C VI 270). For them, surely no realist philosophy, saturated with substances and essences at the heart of things, could capture the dynamic, constant change and flow of reality. Amongst the *philosophes* Denis Diderot is instructive on this point. Diderot maintains that nature is not static but is ever being born anew. In raising certain "Questions" in his work *On the Interpretation of Nature* he writes that if phenomena are not linked, there can be no philosophy. "But if the state of this world of phenomena is one of perpetual change, if nature is still at work on it, then despite the chain that links all phenomena, there can still be no philosophy."[64] Immediately the false dichotomy rises up as one between seeing nature to be static or to be in change, with no middle ground. Diderot's thought denies philosophy the power to provide a categorical interpretation of nature. He rejects any interpretation which admits permanence and stability, while acknowledging development. Instead, Diderot's concept of nature is one of flux and change, ever new and never old. Surely for him no realist philosophy would accommodate such horizons, enmeshed as it appears to be in a static conception of the world as governed and stagnated by a transcendent realm of fixed, immutable essences.

The view of a metaphysical realism that places essences snugly away in a transcendent realm is more consonant with what may be termed the radical essentialism of Plato than the realism of the Aristotle-Aquinas lineage. Aquinas notes "the opinion of Plato, who asserted that the species of things subsisted separately from singular things."[65] For Aristotle and Aquinas the species informs the actual material substance, so denying any metaphysical gulf between the concrete entity and its form. For Plato the sensible world of change and flux is the shadow world of unreality, a faint glimmer of the immutable realm of essence or forms. As discussed earlier, this type of transcendent essentialism is typically and wrongfully seen as most representative of realist philosophy, which invariably gives rise to a static, changeless conception of reality.[66] If anything has emerged through our study of Burke to this point, it should be that he accommodates both change and stability. There is nothing static about his conception of reality in an absolute sense. His metaphysics does provide a framework for change, a change which does not overthrow the timeless and eternal principles of reality or the essences of actual existents, but a change that seeks to improve, to renew, and to perfect these existents.

The real is not a ceaseless, ever new and changing flux; nor is it timeless with a realm of essences aloof from mutability. Things of this world do not gain their reality through some mysterious participation in Platonic Forms. Essences inform and permeate the material realm before us. Yet they do not so determine things as to preclude change within the material existent itself, or, by analogy, within the physical and social order within a commonwealth.

In referring to Burke's conception of essences we have so far generally employed examples from the social order. Thus, Burke's understanding of essences has occurred primarily in the context of discussions on nations and commonwealths. The use of analogy is in operation here because of the difference between the essence of an actual, physical existent and that of a commonwealth. Burke notes this difference when he writes that "commonwealths are not physical, but moral essences. They are artificial combinations, and, in their proximate efficient cause, the arbitrary productions of the human mind" (1LRP V 234). This artificiality does violence neither to the commonwealth nor to the human nature, since it is a tenet of Burke's philosophy that "art is man's nature." So, in producing the commonwealth man helps realize his social nature. And in seeking to understand Burke's metaphysics we are not being misleading to use examples from the social and political order—the focal point of Burke's thought—as he finds reality and its principles analogous between the natural and the social order; between the order of the universe decreed by God, and man.[67]

Room for realization of what one essentially is and potentially can be allows for improvement, as well as degeneration. The fabric of Burke's metaphysics is so suffused with the elements of change and stability as to ensure that "in what we improve we are never wholly new, in what we retain we are never wholly obsolete" (RF III 275). Here surfaces another principle of improvement, further securing the developmental aspect of Burke's metaphysics. This principle is mentioned by Burke in the context of his discussion of the idea of inheritance as including a principle of improvement. In considering inheritance he notes that it secures what it acquires while leaving acquisition free. He refers to this and other principles, such as the one of conservation and transmission, as being maxims upon which the state may proceed. These principles are not solely those of politics, somehow divorced from nature. The state's following of these principles makes its actions analogous to the "pattern of Nature" (RF III 275). And here emerges still another component of Burke's metaphysics, his principle of analogy. Together these principles further clarify the more fundamental ones of change and stability. Just as nature struggles, falls, and improves, so does society. Neither man nor nature starts each day and age *de novo*. Instead, both build on what has gone before, and in building sustain, in sustaining renew. To understand this concept, it will help to look more closely at Burke's position on analogy and to see its importance for understanding his overall metaphysics.

Burke speaks of "the spirit of philosophic analogy" in the context of the idea of inheritance as a factor of social stability. Although he does not specifically discuss "philosophic analogy," he brings this concept forward in the midst of a passage replete with analogies drawn between the "order of the world" and the "method of Nature" (RF III 275). It is important to note these analogies in order to see that Burke's metaphysics bears directly on his political philosophy. It should further our conviction that the language of substance, essence, and nature used in a social or political context by Burke is not removed from, but is the outgrowth of his understanding of reality. These concepts reflect a coherent picture of reality, a reality not speculatively bifurcated from the lived-world of politics, but one that is fundamentally consistent. A review of some of Burke's uses of analogy will be of assistance here.

In *Reflections*, Burke draws parallels with the political scheme of things and nature in five separate references. In succession he refers to the political and social policy of entailed inheritance as the "happy effect of following Nature, which is wisdom without reflection, and above it"; to "a constitutional policy working after the pattern of Nature . . ."; to "the institutions of policy . . . [and] the gifts of Providence" as being handed down "in the same course and order" to the "political system . . . placed in a just correspondence and symmetry with the order of the world"; and, finally, to "a conformity to Nature in our artificial institutions" (RF III 274–76). There is no explication of the meaning of analogy as used here by Burke, but it is apparent that the natural realm and the political realm are analogous to each other in that each reveals a method or design that is orderly yet alterable. We will see later that the ultimate source of order and change transcends this world, yet is present to it, this being God. "Decay, fall, renovation, and progression" are the possible alterations that occur in nature and in the state. This discussion is useful in that it helps demonstrate that metaphysical principles such as those of change and stability, substance and essence, which are grounded in reality, find a ready application to politics for Burke.

All of this is not to deny Burke's guarded use of analogies, especially as providing premises from which to reason. This is particularly the case when the analogies sought are those which occur between physical bodies and political bodies, implying an organicist theory of the state. Burke warns: "I am not of the opinion that the race of men, and the commonwealths they create, like the bodies of individuals, grow effete and languid and bloodless, and ossify, by the necessities of their own conformation, and the fatal operation of longevity and time. These analogies between bodies natural and politic, though they may sometimes illustrate, furnish no argument of themselves."[68] Obviously, Burke wishes to avoid here an analogy that implies that unlike physical bodies, which are destined to grow, then decline and fade away, such may not necessarily be the case with political bodies. Nonetheless, this specific use of an analogy does not invalidate Burke's use of analogy between the method of nature and the social order as Burke makes clear above.

My focus to this point has been upon the elements of change and stability, substances and essences in Burke's metaphysics. It is a fact that individual existents have an essence lending intelligibility to reality. Yet, as we have seen, in recognizing the substantial and essential character of reality, Burke did not slight change as a basic law of nature. This emphasis on change gives a primacy to existence as dynamic activity in Burke's thought. This is not to say that reality is change or process, and nothing more. It is not to deny that things have essences reflecting a stable presence in beings.[69] The effect of Burke's position that the "law of nature is change" is to place a primacy on existence as active as opposed to an essentialism which focuses upon the fixed and static properties of being, to the detriment of its active and dynamic character. To emphasize either extreme, that of existence or that of essence, to the exclusion of either principle is to misrepresent and arbitrarily divide being against itself. This is why the recognition of the primacy of existence as active in Burke's thought is so crucial. The failure to recognize existence as active and dynamic is to risk falling prey to a view of Burke as either a reactionary or a status quo conservative. For this to be the case would be entirely to contradict the thrust of Burke's metaphysics. He holds that change is the dynamic and active aspect of being, and this aspect received first place in Burke's assessment of reality.[70]

Why is this recognition central to things so crucial to our understanding of Burke? It is crucial in that, with a lack of sustained philosophical argumentation on Burke's part, one is forced to isolate those metaphysical principles which occur here and there throughout his various works. Nowhere is there to be found in Burke an explicit anticipation of philosophical existentialism. In part, through the prism of existentialism and from the vantage point of our century, one can better note the emphasis upon actual, concrete existence by Burke. His very hesitancy about all philosophizing and about metaphysics, in particular, is over losing one's intellect in a swirl of abstractions and universals that are peculiar to essentialism. One cannot ignore theory, granted; but one must shun a theory that separates man from existence. This is a recurring theme in Burke. It is this understanding of existence that makes Burke's conservatism different from a conservatism too enthralled with the structures of reality. Although Burke emphasizes order and structures, it is to preserve and ensure the smooth and even flow of change and the direction of the same, rather than to praise order for order's sake.

Yet Burke's "existentialism" is quite unlike a Sartrean view in which existence precedes and determines essence through a freely chosen project. For Burke, in a manner that Maritain would find compatible with his view of existentialism, no existent exists independently of essence, just as no change exists without stability.[71] Beyond this, it is almost impossible to read Burke without beginning to force a philosophical mold upon him foreign to his thought. This understanding of Burke's metaphysics is pivotal to a comprehension of his political philosophy and conservatism. Burke's is a conserving conservatism, not a status quo or reactionary conservatism. His metaphysics reveals an existentialist thrust in that change and activity receive preeminent consideration, and that man is considered in his concrete and historical condition. Yet this is tempered by an accommodation and recognition that existing things have a determinate characteristic about them, a "whatness" that specifically marks kinds of things off from one another. Essences render things intelligible, yet, and Burke notes this danger well, their very intelligibility easily leads the intellect not firmly grounded in existence into a world of abstractions. Thus, Burke claims in *Speech on Conciliation with America* (1775), "Abstract liberty, like other mere abstractions, is not to be found" (SCA II 120).

This brings us near the heart of Burke's metaphysical argument for freedom and liberty.[72] One realizes one's existence in the fullness of freedom by becoming what one most essentially is. Other philosophers feel that it is the rejection of "metaphysical essences" that liberates man and allows him to become that which he chooses to be. In contemporary philosophy Maritain refers to Sartre's "project" as the existentialists' equivalent of essence.[73] But for Burke, "Man is made for Speculation and action; and when he pursues his nature he succeeds best in both" (NB 87). Here, the elements of the metaphysics of change and stability are drawn together in a unified manner. The freedom of an individual, or analogically, a nation, is obtained through activity in accord with one's nature. Burke's philosophy consistently sustains this position, echoing the realist precept that "action follows nature." This is the matrix of a Burkean metaphysics with an emphasis upon the primacy of change in the context of order.

A radical spirit of freedom is often conjoined with a rejection of essences, and this spirit Burke found in the French radicals. For Burke "the spirit of freedom [leads] in itself to misrule and excess" (RF III 276). There is a hierarchy of existence that not only unveils to man his true interests, but his place in the universe itself. And his place is not above or outside of society, in a pre-social state of nature, and possessing a hypothetical freedom. His place is essentially an integral part of the commonwealth where the individual neither reigns supreme, nor is swallowed up by Leviathan, or the commonwealth, or by the levelling spirit of the *philosophes*. Here Burke's metaphysics clearly vitalizes his political philosophy.

Both Burke and the *philosophes* place great emphasis upon change. Yet the latter, as Burke construes their thought, are more expectant of a change that brings inevitable progress, a change more likely to shed the mantle of the past as so much unwanted baggage. In order to understand more fully Burke's metaphysics, it is necessary to take a representative view of the *philosophes* whose thought is in opposition to that of Burke. It is also necessary to note the influence of Locke on the French *philosophes*.

Among certain of the *philosophes* the rejection of essences appears akin to the rejection of metaphysics conjoined with empiricist tenets. This anti-metaphysical impulse for Enlightenment thinkers such as Diderot, d'Holbach, and d'Alembert, leads them to castigate metaphysics for going beyond the bounds of what can be verified by sense experience. As Baron d'Holbach writes in *The System of Nature*, "matter alone is capable of acting on our senses, and without this action nothing would be capable of making itself known to us."[74] Despite Burke's suspicion of the *philosophes* as embracing a rationalistic, deductive metaphysics, many Enlightenment thinkers had been quite taken by Locke's empiricist philosophy, and the success of science and the experimental method.[75] Of course, to designate Locke as an empiricist is not to deny his use of a deductive methodology at times. Obviously, one of Locke's proofs for God's existence starts with an intuitive grasp of the self from which he proceeds by deduction to the rational assent to God's existence.[76] Nevertheless, the mention of Locke's influence is not to deny the rationalism of the *philosophes* for, as Seamus F. Deane remarks, Burke's "attitude had to clash with the plain reason of the *philosophes*, for whom the world was in its essence rational, and, therefore, the true and only home of man. To them Nature was predictable, given sufficient knowledge; to Burke it was esoteric, no matter how extensive human knowledge was."[77]

Locke had a powerful influence upon the French *philosophe* Jean d'Alembert. He announced that "Locke undertook and successfully carried through what Newton found impossible. It can be said that he created metaphysics almost as Newton had created physics."[78]

Now it is true that d'Alembert disparaged "metaphysics" declaring "that this title will soon become an insult for our men of intelligence, as the name 'sophist', degraded by those who bore it in Greece, was rejected by true philosophers, even though it means 'a sage.' "[79] On the other hand, d'Alembert held that Locke "reduced metaphysics to what it really ought to be: the experimental physics of the soul."[80]

Metaphysics for d'Alembert is indeed a "physics of the soul." It is, in truth, a philosophy of mind for him. This reflects the aim of philosophy for d'Alembert, which is "[t]otally immersed in the analysis of our perceptions. . . ."[81] This further shows d'Alembert's restriction of science, "as much as possible, to facts and to consequences deduced from them. . . ."[82] Metaphysics, therefore, insofar as it can lay claim to being a science, and it is only as a science that it can claim certainty, is restricted to the "facts" of the mind, which are universal. D'Alembert holds that "Reasonable metaphysics can only consist, as does experimental physics, in the careful assembling of all these facts, in reducing them to a corpus of information, in explaining some by others, and in distinguishing those which ought to hold the first rank and serve as the foundation. In brief," d'Alembert concludes, "the principles of metaphysics, which are as simple as axioms, are the same for the philosophers as for the general run of people."[83]

"Reasonable metaphysics" for d'Alembert is not the same as classical, Aristotelian-Thomistic metaphysics. For instance, d'Alembert rejects any knowledge of metaphysical essences or natures, referring to these as the "occult qualities" of the scholastics,[84] maintaining, instead, that metaphysics must either remain in vain speculations or illusions, or become a science of facts: " 'Not only do we not know the nature of each being in particular, we do not even have any clear knowledge of the *nature* of that being in itself.' "[85]

In sum, for d'Alembert the realm of phenomena and the empirically verifiable impose a limit to our knowledge; and "essences" and "natures" suggest an airy flight into the unverifiable.[86]

Baron d'Holbach similarly rejects metaphysics, holding in his *System of Nature* that "Matter is eternal, and necessary, but its forms are evanescent and contingent."[87] And what of man, asks d'Holbach? "[I]s he any thing more than matter combined, of which the form varies every instant?"[88] While d'Holbach believes we cannot finally answer the question of whether man is simultaneously eternal with matter, the greater evidence suggests the supposition that as circumstances vary in nature and as motion is conjoined with matter, those varying circumstances imply the fragile existence of man. As "nature contains no one constant form," and as the "universal law" requires that "all shall experience change," d'Holbach asks man why he believes himself "a privileged being in nature" being "subject to the same vicissitudes as all [nature's] other productions?"[89] All that is required for man to perish is a "slight accident, a single atom to be displaced."[90]

Not only is man's existence fragile, threatened, and apparently destined to be absorbed back into the eternal, whirling, motion of matter, while he exists—though he think differently—his existence is in no way superior to the existence of any other being. "In the eyes of Nature, however," reflects d'Holbach, "the oyster that vegetates at the bottom of the sea is as dear and perfect as the proud biped who devours it."[91] Hence, while "Existence is essential to the universe, or to the total assemblage of matter essentially varied that presents itself to our contemplation . . . the combination, the forms, are not essential."[92] Obviously, from d'Holbach's radical materialism it is easy to anticipate his rejection of any substance or "immaterial spirit" animating man or suffusing him with a life-principle. d'Holbach asks, "How can a being without extent be movable and put matter into action?"[93] Such conclusions are mere chimeras of theology, for which there is no corresponding idea made available to us through sense. That which is "without extent, without parts, is nothing more than an absence of ideas," therefore it is nothing.[94]

For d'Holbach, there is only matter and motion, existing eternally, and following the universal law of alteration or change. Things take successive forms, coming to be and perishing, possessing no qualitative distinctions. All things are on a level with one another, as all is matter taking successive appearances. Man's supposed superiority or sense of excellence only reflects a "predilection he has in favour of himself."[95] Nothing is but constant change. The ghost of Heraclitus weaves itself through the genius of the French Enlightenment.

Although Enlightenment thinkers are by no means strictly materialistic in their philosophies, materialism plays a dominant theme for Diderot, d'Holbach, and d'Alembert. This focus upon change, and the disavowal of substances and essences suggests a certain revulsion with "is-ness," which Jeffrey Hart terms a mood of "anti-ontologicality."[96] The language of essences suggests for them a freezing of reality, an imposing of static immutable concepts upon the world of mutability, change and progress. This view of nature, this radical existentialism, in which change is supreme and essences taboo, fuels a philosophy which sees progress as abetted by change. While progress need not necessarily be the outgrowth of change, it appears to be so for Diderot, d'Holbach, and d'Alembert.

The rejection of metaphysical essences has its philosophical antecedent for the Enlightenment thinkers in Locke. The view of essences as fixed and stable and as standing apart from the real world, like Platonic archetypes of which natural things partake, is rejected by Locke as being incompatible with available empirical data. Locke does assert another type of essence as more reasonable, whereby "natural Things . . . have a real but unknown Constitution of their insensible Parts, . . ." and since it is unknown, it is incapable of being abstracted. Yet his thought tends more to nominalism, in which a name is given to individual things having some characteristics in common.[97]

For the *philosophes*, the idea of essence and nature is the idea of something that stands apart from and in opposition to reality, which is a world of flux and change. Instead of being, they opt for becoming, hence their "anti-ontologicality." The choice, however, is not simply between being and becoming, between a fixed and immutable world and a world of change. Neither Parmenides nor Heraclitus exhausts the possibilities. Aristotle offers a middle ground which accounts for both being and becoming, through the elements of being-in-act and being-in-potency. Fundamental to this is the realization that forms and essences do not exist in a world apart, but, together with matter, constitute the metaphysical elements composing substances. This realization is not founded on "the hypthetico-deductive method" that Henry Veatch argues characterizes contemporary philosophy of science.[98] Such a method attempts to secure scientific knowledge following deduction predicated upon hypothetically attained first premises. In this regard, Kant and his transcendental method of philosophy is the exemplar. This is not the method of Aristotle; nor is it the method of Burke, who disdains a rationalistic metaphysics particularly in disregard of experience and empirical data. Thus, Veatch asks the question:

> in the *Physics* does not Aristotle adduce both evidence and argument in support of the fact that substances in the natural world are subject to change, that they do indeed undergo change upon occasion, and that when they change, what is involved is always and necessarily a change *of* something, *from* its having been something, *to* its being something else? Clearly also, for anything thus to undergo change and to become other and different from what it was—be it quantity, quality, place, or even substance—it must have had what can only be called a capacity or a natural potentiality thus to become other and different. Without such a potentiality, the object could not change; it could not become other and different.[99]

It is apparent from Veatch's analysis that a realist metaphysics does not proceed independently of empirical observation. Further, that for Aristotle, his metaphysics in no way relies upon hypothesis followed by deduction. It is firmly grounded in the evidence of sense experience. Therefore, common observation reveals that each substance possesses the potentiality of becoming what it is, a capacity to actualize more completely its form or essence. Aristotle occupies the middle ground between Parmenides and Heraclitus in the sense that he accommodates in his metaphysics both change and permanence. It is this middle ground which Burke's metaphysics occupies, avoiding on the one hand the extremes of radical essentialism and on the other hand radical existentialism. Instead, his thought reveals a metaphysics much nearer the Aristotelian-Thomistic tradition, a tradition enhanced for Maritain, by Aquinas' authentic existentialism.

There is not enough evidence in Burke to make such fine distinctions among the elements of his metaphysics to so warrant the conclusion that his philosophy is exactly in accord with Aristotle, Aquinas, or Maritain. For example, the emphasis placed on *esse*, or the "act of existing" by Aquinas, over *ens*, or being, as signified by the formal element of the substance, is, of course, not explicitly present in Burke. The force of his emphasis placed on the law of nature as being, first of all, change, and his concern with the concrete circumstances, rather than succumbing to arid rationalism, in itself is not sufficient to mark Burke an Existential Thomist as one can mark Maritain. Both Aquinas and Maritain argue for the metaphysical apprehension of *esse* ("to be" or the "act of existing") as primary to all existents. Burke did not speak specifically to such a metaphysical insight, but he did note the dynamic yet structured nature of reality. It is this structured dynamism which we have focused on in the emphasis placed on change and stability in Burke's metaphysics. While generally the Aristotelian elements of act and potency would adequately accommodate Burke's position, Burke is closer to the Common Doctor than to Aristotle due to the Christian influence upon his metaphysics, recognizing the existential, here and now, dependency all creation has upon the conserving action of the Creator.

Thus, it is not too bold to claim that Burke's thought places him squarely within the Aristotelian-Thomistic mainstream of classical, moderate realism. The judicious and cautious affirmation of this point by Canavan is advisable: "The basic premises of Burke's mature political thought . . . strongly resemble those of medieval Christian Aristotelianism."[100]

The evidence from Burke bears out the conclusion that his political thought is based on a firm, classical moderate realist metaphysics. Burke's metaphysics affirms an ordered yet changing reality. Change takes place in conformity with the structuring principles of reality reflecting a fundamental predominance of order over chaos. In short, reality is intelligible, giving evidence of the governance of reason. Furthermore, such metaphysical concepts as essence, substance, and nature, as they structure change and stability, are applied and revealed by Burke in a consistent fashion. And, finally, all of reality is dependent upon the divine action, here and now, which conserves and sustains creation, and beckons it forth in the direction of realizing its purpose. All of this, I have argued, serves to sustain the claim that Burke's political thought is grounded in a moderate realist metaphysical understanding of reality.

Notes

1. Etienne Gilson, *The Christian Philosophy of St. Thomas Aquinas*, trans. L. K. Shook, C.S.B. (New York: Random House, 1966), p. 16.
2. Frederick Copleston, S.J., *A History of Philosophy*, 9 vols. (Garden City, N.Y.: Image Books, 1962–1977) I, Part II, p. 31.
3. *A Letter to a Peer of Ireland* (1782), W IV 228.
4. W. H. Greenleaf, *Oakeshott's Philosophical Politics* (London: Longmans, 1966), pp. 6–9. David Cameron in *Social Thought of Rousseau and Burke* (p. 20) makes use of Greenleaf's typology. This typology is likewise useful for our purposes, in part because it highlights the all too typical failure to include moderate realism in its conceptual net, which, I argue is foundational to Burke's politics.
5. Greenleaf, *Oakeshott's Philosophical Politics*, p. 6.
6. The use of the term "transcendental" in this context should not be construed along Kantian lines, of course. Forms for Plato do not transcend the material realm as transcendental categories of the mind. Their "location" is not mental. Rather, they are somehow "above" the material, in a transcendent realm, a realm of the spirit.
7. Leo Sweeney, S.J., *A Metaphysics of Authentic Existentialism* (Englewood Cliffs, N.J.: Prentice-Hall, 1965), p. 81.
8. Ibid., pp. 59–61.
9. Ayer, *Language, Truth, and Logic* (New York: Dover, 1952), p. 33.
10. Loux, "The Problem of Universals," in *Universals and Particulars: Readings in Ontology*, ed. M. J. Loux (Garden City, N.Y.: Doubleday Anchor, 1970), p. 4.
11. Trans. Lewis Galantiere and Gerald B. Phelan (New York: Vintage, 1966), pp. 15–26.
12. *Preface to Metaphysics* (New York: Mentor Omega, 1962), p. 30.
13. Ibid., pp. 4–5.
14. Ibid., p. 5.
15. Ibid., p. 30.
16. Ibid.
17. Ibid., p. 31.
18. Maritain, *Existence and the Existent*, p. 62.
19. *Metaphysics*, in *The Basic Works of Aristotle*, ed. Richard McKeon (New York: Random House, 1941), V, 8, 1017b13–15, p. 761.
20. *Summa theologica*, Ia, 3, 5, ad 1.
21. *Metaphysics*, VII, 15, 1039b20–22, p. 807.

22. William A. Wallace, O.P., *The Elements of Philosophy: A Compendium for Philosophers and Theologians* (New York: Alba House, 1977), p. 29.
23. John Locke, *An Essay Concerning Human Understanding*, ed. P. H. Nidditch (Oxford: Clarendon, 1975), II, 23, 2, p. 296.
24. John Wild, *The Challenge of Existentialism* (Bloomington: Indiana University Press, 1955), p. 197.
25. Andrew Reck, "Being and Substance," *The Review of Metaphysics*, 31, No. 4 (June 1978), 546–47.
26. *Aquinas* (Baltimore: Penguin, 1963), p. 105.
27. Ibid., p. 34.
28. Sir Ernest Barker, *Essays on Government* (Oxford: Clarendon, 1965), p. 219.
29. Ewart Lewis, "Natural Law and Expediency in Medieval Political Theory," *Ethics*, 50, No. 2 (January 1940), 153.
30. Strauss, *Natural Right and History*, p. 296.
31. Stanlis, *Edmund Burke and the Natural Law*, p. 71.
32. Canavan, *Political Reason of Edmund Burke*, p. 18.
33. Wilkins, *Burke's Political Philosophy*, pp. 32–33.
34. Ibid., p. 34.
35. Ibid., pp. 33–34.
36. Ibid., p. 70.
37. Ph.d. Diss., Cornell University, 1928.
38. *The Speeches of the Rt. Hon. Edmund Burke in the House of Commons and in Westminster Hall*, 4 vols. (London: Longman, Hurst, Rees, 1816), I 151.
39. Cf. Canavan, *Political Reason of Edmund Burke*, p. 197.
40. P. I. Samuels, *The Early Life, Correspondence, and Writings of the Right Honourable Edmund Burke* (Cambridge: Cambridge University Press, 1923), p. 28, and Robert H. Murray, *Edmund Burke: A Biography* (London: Oxford University Press, 1931), p. 27, cited in Canavan, *Political Reason of Edmund Burke*, pp. 198–99.
41. III, pt. 2, pp. 24–25.
42. Ibid.
43. Canavan, *Political Reason of Edmund Burke*, pp. 202–203.
44. Ibid., p. 203.
45. Various authors have noted Burke's compatibility with this tradition through the similarity of his conception of natural law with Aquinas' conception. Note: Whenever reference is made to the realist tradition in this work, the Aristotelian-Thomistic tradition will be the one intended. Concerning the Thomistic conception of Burke's philosophy one should consult: Stanlis, *Edmund Burke and the Natural Law*;

Canavan, *Political Reason of Edmund Burke*; and Wilkins, *Burke's Political Philosophy*.

46. David Cameron confirms this point claiming "there is evidence to show that Burke himself, though he did not personally indulge much in it, had no objection to abstract speculation as such: in fact, not only did he write a philosophical treatise on a non-political subject, but within the field of politics itself, he finds a place for philosophy. . . . It was the misuse of such thought, which is to say its so-called application in political affairs, that he attacked." *Social Thought of Rousseau and Burke*, p. 39.

47. *Speech on the Petition of the Unitarians* (1792), W VII 49.

48. James Boswell, *Boswell's Life of Samuel Johnson*, edd. Anne H. Ehrenpreis and Irvin Ehrenpreis (New York: Washington Square, 1965), p. 244.

49. *Preface to Metaphysics*, p. 5.

50. *Aquinas*, p. 32.

51. Ibid., p. 33.

52. Ibid., p. 34.

53. This is not to deny, as Michael Freeman correctly notes, that "Chance, accident and the caprice of men also contribute to social outcomes." *Edmund Burke*, p. 54.

54. W VII 101. One might reasonably object that such statements made by Burke in the context of a speech before Parliament amount to little more than fashionable pious pronouncements calculated simply to gain a receptive audience. Furthermore, one might also regard such effulgent rhetorical flashes occurring as often as they do within Burke's speeches as characteristically a result of a certain zealousness on Burke's part, and hardly fit evidence for scholarly argumentation. Wilkins, in considering this problem specifically as it pertains to Burke, and especially in the setting of his speeches before Parliament, concludes with a generalization that he applies in Burke's case: "I, therefore, think it wise to assume that an author or speaker means what he says in the absence of overwhelming evidence to the contrary." For Wilkins, such evidence to the contrary does not exist in Burke's case. Wilkins, *Burke's Political Philosophy*, p. 12.

55. A. N. Whitehead, *Adventures of Ideas* (New York: Macmillan, 1954), p. 354.

56. *Letter to Sir Hercules Langrishe* (1792), W IV 296.

57. *Correspondence of the Right Honourable Edmund Burke*, edd. Charles Williams, Earl Fitzwilliam, and Sir Richard Bourke (London: Francis & John Rivington, 1844), IV 465.

58. *Speech on the Plan for Economical Reform* (1780), W II 329.

Not only did Burke consider it wise to attend to the order of things, but in his later years he declared as his goal the preservation of the order of things, as he wrote to Lord Loughborough, January 12, 1794: "... I have but one Idea, in which I wish to be serviceable as long as I live, and can serve which is to preserve the order of things into which I was born" (C VII 518–19).

59. For our purposes these terms will be used, for the most part, interchangeably as they appear to be used by Burke. Substance is more likely to refer to the concrete unit of existence itself, which essence or nature defines. Aristotle demonstrates the relationship of substance and essence in *Metaphysics*, VII, 6.

60. Concerning the etymology of the term "substance," see Sweeney, *Metaphysics of Authentic Existentialism*, p. 47n14.

61. Aquinas, *Disputed Questions on the Power of God* in *The Pocket Aquinas*, ed. Vernon Bourke (New York: Washington Square, 1960), p. 98, editor's note.

62. Cf. Wild, *Challenge of Existentialism*, p. 72.

63. Hume, *Treatise of Human Nature*, I 24.

64. *Diderot's Selected Writings*, ed. Lester G. Crocker (New York: MacMillan, 1966), pp. 86–87.

65. *Summa theologica*, Ia, 129, 2, ad 4, p. 157.

66. See pages 54–57.

67. Philosophic analogy will be discussed on pp. 86–87.

68. *Letter to William Elliot* (1795), W V 124. See Walter D. Love's discussion of various organicist interpretations of Burke and the above quotation as utilized by Alfred Cobban. Love, " 'Meaning' in the History of Conflicting Interpretations of Burke," in *Edmund Burke, the Enlightenment, and the Modern World*, ed. Peter J. Stanlis (Detroit: University of Detroit Press, 1967), pp. 120–22, and 129n10.

69. Cf. Wild, *Challenge of Existentialism*, p. 197.

70. Burke's position is compatible with Wild's as the latter concludes, "The act of existing is dynamic and temporal." Also, existence is contrasted by Wild with essences, which he describes as "fixed and timeless." Ibid., p. 242.

71. Maritain chooses "to affirm the primacy of existence, but as implying and preserving essences or natures and as manifesting the supreme victory of the intellect and of intelligibility." Maritain calls this "authentic existentialism." Maritain contrasts "authentic existentialism" with that of "apocryphal existentialism." The latter also affirms "the primacy of existence, but as destroying or abolishing essences or natures, and as manifesting the supreme defeat of the intellect and of intelligibility. For Maritain the notions of existence

(*esse*, or the "act of existing" of Aquinas) and essence are reciprocally related. To abolish one is to abolish the other. Maritain, *Existence and the Existent*, p. 3.

72. An argument to be discussed more fully in the next chapter.

73. Maritain, *Existence and the Existent*, p. 7.

74. *The System of Nature*, trans. H. D. Robinson, (Boston: Mendum, 1853), p. 48.

75. According to Cameron "Locke twisted his fingers not only round the haft of English intellectual life, but round that of Europe as well." *Social Thought of Rousseau and Burke*, p. 64. See also pp. 61–62.

76. Locke, *Essay Concerning Human Understanding*, IV, X, esp. 1–8, pp. 619–22.

77. "Burke and the French *Philosophes*," *Studies in Burke and His Time*, 10, No. 2 (1968–1969), p. 1134.

78. Jean Le Rond d'Alembert, *Preliminary Discourse to the Encyclopedia of Diderot*, trans. Richard N. Schwab (Indianapolis: Bobbs-Merrill, 1963), p. 83.

79. Ibid., pp. 84–85.
80. Ibid., p. 84.
81. Ibid., p. 96.
82. Ibid., p. 84.
83. Ibid.
84. Ibid., p. 82.

85. *Oeuvres philosophiques, historiques et litteraires de d'Alembert*, ed. J. F. Bastien, 18 vols. (Paris, 1805), II 34–35; quotation found in Ronald Grimsley, *Jean d'Alembert* (Oxford: Clarendon, 1963), p. 231.

86. Grimsley, *Jean d'Alembert*, p. 234.

87. d'Holbach, *System of Nature*, p. 48. The "three basic themes ... [of] d'Holbach's *Systeme de la nature* (1770)," as summarized by Alan Charles Kors, are: "(1) that the only coherent deduction from a sensationalistic epistemology was a rigorous materialism, (2) that the only coherent conception of matter was of an uncreated substance containing motion as an essential property, obviating the need for a First or Immaterial Cause, and (3) that the only humane and beneficial morality was one deduced from the imperatives for the happiness and survival of mankind...." *D'Holbach's Coterie: An Enlightenment in Paris* (Princeton: Princeton University Press, 1976), p. 45.

88. D'Holbach, *System of Nature*, p. 44.
89. Ibid., pp. 46–47.
90. Ibid., p. 46.
91. Ibid., p. 47.

92. Ibid., p. 44.
93. Ibid., p. 48.
94. Ibid., p. 80.
95. Ibid., p. 47.
96. "Burke and Radical Freedom," *The Review of Politics*, 29, No. 2 (April 1967), 227.
97. Locke, *Essay Concerning Human Understanding*, III, 3, 17, p. 418.
98. Henry B. Veatch, *Human Rights: Fact or Fancy?* (Baton Rouge: Louisiana State University Press, 1985), pp. 235–44.
99. Ibid., p. 244.
100. Canavan, *Political Reason of Edmund Burke*, p. 205.

4
The Philosophy of God and Human Nature

Now that the fundamental metaphysical principles of order, change and stability, and substance and essence have been defined in the previous chapter, it is possible to develop further the specifics of Burke's metaphysics. Turning to his treatment of God—the first principle and cause of all reality—and human nature, we see the constancy of order both in the designs of God and in the nature of man. These thematic elements of Burke's metaphysics will be more fully elaborated.

Our present focus upon God and human nature will bring us closer to the contingent realm of politics which Burke's metaphysics makes more intelligible. The final portion of this chapter will treat Burke's conception of human liberty and equality, still in the context of human nature. First, we will consider the existence of God and His rational knowability.

Philosophy of God

Burke affirms the existence of God through both his intellect and his feelings. Burke holds that "atheism is against, not only our reason, but our instincts . . ." (RF III 351). This interdependence of reason and instinct is well summarized by Francis Canavan, commenting on this passage: "Both reason and instinct (or feeling, or sentiment) play a part, and play it conjointly, in our deepest convictions. One does not cancel the other, and without both, while a man may become a rationalist or a romantic, he will not think well or rightly."[1] Burke's statement that "atheism is against . . . our reason" implies that given a rational demonstration, man's natural light of reason can affirm God's existence independent of faith and revelation.

Moreover, Burke supplies arguments for the existence of God in the *Inquiry*, making use of traditional philosophical principles.

Burke affirms the principle of causality. He does so in the *Inquiry* by a *reductio ad absurdum* argument:

> But as there will be little doubt that bodies present similar images to the whole species, it must necessarily be allowed, that the pleasures and the pains which every object excites in one man, it must raise in all mankind, whilst it operates naturally, simply, and by its proper powers only: for if we deny this, we must imagine that the same cause, operating in the same manner, and on subjects of the same kind, will produce different effects; which would be highly absurd [ISB I 82-83].

Burke maintains that it is possible, through the effects of nature, to come to know God's existence and attributes, thus again affirming the causal principle of reality.[2] That we can know God's attributes through His works is shown in this passage by Burke in the *Inquiry*: "It is by a long deduction, and much study, that we discover the adorable wisdom of God in his works" (ISB I 185). Elsewhere in Burke's *Inquiry* we find another example: "But because we are bound by the condition of our nature, to ascend to these pure and intellectual ideas,"—that is, the ideas of God's attributes—"through the medium of sensible images, and to judge of these divine qualities by their evident acts and exertions, it becomes extremely hard to disentangle our idea of the cause from the effect by which we are led to know it" (ISB I 142). While affirming Burke's belief that God can be known through his effects, this passage, nonetheless, reveals his hesitancy over the excessive reliance upon speculative reason. This hesitancy is confirmed elsewhere in the *Inquiry* by referring to that "great chain of causes, which, linking one to another, even to the throne of God Himself, can never be unravelled by any industry of ours" (ISB I 209). Nonetheless, a sufficient intellectual industry utilized in reflecting on the human mind itself leads to an affirmation of God's existence: "The more accurately we search into the human mind, the stronger traces we everywhere find of His wisdom who made it" (ISB I 126).

With Burke's conclusion that God's existence can be affirmed by speculative reason, one wonders how Rodney W. Kilcup can declare that for Burke reason is "impotent when it moves to matters beyond the realm of the sensible world?"[3] There is a difference between urging considerable caution, "long deduction, and much study" as Burke does in seeking to discover God's wisdom "in his works," and simply asserting the sceptic's charge that reason is impotent to discover supra-sensible truths. Kilcup ignores this difference.

Beyond Burke's basic acceptance of the knowability of God by speculative reason's reflection on the data of the sensible world lies his assent to the teachings of the Church.

It is evident that Burke held to the traditional teachings of Christianity, especially as confessed by the Church of England. "I am by choice and by Taste," Burke writes in a letter to Dr. John Erskine, June 12, 1779, "as well as by Education, a very attached Member of the Established Church of England" (C IV 84).[4] His attachment was more than just to the "Established Church of England"; it was of a very personal nature to divinity itself: "I bequeath my Soul to God; hoping for his Mercy thro' the only merits of our Lord and Saviour Jesus Christ" (C IX 375). Beyond the Church of England Burke indicates his respect for the "whole Christian Church" by which he means "the Great Bodies of the East and West, including all their particular descriptions, which I am willing to consider, rather as divisions, made for convenience and order, than Separations, from a diversity of Nature, or from irreconcilable contradiction in principles" (C IV 85). Underscoring Burke's breadth of respect for even the "divisions" of Christianity, he declares: "I am attached to Christianity at large; much from conviction; more from affection" (C VI 215). He indicated to the Quaker, Richard Shackleton, that though it is true that "we take different Roads," and "indeed it is a melancholy thing to consider the Diversities of Sects and opinions amongst us," still "as there is but one God so there is but one faith, and one Baptism" (C I 32–33).

Christian doctrine included for Burke belief in a transcendent Deity, a Creator God who is a Provider for His creation. In other letters to Shackleton he refers to "the word of the creator sufficient to create the universe from Nothing," and to "the wise and all powerfull providence of God" (C I 18 and 22). Reference to God and His providential care for the world occur throughout Burke's works. As a youth Burke writes in another letter "of the great Shepherd of all, on whom Let us Cast all our Care for he Careth for us" (C I 39)!

These references to divinity especially emerge in Burke's battle with the Jacobins of the French Revolution who, by way of their radical atheism, as Burke saw it, sought to undermine the very foundations of society. These foundations are ultimately rooted in God. God is not only intimately linked to individual man as the cause of his existence, but God is the "great Master, Author, and Founder of Society" (RF III 354). He has created man in His image, denoted by man's nature as a rational animal.

God creates man in His image and imprints upon him his unique character. Burke refers to "Him who gave us our nature, and in giving impressed an invariable law upon it" (TPL VI 322). God does not create man to turn him loose upon his own designs; He creates man according to His own plan. God is a God of order, and, as cited previously, Burke states, "I know that there is an order that keeps things fast in their place: it is made to us, and we are made to it."[5] How does Burke know this? Primarily all knowledge of these matters pertaining to God stems from religion, which he labels that "grand prejudice . . . which holds all other prejudices together."[6] To speak of religion as a prejudice is not to suggest an irrationally held opinion. When speaking of religion or the "Church Establishment . . . [as] the first of our prejudices," Burke adds that such a prejudice is not "destitute of reason, but involving in it profound and extensive wisdom" (RF III 352).[7] The "prejudice" of which Burke speaks is the ancestral wisdom that is the living deposit passed on from one generation to the next. It is this wisdom that is the product of man's nature, and this "Nature . . . is wisdom without reflection and above it" (RF III 274). Burke believes that this nature, being man's instinctive response to moral values and religious assent, proves that God exists.

As we reflect on Burke's argument and statements concerning the existence of God and His nature, it is apparent that on the whole he is not writing as a philosopher or theologian but as a practical politician or political essayist urging action. The significant exception, of course, is the *Inquiry*. For the most part he assumes the basic premises of what I have pointed to as his philosophy of God, although not entirely. However unsatisfactory this might be for the academic philosopher, Burke is being faithful to his vocation and purpose. Still, to fully comprehend his position on politics requires attention being given to his philosophy of God.

In recognizing that God creates in us a particular nature and orders us for a specific end, Burke may seem to imply that God determines our specific acts. Some of his writings, in fact, give this impression. In Burke's *Appeal from the New to the Old Whigs*, he writes:

> ... I may assume that the awful Author of our being is the Author of our place in the order of existence,—and that, having disposed and marshalled us by a divine tactic, not according to our will but according to His, He has in and by that disposition virtually subjected us to act the part which belongs to the place assigned us [ANW IV 165–66].

Even more to the point, while despairing over Pitt's hesitation to appoint Lord Fitzwilliam as Lord Lieutenant of Ireland, Burke declares: "However, we must still use our poor human prudence and our feeble human efforts, as if things were not, what I greatly fear they are, predetermined" (C VIII 35). We may ask ourselves, has God created an automaton? Does the "divine tactic" order our every move, or does He invite us to cooperate in His plan and by a free acquiescence to participate in the ends He has ordained for us?

Burke's God is the God of classical theism.[8] Not only has God brought the world out of nothing into existence, but all of existence, down to the minutest details, remains in a state of dependence upon its Creator (C VIII 364). In assessing Burke's position on this point, Canavan concludes, "It follows that the actions of all creatures, even the free actions of men, are fully under the dominion and direction of God, and this direction is called divine providence."[9] Canavan continues by identifying two features of Burke's doctrine of providence. They include man's freedom of choice and God's "supreme and ineluctable guidance of history."[10] Burke, as is the case in most of his philosophy both political and otherwise, assumes this doctrine of Providence, making no attempt to prove it. Nonetheless, man's "natural feelings" confirm Burke's belief in Providence. Burke advances this position in his *Notebook*:

> The Arguments against Providence are from our *Reasonings*, observing a certain order in the works of God. There is nothing at all in our natural feelings against it.
>
> There is a great deal in our natural feelings for it.
>
> All Dependant Beings that have a Sense of their Dependence naturally cry out to their Superiour for assistance [NB 71].

Burke continues by arguing against a fatalistic determinism: "No man can act uniformly as if a fatality governed everything. Men do not naturally conceive that, when they are strongly actuated to call upon a Superior, that [sic] they cannot be heard; they do not conceive that they have Passions which have no Purpose" (NB 71). Therefore, as Canavan summarizes matters on Providence for Burke, he "believed both in God's supreme dominion over history, and in a genuine, though limited, human freedom within history."[11] Canavan's conclusion appears to be confirmed in Burke's letter to his son Richard who had gone to Ireland to aid the Catholics: "Be content to have done your best and leave the rest to the disposer of Events" (C VII 17).

In speaking of God in such magisterial ways as "the Sovereign Disposer," "The Awful Author of our nature," and the "great Master, Author and Founder of Society," Burke is not indicating a God who superimposes His will upon man. Man is free to respond to God's will. Thus it is that God orders the basic course of mankind's march through history. Man's own individual behavior and his practical knowledge of what is just and good are informed through several sources such as Holy Writ, the traditional teaching of Christianity, the manifest wisdom of civilization, and society's manners, customs, and chartered rights of man. Additionally, man is in possession of fundamental moral instincts. All of these sources provide ways in which man gains a partial insight into the designs of Providence. As Gerald Chapman remarks: "The idea of Providence working in history

... never lost its hold on Burke, who believed that emergent situations in the historical process, though their causal origins may be obscure, always stand under a judgement, a disposing law and intention, with which it is willful disaster not to cooperate."[12]

Chapman's observations are confirmed in two letters Burke wrote to his son Richard, Jr. In one, dated August 18, 1791, he writes that ". . . we must not struggle with the order of Providence . . ." (C VI 358). To struggle against the order of things according to Providence is really to capitulate to our passionate nature, as Burke relates in another letter to his son, dated October 28, 1791: "Most assuredly it will be wise in us to conform ourselves to that state of things which providence is pleased to direct or permit. To act otherwise is not to make sacrifice to our principles but our passions" (C VI 439).

God creates for a purpose. His existence ensures the stability of the moral law as a defense against the caprice of brute force. Burke writes that "if no Supreme Ruler exists, wise to form, and potent to enforce, the moral law, there is no sanction to any contract, virtual or even actual, against the will of prevalent power" (ANW IV 205). God has given us a particular nature: "the Author of our nature has written it strongly in that nature, and has promulgated the same law in His written word, that man shall eat his bread by his labor."[13]

Through the mysterious and unknown dispensations of Providence, we find ourselves placed within an historical epoch, a situation and environs apart from any choice of our own. As Burke writes to Earl Fitzwilliam: "There is much in Fortune, or in more proper Language, in the overruling and mysterious disposition of Providence" (C VI 37). Burke leaves no doubt that God's Providence applies directly to himself and that it is received as a trust: "God is the distributor of his own blessings. I will not impiously attempt to usurp his throne, but will keep according to the subordinate place and trust in which he has stationed me" (C VI 95). He clearly ratifies his trust in God's Providence in a letter to his brother, Richard Burke, Sr., on November 21, 1787, declaring that "God is all sufficient; and that we exist with any degree of hope at all, is a proof of it—for everything else that comes in the ordinary Course is such that it is half a miracle renewed every day and every hour that we can talk to one another in the Land of the living and have even this melancholy. But I trust in the same providence very sincerely and very fully" (C V 359). Burke finds that the situations and horizons that surround his life are decreed by God, situations which determine his duties. This is not to say that men are not free to choose, but even free acts fall within the designs of Providence.[14] Burke often calls attention to our duties—duties not chosen but nonetheless incumbent upon us to perform. We may ignore them, but we do so by contravening our own nature, natural feelings and dispositions. In this regard we find a moving letter which reveals Burke's deep religious convictions. Burke replies to Earl Fitzwilliam's letter of condolence on the death of Burke's son, Richard, and refers to the "common Providence of God," and to the feelings "that God and nature have implanted in me." Also, he alludes to the things he must do as God has ordained which he will submit to with God's grace (C VII 568–69).

Although history to some thinkers seems to betray a certain dynamism in obedience to a law of nature, Burke would not go so far as to conclude that every nation is inevitably succumbing to a predetermined destiny, although, as he pondered the events of the Revolution in France, he expressed his fear that things were "predetermined" (C VIII 36). If God allows a civilization to decay and disintegrate, He may well be doing so as a punishment to rebellious man. Burke wrote, "But tell me, has not God himself commanded or permitted the storm to purify the elements?" (C VI 154). Regardless, he believed "There is still a God; and that is a consolation" (C VII 523). Still, Burke does not assent to a type of Providence resulting in historical determinism:

> I doubt whether the history of mankind is yet complete enough, if ever it can be so, to furnish grounds for a sure theory on the internal causes which necessarily affect the fortune of a state. I am far from denying the operation of such causes: but they are infinitely uncertain, and much more obscure, and much more difficult to trace, than the foreign causes that tend to raise, to depress, and sometimes to overwhelm a community [1LRP V 235].[15]

If states and civilizations follow some ineluctable pathway from inception and development through pre-eminence, decay and, finally, destruction, this pathway remains obscure to man. Whatever may be the case, we are each called to "perform," as Burke wrote to Lord Fitzwilliam near the end of his life, "a present Duty—and as to the future it must be committed to the disposal of Providence" (C IX 317). This expression of Christian resignation by Burke does not eliminate for him the incredible influence the lives of single individuals can exercise upon the destiny of nations: "The death of a man at a critical juncture, his disgust, his retreat, his disgrace, have brought innumerable calamities on a whole nation. A common soldier, a child, a girl at the door of an inn, have changed the face of fortune, and almost of Nature" (1LRP V 236). That such individuals emerge to lead further manifests God's mysterious Providence: "As to great and commanding Talents they are the Gift of Providence in some way unknown to us" (C VI 242). One might wonder if such potential on the part of the individual does not jeopardize the law of nature as it comes from God.

To make such a bold claim on behalf of the importance of the individual does not invalidate the natural law. First, the natural law gives substance to right and wrong but does not detract from free choice. It is not a deterministic force in the life of man, save that the violation of the law comes at a price. Second, Burke's regard for the impact of the single individual is an acknowledgement of the dignity through freedom which man possesses. When the circumstances are fitting, the individual, through his choices, can effect for good or evil the course of a nation. Thus, Burke's view of history and God's providential role in it, again, does not conflict with the freedom of the individual.[16]

God has created the universe and has placed man therein with a nature that is both fixed and alterable. Burke writes in the *Reflections*, referring to two types of men, the "learned and reflecting part of this kingdom," and the "less inquiring," that "they conceive that He who gave our nature to be perfected by our virtue willed also the necessary means of its perfection: He willed therefore the state: He willed its connection with the source and original archetype of all perfection" (RF III 360–61). God gave man his nature and the means to its perfection. This brings us to a consideration of Burke's philosophy of human nature.

Philosophy of Human Nature

The complexity of man's nature is readily apparent. Ultimately, he is composed of body and soul, passion and reason. Man, a reasoning being by nature, may allow his passionate nature to enslave his reason. Burke writes, "Strong passion under the direction of a feeble reason feeds a low fever, which serves only to destroy the body that entertains it" (2LRP V 407). Burke warns that no one is immune from a flawed nature: "But we have no charter of exemption, that I know of, from the ordinary frailties of our nature" (LSB II 203). Here rings the note of a fundamental struggle at the core of man's being, his passionate nature threatening to disrupt a precarious balance between itself and reason. But complexity, inward struggle, and strife express only one side of human nature. Out of this struggle between reason and the passions can emerge a harmony. This is not meant to be a harmony where the passions are completely suppressed in deference to rationality. This would deny a crucial component in man's complex nature. Rather, the passions can and should be placed in service to reason, and through this service can emerge at least a partial harmony. Burke continues: "But vehement passion does not always indicate an infirm judgement. It often accompanies, and actuates, and is even auxiliary to a powerful understanding; and when they both conspire and act harmoniously, their force is great to destroy disorder within and to repel injury from abroad" (2LRP V 407).

Peter Stanlis sees Burke's typification of man's nature as being so complex and variable as almost to defy generalization.[17] Burke himself notes in his *Reflections*: "The nature of man is intricate; the objects of society are of the greatest possible complexity; and, therefore, no simple disposition or direction of power can be suitable either to man's nature or to the quality of his affairs" (RF III 312). How does this complexity affect the moral nature of man?

Man, for Burke, comes into being neither totally corrupt nor sublimely good. He has an intricate, complex nature modified by his environment, religion, habits, and a myriad of other variables, all informing his existence. Man finds a proper development of his potential for goodness through the enrichment of his social nature.[18] His nature and God's will ordain his sociability. This is confirmed by Burke: "Men are not tied to one another by paper and seals. They are led to associate by resemblances, by conformities, by sympathies. It is with nations as with individuals. Nothing is so strong a tie of amity between nation and nation as correspondence in laws, customs, manners, and habits of life" (1LRP V 317). Burke denies any anarchical claims to extreme individual freedom. Anarchy tends to absolutize individual freedom at the expense of society's claims on the individual, thereby ignoring man's social and political nature. Yet man's social nature is inescapable. "Men are never," Burke says, "in a state of *total* independence of each other. It is not the condition of our nature" (1LRP V 321). Further, what nature declares must be submitted to, for "an attempt . . . to force nature, will only bring on universal discontent, distress and confusion" (C III 434).

Through a common social nature, all men maintain an identity with one another that does not preclude differences. The question is, how can mankind be united to one another by a common nature while the world bears witness to so much pluralism among customs, traditions, and laws? Burke tackles this problem when he considers the role of the ancient legislators as they addressed the problems of their times. Burke writes that the ancient legislators

> . . . had to do with men, and they were obliged to study human nature. They had to do with citizens, and they were obliged to study the effects of those habits which are communicated by the circumstances of life. They were sensible that the operation of this second nature on the first produced a new combination,— and thence arose many diversities amongst men, according to their birth, their education, their professions, the periods of their lives, their residence in towns or in the country, their several ways of acquiring and of fixing property, and according to the quality of the property itself, all which rendered them as it were so many different species of animals [RF III 476–77].

This passage from the *Reflections* is crucial to resolve the problem that Weston poses for Burke: "Does human nature change or is it everywhere the same?"[19] Weston's resolution of the problem, after advancing quotations from Burke which appear both to support a universal human nature, and to deny it, is the following: "Taking all the evidence together, it is suggested here that Burke believed that in any particular society human nature was the same, that Burke derived that human nature was everywhere the same, and that near the end of his life Burke perceived that even in a particular society human nature can change fundamentally."[20] But, in fact, Weston has not taken all the evidence together for he did not consider this crucial passage from the *Reflections*, a work written in the latter stages of Burke's life.

The vacillation by Weston on whether or not Burke held to an underlying, permanent human nature is echoed by other Burke scholars. Kilcup argues that though Burke held "in the area of personal morality [that] human nature changes," and so "refused to believe in a radically historicized fundamental human nature" he is, nonetheless, "committed to a view that entailed the historicization of political ethics."[21] J. G. A. Pocock finds in effect human nature for Burke to be subsumed within his doctrine of traditionalism, and disclosed through the progress of history and its instantiation in custom, and promulgated in the "ancient constitution."[22] More recently, Pocock concedes the importance of "nature" for Burke, but contends that the importance of "history" in Burke's political philosophy has been short-changed by certain Burke scholars. Pocock argues that Burke "was, of course both . . . a philosopher of nature" and a philosopher of history.[23]

So, based on the critiques of Weston, Kilcup and Pocock, how do things stand? Weston resolves the matter by leaving things unresolved, implying thereby Burke's position is inconsistent despite his own protestations in his *Appeal from the New to the Old Whigs* that his work is consistent throughout. Kilcup divides the matter, arguing that Burke held to a permanent human nature in the area of "personal morality," but succumbed to a relativism and historicism in the area of "political ethics."[24] Thus, Kilcup concludes that for Burke "Natural moral sentiment is safe from the ravages of historical change, but the principles that guide men in public affairs are historically relative."²⁵ To claim that the principles animating our "personal" or private morality differ from those "principles that guide men in public affairs" is opposed to Burke's own remarks on the subject. Burke avowed that "the principles that guide us in public and private, as they are not of our devising, but moulded into the nature and essence of things, will endure with the sun and the moon" (C II 282). The dramatic split between the principles of personal or private morality, and those guiding us in public affairs are not malleable, but "moulded" into the very nature of things for Burke. There is neither diffidence about nor distinction between the personal and the political at the level of principles for Burke.

As for Pocock, in later works he has accorded a place for "nature" and "history" in Burke. Yet Pocock fails to argue for the priority of one over the other, thus risking the dissolution of nature into history. For Burke the priority is clearly given to nature, as he asks, concerning man and his affairs, "Does it suit his nature in general?—does it suit his nature as modified by his habits?" (SC VII 97).

It is clear that for Burke man's so-called first nature, his human nature, entails his second nature, his activity as a citizen of society. Man is naturally social and his sociability, and the varying circumstances in which the plurality of men find themselves, result in a diversity of habits and customs.²⁶ "Man, in his moral nature becomes, in his progress through life," according to Burke, "a creature of prejudice, a creature of opinions, a creature of habits, and of sentiments growing out of them. These form our second nature, as inhabitants of the country and members of the society in which Providence has placed us."²⁷ The specific relationship between nature and custom is noted by Burke in his *An Abridgement of English History* (1757), in which he writes: "If people so barbarous as the Germans have no laws, they have yet customs that serve in their room; and these customs operate amongst them better than laws, because they become a sort of Nature both to the governors and the governed."²⁸ The compatibility with Burke and Aquinas on this point is striking: "Custom, and especially custom in a child," St. Thomas states, "comes to have the force of nature. As a result, what the mind is steeped in from childhood it clings to very firmly, as something known naturally and self-evidently."[29] In effect, both for the realist Aquinas and for Burke the development of a second nature, shaped by habit, custom and tradition, is not only consistent with, but a natural outgrowth from, our first or essential human nature.

The Aristotelian categorical distinction between substance and accident has a ready application here. The fusion of man's circumstantial or conditional nature, as one might call this second nature, and his human nature, or first nature—which *is* a social nature—does not eliminate the priority and the most fundamental aspect of this first nature. Indeed, the very peculiarity of man's first nature, its social quality, lends itself to the constant development that he undergoes in the infinite diversity of the social world. Writing of Burke's notion of human nature Cameron concludes:

> Human nature (although it can be taken as constant for practical purposes) does indeed change in the course of time, and man himself can discern this in the long run; what does not change is the principle of man's proper development, which may be known in fragmentary fashion by men, but which is entirely comprehended only by God. There can be both radical historical diversity among the peoples of the world and a universal moral order.[30]

Through this development of his social nature, man substantially retains his distinctiveness as man.

All of this is compatible with Burke's metaphysical principles of change and stability. Essentially, human nature is fixed. Writing to Adam Smith he refers to "the Nature of man, which is always the same . . ." (C I 130). In the *First Letter on a Regicide Peace* (1796), he claims that, in the area of morality, "men are not changed, but remain always what they always were . . ." (1LRP V 249). There is no dimension of process on the level of the essential nature of human beings. But the dynamic, developmental aspect of reality is accommodated by man's social nature, or second nature. This social nature permits social differentiation, accounting for distinction of peoples through custom, clime and habit. Through the confluence of a variety of forces impinging on him, together with the choices he makes, the individual becomes something distinct, something unique, while retaining his essential humanity. The entire social order is created and exists for the purpose of man's perfecting of his being, that is, for the dignity of man. Burke ties together these notions:

> Every sort of moral, every sort of civil, every sort of politic institution, aiding the rational and natural ties that connect the human understanding and affections to the divine, are not more than necessary, in order to build up that wonderful structure, Man,—whose prerogative it is, to be in a great degree a creature of his own making, and who, when made as he ought to be made, is destined to hold no trivial place in the creation [RF III 353].

Two things now become clear. First, Burke affirms causality. God is causally present to the universe not only in His role as Creator, but also as sustainer and, beyond that, as the end of the universe, urging man toward perfection, and calling for man's cooperation in the pursuit of justice. Second, the effect of God's causal presence is intelligible to man. Man can recognize through reason God's hand in the universe, although, more important for Burke, man apprehends God's handiwork according to his natural feelings. Further clarification on Burke's philosophy of human nature regarding man's rationality is needed.

Man is a rational animal.[31] Burke makes this clear in the following: "For man is by nature reasonable; and he is never perfectly in his natural state, but when he is placed where reason may be best cultivated and most predominates" (ANW IV 176). This claim of man's rationality does not preclude irrational behavior, or suggest that human reason is always in firm and dispassionate control of human conduct.[32] It does assert, as Canavan notes, "that man is, with all his faults and weaknesses, a rational animal. . . ."[33]

Man is not only a rational animal. To claim that man is purely rational is to strip him of other characteristic properties; it is to distort and oversimplify his existence. His rationality affirms his essence, but his essence is to be a human being of flesh and blood, not to exist as pure intellect. This point is amply illustrated in Burke's discussion of the successful repeal in 1766 of Grenville's Stamp Act by the Rockingham administration and its simultaneous upholding of Britain's right to tax the American colonies. "Whether all this can be reconciled," Burke argues, "in legal speculation is a matter of no consequence. It is reconciled in policy; and politics ought to be adjusted, not to human reasoning, but to human nature; of which the reason is but a part, and by no means the greatest part."[34] This historical event and Burke's position on it are an important example of his rejection of a political stand based on nothing more than an abstract principle. To tax the colonies based only on a "right" to tax, divorced from all circumstance, is imprudent and unjustified. One may accept the right, as Burke did, but in examining the likely consequences determine not to exercise the right.

When Burke claims that reason is "by no means the greatest part" of human nature, he may appear to contradict himself when he states that "man is by nature reasonable." The context which elicited Burke's response makes it clear that Burke has reference to a type of abstract reason, which moves from a fixed principle, deductively, to a logical conclusion without reference to any social or political context in which the principle is to be applied. Parliament, to Burke's mind, was being duped by a type of reason which was inappropriate to politics and by the mentality of an abstract notion of its "right" to tax. While abstract reasoning is an important part of human nature, "it is by no means the greatest part," especially when one considers the life of a political and national institution such as the British Parliament.

Burke wars with those students of politics who determine what the political state of affairs ideally should be in stark contrast to what in fact they are. Such is the case with the Jacobin writers of the French Revolution. They draw up blueprints for society, analytically consistent, yet devoid of an historical appreciation of man. To Burke's mind, the Jacobins ignore the weight of traditions and customs which, while limiting man's political horizons and restraining the itch for novelty, nonetheless ground man in his past.[35] These traditions preserve men from the machinations and designs of utopian political writers. Thus, when Burke denigrates the use of abstract reason in the realm of politics, he generally does so to rebuke those writers who ignore the whole complex creature who is man.

Reason belongs to a being who retains much of that animality shared with the brute world. Human reason is not a faculty independent of one's physical or emotional state, or able to separate itself from environmental influences. Yet reason can, at least in part, transcend its own creaturely existence—to a greater extent in its speculative function, to a lesser extent in the political realm as political reason.

When Burke calls for the subjection of reason, he means a reason which divorces itself from the concrete, being-in-the-world existence of man. Such abstract reasoning is *a priori* in character and reflects more man's wishful thinking than his actual state (RF III 311). So the force of the quotation from Burke in which reason is cited as "by no means the greatest part" of human nature is to urge us not to isolate one aspect of man, however significant, at the expense of the entire individual. There is no sense in which Burke is proposing an opposition between nature and reason. "Never, no, never," Burke remarks, "did Nature say one thing and Wisdom say another" (3LRP V 407). In fact, in the *Reflections*, nature is seen to be the unreflecting embodiment of reason: "nature . . . is wisdom without reflection, and above it" (RF III 274). For Burke, our natural feelings and affections are implanted in our nature by God, as are our reasoning abilities; hence they are not at variance with each other by God's design—rather, they are complementary. This is not to oversimplify matters for as Burke states in the *Reflections*: ". . . The nature of man is intricate . . ." (RF III 312). Furthermore our natural feelings and instincts can become corrupted and they need to be checked at the bar of practical reason. For example, we naturally "shun disgrace." To do so "is an instinct; and under the direction of reason, instinct is always right."[36]

In considering the essence of human nature, we cannot ignore the complexity of man's existence that, through a ceaseless array of changes, modifies and develops man's social nature. When we speak of human nature, we are calling to mind those qualities which apply to all human beings, not just to some. Burke maintains that we are both rational and religious by nature. This too is but one essential aspect of our complex nature. Regarding man's religious nature, Burke states, "We know, and it is our pride to know, that man is by his constitution a religious animal; that atheism is against, not only our reason, but our instincts; and that it cannot prevail long" (RF III 351). The person who denies that which is by nature part of his very being does so at a price. He is at war with himself. And, as a consequence, he is at war with all mankind. Atheism, for Burke, gnaws at the very foundations of society. So basic to man's being is his religious nature that religion holds first place among the values of life. "On [the Christian] religion, according to our mode, all our laws and institutions stand, as upon their base. That scheme is supposed in every transaction of life . . ." (4LRP VI 112). Burke confirms this point in the *Reflections*: "We know, and, what is better, we feel inwardly, that religion is the basis of civil society, and the source of all good, and of all comfort" (RF III 350). From these reflections on human nature emerges a further consideration.

Does Burke consider man good, evil, or morally indifferent by nature? Is man's fundamental tendency in the direction of a self-centered egotism or of a natural harmony with his fellow-man? Burke provides a general answer to this question in *Thoughts on the Cause of Our Present Discontents*: "We must soften into a credulity below the milkiness of infancy to think all men virtuous. We must be tainted with a malignity truly diabolical to believe all the world to be equally wicked and corrupt. The elevation of the one, and the depression of the other, are the first objects of all true policy."[37]

Other political philosophers, such as Hobbes and Rousseau, suggest different viewpoints. Hobbesian man is driven primarily by the desire for self-preservation, haunted as he is by insecurity and fear of death. Consequently he seeks power: "I put for a general inclination of all mankind, a perpetual and restless desire of power after power, that ceaseth only in death."[38] As all men have a thirst for unlimited power, they are thrust in opposition one to the other, reducing each person to an isolated state seeking his own self-interest. Hobbes is led to his famous epigram on man, whose life he regards as "continual fear, and danger of violent death; and the life of man, solitary, poor, nasty, brutish, and short."[39] In the Hobbesian state of nature, man is locked in a continual condition of war, a condition which only the emergence of the state can amend.

Equally famous is the opening line of Rousseau in *The Social Contract*: "Man is born free, and everywhere he is in chains." The initial import of this statement, separated from the complexity of Rousseau's social thought, is that the natural condition of man is liberating and felicitous, while the unnatural condition is enslaving and corrupting. David Cameron characterizes the position of natural rights theorists and Rousseau thusly: "Natural man, according to most exponents of natural rights, was not wicked, and for many of them he was positively good. The origin of evil was found not in the constitution of man, but in the composition of society."[40] Both Cameron and Arthur O. Lovejoy, though, point out that Rousseau holds natural savage man to be hardly different from an animal, living by instincts. These instincts are not so violent as Hobbes speculates, as man has a natural compassion for others, and a desire for self-preservation. What he lacks is a developed reason or a moral sense. He lacks a reflective sense of self, and therefore has not yet achieved a level of humanity that may only be achieved in civilized society. As Lovejoy remarks, "True it is . . . that Rousseau asserts the 'goodness' of man in his primitive state," but "in the state of nature man has not the status of a moral agent." For Rousseau man "was originally a non-moral but good-natured brute."[41]

Burke disavows the extremes of both Hobbes and Rousseau. As a naturally social being, man does not suffer from the regimentation that falls to him while living in community, under the governance of laws. In fact, without society and on his own, man lacks the ability to develop and perfect his personality. At the same time, since he is not totally and naturally depraved, too much social regulation bridles unnecessarily the individuality of man. A balance is to be struck. Human nature, after all, is a product and reflection of divine intelligience. Man is an intelligent being—created in God's image—not simply a bundle of passions. He has the potential for good. Further, man's social or second nature, an extension of his human nature, helps make him an adaptable rather than a rigid, inflexible being. He possesses a nature of ordered proportions. Yet his nature invites uniqueness and change without dissolving into an amorphous existence that rescinds man's humanity. It combines identity and difference. Man as man has a common nature, yet each person develops uniquely in society, not uniformly.[42] Again, Burke's metaphysics of change and stability, with the emphasis upon order and development, draws together the elements of his philosophy. The possibility of the passions giving way to chaos remains. For social order to prevail as is meant, man must freely choose to cooperate in society.

In light of man's nature as a reasoning, religious, social being, how does Burke connect his metaphysical principles with his political philosophy? As previously mentioned, two crucial concepts emerge here, both being important for an understanding of Burke's philosophy of human nature and his political philosophy. These are the political concepts of freedom and equality. Burke's thought on these concepts serves to illustrate further, in a different context, his principles of order, change and stability, and essence and nature.

Human Freedom

In this section I will discuss the nature of human freedom as it exists both on the personal and on the social level for individuals. My purpose is to show further how human nature, reflecting Burke's metaphysical principles of change and stability and of a lawfully ordered reality, comes to bear in a more specific way in his political philosophy.

Freedom for Burke is natural to man. It flows from his very nature as an intelligent reasoning being. Burke writes of "the rational and moral freedom of individuals . . . that personal liberty" that contributes so much "to the vigor . . . and dignity of a nation" (LNA IV 49). Not only is freedom natural to man, it is the right of all men. In his *Letter to the Sheriffs of Bristol* (1777) he makes clear that "Liberty, If I understand it at all, is a *general* principle, and the clear right of all the subjects within the realm, or of none. Partial freedom seems to me a most invidious mode of slavery" (LSB II 198). We are not compelled to behave in any determined fashion. There is nothing about our nature which denies us freedom. Created to be free by God, to enjoy liberties as social beings, we are not created to be free without restraints. Burke remarks that "Liberty, too, must be limited in order to be possessed" (LSB II 229). Our freedom is not by nature infinite, but rather finite and structured. Freedom is vital, not static.

Freedom is not simply limited by the order of the universe; rather it is secured by the same. Because of its finitude, man's intellect is limited in its range of knowledge, consequently reducing that upon which he can act. We cannot come to know completely the entire panorama of life which places demands upon us. Man is restricted in the scope of his activity and the knowledge upon which he can act. Consequently, Burke's conception of liberty is one of limited freedom. Freedom without limits and structure spells license and chaos. The theme of limit brings order to man's freedom. Sartre draws the following conclusion: "I am condemned to be free. This means that no limit to my freedom can be found except freedom itself or, if you prefer, that we are not free to cease being free."[43] The Sartrean view of freedom, denying all limitation as a circumscription on being-for-itself, has no analogue in Burke. Nor is a Marxian-type man, whose social consciousness is a reflection of extant material and economic conditions, compatible with Burke's viewpoint. Instead, man has by nature a structured freedom. What about his structure?

The essence of man's freedom is structured for society. Man's metaphysical structure makes of him a being located in space and time, a structure that demands realization, not at an ideal level of abstraction, but within the historical and social moorings unique to each individual. These limits, or determinations of our metaphysical structure, provide a backdrop which roots us and provides order. We are at the interstices of the physical, social, and spiritual dimensions of a reality which, though universal, is uniquely experienced as ours. And these real dimensions of our lives impose a boundary which does not suffocate our natural freedom rooted in rationality. Rationality structures freedom, reminding us that there are limits to this uniquely human possession called freedom. Our human nature places us squarely within the social arena in which, as Burke concludes, we are never totally independent of one another (1LRP V 321).

Man is radically free in that his freedom is at the very core of his essence. Freedom is man's birthright, his dignity as man. It is not earned; it is a gift due him as a rational being. Speaking of liberty, Burke states his belief, in a letter to Depont in 1789, "that all men who desire it, deserve it. It is not the reward of our merit, or the acquisition of our industry. It is our inheritance. It is the birthright of our species. We cannot forfeit our right to it, but by what forfeits our title to the privileges of our kind. I mean the abuse, or oblivion, of our rational faculties . . ." (C VI 41).

This freedom, with its potential for excess, is mediated on the social plane, becoming what it is meant to be, a social freedom. This is not an unnatural abridgement of what is otherwise an absolute freedom, but it is the necessary requirement for the realization of man's essence. Man's social interdependence is a condition of his fulfillment and his self-realization. Here, the continuity of man's essential nature affords the backdrop for his development as man; while retaining its essential sameness, man's existence expresses itself dynamically. The freedom of man is a positive good for it permits moral perfection. Still, freedom in itself is not an unlimited good for without the restraint of law and wisdom freedom becomes an evil force. Burke states in the *Reflections*, "I shall always, however, consider that liberty as very equivocal in her appearance which has not wisdom and justice for her companions" (RF III 409); and in a *Letter to the Sheriffs of Bristol* (1777) he holds that "among a people generally corrupt liberty cannot long exist" (LSB II 242). Freedom cannot exist in man unbounded, unrestrained, unlimited. It must be limited to be possessed. Further, as Burke makes clear in his *Letter to a Member of the National Assembly* (1791), those who fail to self-impose restraints will have externally imposed restraints by society: "Men are qualified for civil liberty in exact proportion to their disposition to put moral chains upon their own appetites. . . . Society cannot exist, unless a controlling power upon will and appetite be placed somewhere; and the less of it there is within, the more must be without. It is ordained in the eternal constitution of things, that men of intemperate minds cannot be free. Their passions forge their fetters" (LNA IV 51–52). Clearly, the unlimited nature of freedom-in-itself leads to an overthrow of the vital structures of the social life of the person. That freedom must be curbed as a condition of man's social existence is not only the province of Burke's political philosophy, but also central to his philosophy of human nature.[44]

The fusion of the themes of limit and the unlimited—of freedom according to one's nature and absolute freedom—find their analogue in the twin features of Burke's metaphysics, stability and change. Stability, permanence, and continuity of one's nature—all of these echo the theme of limit, while change echoes that of the unlimited. The universe as orderly underscores the theme of restraint, moderation, or limitation. On this point Burke writes, in a letter to the Archbishop of Nisibis, in 1791: "I love order so far as I am able to understand it . . . for the universe is order" (C VI 460). The universe is order, yet order can be threatened by its opposite, disorder. In the political realm, disorder prevails when freedom is admitted without limit. Burke warns of "the spirit of freedom, leading in itself to misrule and excess . . ." (RF III 276). For Burke, freedom in its unbridled form spells chaos. He warns that to make freedom a gift "only requires to let go the rein." Yet he continues by emphasizing that true freedom demands tempering "together these opposite elements of liberty and restraint in one consistent work . . ." and this requires "deep reflection, a sagacious, powerful, and combining mind" (RF III 559–60).

From this the following conclusions emerge. First, freedom in itself is unlimited, and is potentially destructive if not checked by some restraining limit. As Burke writes in a letter to Depont in 1789, "The Liberty I mean is *social* freedom. It is that state of things in which Liberty is secured by the equality of Restraint. . . . This kind of liberty is indeed but another name for Justice, ascertained by wise Laws, and secured by well constructed institutions" (C VI 42).[45] Second, the extreme of limitation and restraint without freedom is equally destructive. In this vein Burke states, "It is better to cherish virtue and humanity, by leaving much to free will . . . than to attempt to make men mere machines. . . . The world on the whole will gain by a liberty without which virtue cannot exist" (RF III 368–69). Third, freedom and restraint, the unlimited and limited, are best brought together in a tempered harmony. The universe reveals a clash of opposites which may be reconciled on both the physical and political planes of existence. Burke reminds the French that under the old regime they "had that action and counteraction which, in the natural and in the political world, from the reciprocal struggle of discordant powers draws out the harmony of the universe" (RF III 277).

Co-active principles of reality such as the limited and the unlimited are perennial in metaphysics. The most fundamental Pythagorean doctrine was, as Kirk and Raven note, "the ultimate dualism between Limit and Unlimited, ..." principles which "underlie the whole universe."[46] From this pair of opposites the principle of the limited gives rise to the good, while the principle of the unlimited is represented by the answering evil, according to the Pythagorean table of opposites. Limit, therefore, includes "unity, rest, goodness and so on."[47] My purpose here is to note a metaphysical parallel in the history of ancient Greek philosophy with the philosophy of Burke. While Burke does not hold to the existence of two co-equal principles, the good and the evil, he does consider the spirit of freedom, unlimited and without restraint, to lead to chaos. Instead, the spirit of freedom must be tempered and restrained by the virtues, which limits the otherwise unlimited spirit of freedom.

In light of the characterization of Burke's thought, offered by Canavan, as resembling "medieval Christian Aristotelianism," it may seem curious that parallels with Burke's philosophy would be sought in pre-Socratic thought. Clearly, the pre-Socratics bear a similarity with Aristotle. As stated, limit includes unity and goodness. These ideas in effect suggest the transcendentals of being, and it is clear that Aristotle held to certain transcendentals. Furthermore, matter, considered in itself, is unlimited, unformed, prone to nothingness save structured by form, which limits and specifies. So, Aristotle's metaphysics, stressing such concepts as form and matter, certainly bear a continuity with the pre-Socratics, as the first book of his *Metaphysics* makes clear.

Moreover, the concepts of form and matter are pivotal to the metaphysics of Aquinas, although they are incorporated into a more profound reflection, underscoring the creative acts of God. So, to draw parallels in the history of ancient metaphysics is not to circumvent the depiction of Burke as a "Christian Aristotelian," but to buttress the claim by way of the tradition that nurtures the perennial philosophy which finds Aristotle to be the most respected of founding fathers.

Thus, for Burke, man is possessed of a reasoning capacity, but man's passionate nature too often chafes at the controls of reason. Yet these very controls channel the passions of man in a way that lends harmony both individually and socially to man's being. For Burke, the potential metaphysical rupture at the heart of man is the very secret of man's success as man. The unlimited thrust of the passions and the spirit of freedom desire and seek fulfillment in the just rule of reason. As Burke points out, society demands the subjugation of the passions; such a subjugation is a condition of man's social existence, and such an existence is the natural realization of his nature. Even more to the point, this subjugation of our passions can be considered one of our rights. Burke contends in the *Reflections* that

> Government is a contrivance of human wisdom to provide for human *wants*. Men have a right that these wants should be provided for by this wisdom. Among these wants is to be reckoned the want, out of civil society, of a sufficient restraint upon their passions. Society requires not only that the passions of individuals should be subjected, but that even in the mass and body, as well as in the individuals, the inclinations should be frequently thwarted, their will controlled, and their passions brought into subjection. This can only be done *by a power out of themselves*, and not, in the exercise of its function, subject to that will and to those passions which it is its office to bridle and subdue. In this sense the restraints on men, as well as their liberties, are to be reckoned among their rights [RF III 310].

What has been said about freedom as a part of Burke's philosophy of human nature applies universally to man, entailing an essential, natural equality between men. Understanding Burke's theory of equality is a key to furthering our grasp of the metaphysical foundations of his political philosophy.

Human Equality

Man as man is born into society, and from this common social bond a rich variety of differentiation emerges, a process which is pivotal for the growth of society. If metaphysical speculation ignores or denies this process of differentiation, then the purpose of metaphysics—to make known the principles of reality—is truncated, and metaphysics fails its goal. Metaphysics cannot falsify or obscure reality; rather it must reveal reality. A false metaphysics, which reduces us to a contrived egalitarianism, such as the Jacobins perpetrated, cannot for Burke be accepted.

At certain levels of reality men share natural equality, at others a natural inequality. In terms of equality, men all share in a common nature, possessed of reason, having a natural tendency toward society, and under the governance of the law of nature (TPL VI 323). Though the rudimentary endowments alluded to in this list are shared by all, the degree to which they are possessed varies sharply. So it is acknowledged as true, and as a fundamental tenet of Burke's theory of equality, that all men are born equal. One way in which this equality is made manifest is man's equal subjection to the pre-existent natural law of which God is the source. But again, inequality emerges, as not all men are actually, or by design, meant to be fused together in a monotonous similarity. How does a natural equality on the level of a common human nature give way to a natural inequality? Does the apparent discrepancy occur at two different levels of existence? In order to answer these questions we must first consider Burke's treatment of human rationality as it relates to equality.

It is true that all men possess the ability to reason. It is just as true, however, that the ways individual men have cultivated their powers of reason, or the ways in which they have corrupted or abused reason result in a permanent alteration of one's nature. Sound reason, Burke maintains, is a condition of a virtuous life. To live without reason is to invite the madness of a mean and wretched existence (LNA IV 24). Such a life may not completely annul man's basic human nature, but it does degrade him. Moreover, a life of intemperance and immoderation, where all reason and lawfulness are disavowed, leads to the loss of freedom and to personal enslavement (LNA IV 52). In short, men must "put moral chains upon their own appetites . . ." (LNA IV 51). Our experiences permanently affect the kind of persons we are. Here we see that our social or second nature impinges upon and affects, without essentially altering, our human nature.

So we have equality with inequality. Circumstances may affect the natural equality that prevails between men through their possession of a common nature. This is not to say that circumstances alone alter a natural equality. Men naturally vary in abilities. Circumstances, conjoined with man's exercise of his abilities, permanently enhance or diminish him. Whatever these actual variations—some men being more dexterous of hand, others of mind—it is natural for men to manifest a variety of abilities. There is, quite obviously, the superior and inferior in nature and in society. A simple levelling of conditions, a uniformity of experiences, and equalization of social conditions, would not, and should not, eliminate this natural inequality between men. Why is this the case?

A levelling of social conditions to obtain a social equality is not only utopian idealism, but it defies a natural inequality realized in the order of nature itself. For Burke, the idea of the natural order of things requiring each of us to occupy a definite place in the hierarchy of nature, is expressed in the metaphor of "the great primaeval contract of eternal society, linking the lower with the higher natures, connecting the visible and invisible world, according to a fixed compact sanctioned by the inviolable oath which holds all physical and all moral natures, each in their appointed place" (RF III 359). Not only does the physical, natural order of things find itself linked and ordered to the rest of nature, but so does the moral and social world. We are naturally and fruitfully subordinated by convention and by nature one to another, giving evidence of a proper and fitting social inequality. How else could true *politeia* be obtained save that some should lead and others follow? It is the natural condition of man, society, and physical reality itself to be interdependently related to some distinction of rank or chain of being that superordinates some things and subordinates others. And, for man and society, such conditions help achieve the common good. We are, for Burke,

> to recognize the happiness that is to be found by virtue in all conditions,— in which consists the true moral equality of man-

kind, and not in that monstrous fiction which, by inspiring false ideas and vain expectations into men destined to travel in the obscure walk of laborious life, serves only to aggravate and embitter that real inequality which it can never remove, and which the order of civil life establishes as much for the benefit of those whom it must leave in a humble state as those whom it is able to exalt to a condition more splendid, but not more happy [RF III 279-80].

It is not only just but necessary for there to be a hierarchical arrangement for society. This hierarchy should not be one of increase in privilege and status alone, but one in which higher status brings increased social responsibility.

Just as reality possesses an ordered diversity, a hierarchy of being, there likewise is a social grading that in part reflects the needs of society and the condition of persons. Burke recognizes an ancient order in society that assists individuals in knowing their station and consequent duties. He writes: "Our country is not a thing of mere physical locality. It consists, in a great measure, in the ancient order into which we are born. . . . The place that determines our duty to our country is a social, civil relation" (ANW IV 167). It is the existence of this order that structures change and permits a purposeful development within society, achieving an equality that equally meets the needs of man as man, and man in society. A social hierarchy suggests for Burke a natural equality and inequality. That Burke's theory of equality reveals both a natural equality and inequality does not imply a contradiction within Burke's philosophy. Equality and inequality occur at two different levels. Man's natural equality occurs at the level of his humanity. We all share in those singular qualities which make us human. Yet our humanity bears in its essence those very qualities which lead to a natural inequality.

We are by nature social beings. More specifically, "we are creatures designed for contemplation as well as action; since solitude as well as society has its pleasures; as from the former observation we may discern, that an entire life of solitude contradicts the purposes of our being, since death itself is scarcely an idea of more terror" (ISB I 116). Human nature is expressed in a social nature which flourishes and realizes itself uniquely in each person. It is the Jacobins who go awry, led in their ideological fervor by a falsely construed metaphysics, to seek an equalization of conditions among individuals, and thinking thereby that they serve some metaphysical imperative. Who are these Jacobins? For Burke, they are those who ". . . resolved to destroy the whole frame and fabric of the old societies of the world, and to regenerate them after their fashion. . . . As the grand prejudice, and that which holds all the other prejudices together, the first, last, and middle object of their hostility is religion."[48] The Jacobins err in terms of their theories both of equality and of liberty. In their championing of the natural rights of men, they posit what for Burke is that infamous state of nature where all men equally possess liberty. They assume, forthwith, it is the nature and mandate of government to liquidate all inequalities in order to unleash this primal state of equality amid a putative state of natural liberty. Whoever the Jacobins were and whatever their philosophy could be, there were basic tendencies to their thought that Burke conceived of as extreme. A spirit of radical egalitarianism was one of these tendencies—this desire to reduce all levels of society to a basic equality could only have squalid results. Burke notes that from the movement toward egalitarianism "a perfect equality will, indeed, be produced,—that is to say equal wretchedness, equal beggary, and, on the part of the partitioners, a woeful, helpless, and desperate disappointment. Such is the event of all compulsory equalizations. They pull down what is above; they never raise what is below; and they depress high and low together beneath the level of what was originally the lowest."[49] This fear that the movement towards egalitarianism leads to a greater impoverishment of the masses is confirmed by Burke in a letter to William Cusac Smith, July 22, 1791: "but that process of reasoning, which would shew to the poorest how much his poverty is comparative riches in his state of subordination, to what it would be in such an equality as is recommended to him, is quite out of his reach, even if it were pleasing to his pride" (C VI 304).

There are different reasons one may have for rejecting the spirit of egalitarianism. The Danish existentialist, Søren Kierkegaard, rejected it based on the threat it posed for the individual and sketches a more extreme position than Burke's. For Kierkegaard all forms of society and association carry within them the levelling virus. In *The Present Age* he argues: "No society or association can arrest that abstract power [the process of levelling] simply because an association is itself in the service of the levelling process. . . . The abstract levelling process . . . is bound to continue, like a trade wind, and consume everything."[50] Like Kierkegaard, Burke also feared that the very force that was to free the individual from social servitude, namely the spirit of equality, would be the force that reduces the individual to an indistinguishable number among the teeming masses of the state. But in opposition to a position such as Kierkegaard's existentialism, Burke does not believe that all association results in the annulment of the individual, Kierkegaard's prized existential category. To associate in society is basic to human nature. What is not basic to human nature for either Burke or Kierkegaard is to lump mankind together without distinction as to position or station in life.

The speculative thinker who fails to see a natural inequality and diversity between human beings is one blinded by misconceived social theories. In the *Reflections* Burke claims that the ancient legislator

> would have been ashamed that the coarse husbandman should well know how to assort and to use his sheep, horses, and oxen, and should have enough of common sense not to abstract and equalize them all into animals without providing for each kind an appropriate food, care, and employment,—whilst he the economist, disposer and shepherd of his own kindred, subliming himself into an airy metaphysician, was resolved to know nothing of his flocks but as men in general [RF III 477].

To treat all people alike as if there are no differences between them is an error. Consider the area of employment. Burke holds that while all honest occupations are worthwhile and deserving of the state's respect, not all are honorable. For to claim a position as honorable, he remarks, is to "imply some distinction in its favor" (RF III 296). But some occupations are servile in nature. To consider individuals employed in these occupations as equal to individuals with truly honorable occupations is to be "at war with Nature," rendering in fact a false equality (RF III 296).

The spirit of equality, of course, serves as a convenient ideological weapon against the monarchy and nobility because, if men are indeed equal, then the social differences between them demands a justification nature does not provide. There are differences between individuals which are a result of prevailing social conditions. But these differences are not unnatural; it is not unnatural for there to be gradations within society. "Some decent, regulated pre-eminence, some preference (not exclusive appropriation) given to birth is," Burke writes, "neither unnatural, nor unjust, nor impolitic" (RF III 299). It may be quite fortuitous for some people to receive noble parentage while others do not. The refinement that comes with such a noble birth—or at least Burke hoped such refinement would follow—attests to the welding of man's two natures together making for a real difference. Without this inequality society cannot exist and man's social nature and his very existence are wanting. The question is whether or not the levels of society harmonize together to make for a healthy social entity, in pursuit of the common good, and allowing each man an arena within which he can perfect himself.

The metaphysicians who incur Burke's wrath are those who in their efforts to equalize, instead, pull down the scaffolding of society and mankind with it. Burke condemns these levellers thus, and singles out their false metaphysics of equality:

> They have attempted to confound all sorts of citizens, as well as they could, into one homogeneous mass. . . . They reduce men to loose counters, merely for the sake of simple telling, and not to figures, whose power is to arise from their place in the table. . . . The troll of their categorical table might have informed them that there was something else in the intellectual world besides *substance* and *quantity*. They might learn from the catechism of metaphysics that there were eight heads more, in every complex deliberation, which they have never thought of . . . [RF III 478].

False theories of equality attempt to do the impossible—imposing an equality on men, removing all differences between them, opting for masses over classes. All of this continues to underlie the fundamental distinction between Burke and the Jacobins on the nature of society. For the latter, as Burke viewed them, society is a convention, an artifice which constricts the natural freedom of man. Being artificial, hence unnatural, the social differences that exist within society do violence to man's nature. The rule of one class over another imposes a hegemony by convention that does not obtain in a state of nature where man is naturally free. This constitutes a restatement of the dilemma which remains at the very center of Burke's controversy with the Jacobins, a controversy which Burke's metaphysics seeks to overcome.

Burke holds that the legitimate and natural social inequalities, such as those found in class distinctions within society, are conducive to the common good. He writes "that every such classification, if properly ordered, is good in all forms of government, and composes a strong barrier against the excesses of despotism, as well as it is the necessary means of giving effect and permanence to a republic" (RF III 478-79). As a buffer against despotism and a buttress to a sound republic, social classes and the distinctions they entail are necessary to a nation. Furthermore, a hierarchy of social classes does not suppress those who should lead, or elevate those who should follow. Instead, such suppression results from the levellers of society, the enforcers of equality, such as the revolutionaries in France. They would "lay low everything which had lifted its head above the level," and while attempting to level, fail to equalize (RF III 475). Burke states "Believe me, Sir, those who attempt to level never equalize. In all societies consisting of various descriptions of citizens, some description must be uppermost. The levellers, therefore, only change and pervert the natural order of things: they load the edifice of society by setting up in the air what the solidity of the structure requires to be on the ground" (RF III 295).

For Burke, there is a class of people, the aristocracy, who provide natural leadership for a nation. Primarily, one is a member of his class by birth; the aristocracy and its position are ensured through hereditary wealth and the disproportionate share of the nation's property that belongs to them. Such a state of affairs Burke holds natural: "The characteristic essence of property, formed out of the combined principles of its acquisition and conservation, is to be *unequal*" (RF III 298). Burke writes that "the power of perpetuating our property in our families is one of the most valuable and interesting circumstances belonging to it, and that which tends the most to the perpetuation of society itself" (RF III 298). Among the duties of leadership belonging to aristocracy is "to be employed as an administrator of law and justice, and to be thereby amongst the first benefactors to mankind" (ANW IV 175). Society should protect and perserve the aristocracy in this role, while aristocracy should offer principled direction for the nation, tapping the vast reservoirs of wisdom that tradition has delivered intact to society. And it is this natural leadership which reflects the dictates of reason over passion, of man's higher nature over his lower nature. It is an inequality that is equitable for it reflects the nature, not only of man, but of an ordered universe whose order is the design of the Creator himself.

The metaphysical elements of Burke's philosophy discussed in Chapter 3 are reflected in his philosophy of God and human nature, liberty and equality. Burke's thought on God and man sustains the thesis of a developmental conception of reality, one that is not essence-free. The metaphysical principles developed in Chapter 3 find a ready application to the political concepts of liberty and equality. Liberty assists man in realizing his essential nature in becoming what he potentially is. His choices, to be truly free, are made according to what is consonant with his nature. Concerning equality, we see Burke's disavowal of any movement toward egalitarianism that would violate the hierarchically structured nature of reality. Each thing has its place and its purpose, including man. Burke's view of reality discloses a lawful and purposive design, forming an important element in the fabric of his metaphysics. The elements of teleology and natural law as they pertain to Burke's metaphysics are our next concern.

NOTES

1. Canavan, *Edmund Burke: Prescription and Providence* (Durham: Carolina Academic, 1987), p. 64.
2. See the discussion in Wilkins, *Burke's Political Philosophy*, pp. 126–27, and in Canavan, *Political Reason of Edmund Burke*, pp. 44–45 for agreement with this claim.

3. "Reason and the Basis of Morality in Burke," *Journal of the History of Philosophy*, 17 (1979), 275. Cf. Kilcup's "Burke's Historicism," *Journal of Modern History*, 49, No. 3 (September 1977), 397, 408–409.

4. Cf. C VIII 146.

5. *Speech on the Representation of the Commons in Parliament* (1782), W VII 101.

6. *A Letter to William Smith on the Subject of Catholic Emancipation* (1795), W VI 367.

7. Canavan writes that "prejudice, in the sense in which Burke praises it, is not irrational. Yet there is a sense in which it is opposed to reason. The reason to which it is opposed is that of the thorough individualist, who is primarily concerned with his own rights and interests. . . ." Canavan, *Political Reason of Edmund Burke*, p. 75. Russell Kirk considers "prejudice" to refer to "the supra-rational wisdom of the species. . . ." "Burke and the Philosophy of Prescription," *Journal of the History of Ideas*, 14 (1953), 365.

8. The label "classical theist" is the one given by Charles Hartshorne to those philosophers who conceive God to be "Eternal Consciousness. Knowing but not including the world." Philosophers included by Hartshorne in this tradition include Philo, Augustine, Anselm, al'Ghazzali, Aquinas, Leibniz, et al. *Philosophers Speak of God*, edd. Charles Hartshorne and William L. Reese (Chicago: The University of Chicago Press, 1969), p. 17.

9. Canavan, *Political Reason of Edmund Burke*, p. 178.

10. Ibid.

11. Ibid.

12. Gerald Chapman, *Edmund Burke: The Practical Imagination* (Cambridge: Harvard University Press, 1967), p. 271. See also Canavan's thorough study of Burke on divine providence in *Edmund Burke: Prescription and Providence*, chap. 7.

13. *Two Letters to Gentlemen in Bristol* (1778), W II 260.

14. Canavan, *Political Reason of Edmund Burke*, p. 180.

15. John C. Weston, Jr., argues that Burke's understanding of history offers "a theory of growth, saved from becoming a deterministic organic theory of society by Burke's insistence upon the necessary operation of the free human mind." Weston, "Edmund Burke's View of History," *Review of Politics*, 23, No. 2 (1961), 212. See also Stanlis in *Edmund Burke: The Enlightenment and Revolution* (New Brunswick: Transaction, 1991), esp. pp. 104–106, 198–99, and 236–37.

16. Weston summarizes the relationship between the Providence of God and human history in "Edmund Burke's View of History," 212.

17. Stanlis, *Edmund Burke and the Natural Law*, p. 286n39.

18. Concerning this aspect of man's nature and its implications for freedom, Stanlis writes: "Like Aristotle, Burke believed man was by nature a political animal, so that true liberty must be 'social freedom', a condition which required restriction on raw will and prevented anyone from exercising arbitrary power." Stanlis, *Edmund Burke and the Natural Law*, p. 67.

19. Weston, "Edmund Burke's View of History," p. 214.

20. Ibid., p. 216.

21. Kilcup, "Burke's Historicism," p. 409.

22. Pocock, "Burke and the Ancient Constitution," in *Politics, Language and Time: Essays on Political Thought and History* (New York: Atheneum, 1971), pp. 202–32.

23. Pocock, "Introduction," in Edmund Burke, *The Reflections on the Revolution in France*, ed. Pocock (Indianapolis: Hackett, 1987), pp. xlvii–xlviii.

24. Kilcup, "Burke's Historicism," pp. 408–409.

25. Ibid., p. 409.

26. Cf. Bruce James Smith, *Politics and Remembrance: Republican Themes in Machiavelli, Burke, and Tocqueville* (Princeton: Princeton University Press, 1985), p. 120. Burke refers specifically to the "social nature of man" in 2LRP V 361.

27. Burke, *Speeches in the Impeachment of Warren Hastings*, W XII 164.

28. Burke, *An Essay towards an Abridgment of the English History* (1757), W VII 292.

29. Aquinas, *Summa contra gentiles, Book One: God*, trans. Anton C. Pegis, F.R.S.C. (Notre Dame: University of Notre Dame Press, 1975), ch. 11, p. 81.

30. Cameron, *Social Thought of Rousseau and Burke*, pp. 84–85.

31. In *Inquiry* Burke claims that "We are rational creatures. . . ." ISB I 186. In discussing this aspect of human nature I am necessarily prescinding from what Stanlis rightly refers to as Burke's view of "man as a rational and emotional being. . . ." Stanlis, *Edmund Burke and the Natural Law*, p. 161.

32. Wilkins records that Burke sometimes speaks of a struggle between reason and the passions. Wilkins concludes, though, that "Burke believed in a fundamental accord or harmony between reason and the passions." Wilkins, *Burke's Political Philosophy*, pp. 102–103.

33. Canavan, *Political Reason of Edmund Burke*, p. 80.

34. *Observations of a Late Publication on the Present State of the Nation* (1769), W I 398.

35. Cf. Anthony Quinton, *The Politics of Imperfection* (London: Faber & Faber, 1978), p. 16. Quinton considers "traditionalism" to be one of three fundamental "principles of conservatism."

36. *Letter to a Noble Lord* (1796), W V 208-209.

37. Contrast this with Frank O'Gorman's mistaken notion of Burke's position: "Burke believed in the essential weakness and corruptibility of human nature, in the incapacity of the average man to resolve his problems in a rational manner, in the irrelevance of most 'rational' solutions to political problems. . . ." O'Gorman, *Edmund Burke: His Political Philosophy*, p. 142. Cf. Charles Parkin, *The Moral Basis of Burke's Political Thought* (Cambridge: Cambridge University Press, 1956), p. 56.

38. Thomas Hobbes, *Leviathan*, ed. Michael Oakeshott (Oxford: Blackwell, 1946), Pt. I, Bk. 11, p. 64.

39. Ibid., Pt. 1, Bk. 13, p. 82.

40. Cameron, *Social Thought of Rousseau and Burke*, p. 49. Cf. p. 189 *n*17.

41. Arthur O. Lovejoy, "The Supposed Primitivism of Rousseau's *Discourse on Inequality*," *Modern Philology*, 21, No. 2 (November 1923), 171.

42. According to Dreyer, "When Burke wrote *The Sublime and Beautiful*, he assumed that human nature was in certain respects constant and unchanging. . . . Burke never seriously repudiated this assumption of human identity. In the impeachment of Hastings he might sometimes argue as if the English and the Indians were fundamentally different . . . but however sensitive he was to the peculiarities of Indian culture, Burke's basic argument in the impeachment was that Indians and Englishmen exhibited a common human nature. . . . From the beginning to the end of his career, Burke asserted the reality of an abstract and uniform human nature." *Burke's Politics*, pp. 55-56.

43. *Being and Nothingness*, trans. Hazel Barnes (New York: Washington Square, 1966), p. 566.

44. Osborn remarks that "For Burke . . . freedom was to be regarded in the light of the means whereby the state could achieve its end. Indispensable as it was, liberty was not in itself the end of the state." Osborn, *Rousseau and Burke* (London: Oxford University Press, 1940), p. 130.

45. According to a newspaper account of his day, Burke reportedly made the following reply to a toast at a dinner honoring Charles James Fox, October 10, 1787, whereby he again connects freedom and justice, contrasting it with passionate excess: "Nothing could be more truly deserving the attention of those who loved freedom than the pursuit of

justice and humanity. Where these were wanting, freedom might be no more than a popular mask to cover ambition and the baser passions" (C V 351n1).

46. G. S. Kirk and J. E. Raven, *The Presocratic Philosophers: A Critical History with a Selection of Texts* (Cambridge: Cambridge University Press, 1969), p. 229.

47. Ibid.

48. *A Letter to William Smith on the Subject of Catholic Emancipation* (1795), W VI 367.

49. *Thoughts and Details on Scarcity* (1795), W V 142–143.

50. *The Present Age*, trans. Alexander Dru (New York: Harper & Row, 1962), pp. 55–56.

5
The Metaphysical Elements of Teleology and Natural Law

Teleology

THERE IS AN END or goal for which things exist. In realist metaphysics this has been spoken of as final causation. God creates for a purpose, not capriciously, and consequently the universe as God's creation is purposive. Mention has already been made of the role of divine purpose in history, which is manifested in the telic nature of man and society. Thus, it is necessary to consider the teleological dimensions of Burke's thought, especially as they pertain to his political philosophy.

For Burke the telic quality things possess reflects the objective order of reality. The purpose of one's life or of a civilization is not simply what any person or collectivity determines it to be. It is in the order of things that all creation should by its very nature be created with a purpose. In a letter to an unknown correspondent in 1795 Burke states:

> If the Creator never can be absent from the minutest as no more than from the greatest of his Works; If it be true, that he must see them in every state of their existence with the Eye of the same Reason and design with which he first made them—if the whole scale of Nature is subservient to a moral End, then it is most sure that as no sparrow falls to the Ground without a purpose so no being is preserved in its vital Energies but for some purpose too [C VIII 364].

This purpose is not simply the expression of an epoch or moment in the historical unfolding of reality. Teleology, therefore, is an element of Burke's metaphysics because it concerns the purposive nature of creation as ordained by God.

Reality is not simply a random or even a lawful mechanistic

interplay of parts. Embedded in the essential structure of things is the purpose for which things exist. This purpose is not experienced in isolation in which each being somehow fulfills its design in ontic, monadic autonomy from all the rest. Things exist in interaction and interplay. Society, for example, is not simply what we experience today. It is a living social body: "[Society is] a partnership in every virtue and in all perfection. As the ends of such a partnership cannot be obtained in many generations, it becomes a partnership not only between those who are living, but between those who are living, those who are dead, and those who are to be born" (RF III 359). What *has* been is part of what *is* today. It is constituted by an intricate and vast network of relationships connecting the customs and manners from the past with the interchange of peoples past and present in a bonded unity. This unity does not simply exist; rather, it exists for a purpose. The purposive quality of its being may or may not be realized. A nation, comprising an organic unity of constituent parts, is informed and infused in its essential core with a reason for being. This reason exists within it and before it urging it to growth, development, and change. The ideal of its growth, the felicity of the parts and the whole, is achieved in degrees. The virtuous perfection of the person and the realization of the common good by societies represent ends to be achieved, and a nation's reason for being.

There is a twofold aspect to this telic quality of reality. As an aim for existence and a goal to be achieved there are both transcendent and immanent aspects of existence. The *telos* for human nature and its natural expression, society, transcends man in a dual way. It does so in that the purpose for man's existence is ordained by God. As the cause of man's reason for being, this telos, as residing in God, transcends man. This constitutes its ideal component. Man, fallible by nature, an admixture of both good and evil, will never in this life become fully what he was created to be.[1] There can be no utopian expectations indulged by man while being true to his condition. The second aspect of the transcendent quality of man's purpose resides in the immanent telos to be aimed for. The ideal of human nature, being an ideal which transcends what reasonably can be obtained, entails for Burke the subordination of the passionate side of man's nature to his moral reason. Burke claims that "the passions give zeal and vehemence. The understanding bestows design and system. The whole man moves under the discipline of his opinions" (2LRP V 361).

An immanent aspect also reveals itself. Both man and society actually possess the potential to improve and to more nearly achieve their own essential purpose here and now. It is reasonable to seek the fulfillment of one's nature, a nature that reveals the telos of one's being. And the ability to become what one potentially is constitutes a fundamental aspect of what the essence of a thing is.

Burke's metaphysics, therefore, has a teleological component. The pertinent aspect of this point for Burke lies not in the realm of cosmology, but in his understanding of man and society. First, I shall consider the telic quality of human nature, and second, that of society. This should serve as another link between Burke's metaphysics and his political thought.

In examining human nature Burke concludes in a very early writing that "man is made for Speculation and action; and when he pursues his nature he succeeds best in both" (NB 87). The end of human nature is twofold: the discovery of truth and activity aimed toward the common good. This twofold end of human nature is best stated through contrasting the end of the speculative philosopher and that of the philosopher in action. In the realm of speculation, only truth will suffice. As noted earlier, the speculative philosopher's purpose is to mark the ends of government, whereas the philosopher in action is concerned with the proper means to those ends. For Burke, both the speculative and the practical side of human nature serve a purpose in the realization of the individual and society.

Man is obliged to submit to the truth and choose the good, reflecting the natural order of things. This order binds the entire universe together into one integrally linked "eternal society." Burke writes of

> . . . the great primeval contract of eternal society, linking the lower with the higher natures, connecting the visible and invisible world, according to a fixed compact sanctioned by the inviolable oath which holds all physical and all moral natures each in their appointed place. This law is not subject to the will of those who,

by an obligation above them, and infinitely superior, are bound to submit their will to that law [RF III 359].

This unity is found in the natural law. Man perfects his nature only when he acts in accordance wth the law of nature. To elevate one's will over nature's law as ordained by God Burke considers folly. Burke writes, "We may bite our chains, if we will, but we shall be made to know ourselves, and be taught that man is born to be governed by law; and he that will substitute *will* in the place of it is an enemy of God."[2] God has placed all natures, Burke reminds us, in their appointed places, in proper relationship to one another.

For Burke, "This is the true touchstone of all theories which regard man and the affairs of men.—Does it suit his nature in general?—does it suit his nature as modified by his habits?" (SC VII 97). This indicates that the standard of human endeavor is itself human nature, not in abstraction, but as it actually is realized in society.

In speaking of man's nature "as modified by his habits," Burke is referring to man's second or social nature. The imperative of his rational social nature to seek a prudential, virtuous happiness in society finds its realization in the particular, contingent moment of this lived-world. This emphasis upon the actual, concrete world underscores the existential thrust in Burke's thought. His political philosophy is not utopian, or abstract in character, charting some ideal view of man and his destiny. His political thought is conditioned by the present moment, ripe with all the dilemmas, anxieties, and joys that this entails. Burke would agree with John Macquarrie that "man is temporal through and through."[3]

This realization of one's nature requires both the social context which supplies the condition of man's fulfillment, and liberty and virtue as the proper way to realize one's *telos*. It is necessary to consider in more detail the purpose civil society provides for man.

Civil society exists for the express purpose of providing man with the means and conditions of enjoying his natural rights. This, for Burke, is the "ultimate purpose of civil society" (TPL VI 333). But man has no right inconsistent with virtue, especially prudence. Rights must be consistent with nature. Burke holds that "Men have no right to what is not reasonable and to what is not for their benefit" (RF III 313). Hence, as the goal of civil society, rights are natural human goods recognized by reason. It is a social purpose and not an expression of bourgeois individualism which is implied by Burke's mention of "natural rights." The rights of men in society are not absolute, demanding fulfillment without qualification. Rather, "the restraints on men, as well as their liberties, are to be reckoned among their rights" (RF III 310).[4] Man does not renounce certain freedoms to obtain the security of group affiliation; instead, the freedoms man possesses are social freedoms, not freedoms antedating some mythical entry into society through a social contract. Granted, Burke does acknowledge the existence of a contract as fundamental to society, but it is not the type of social contract admitted to by Locke or Rousseau.[5] "Society is indeed a contract," concedes Burke. But it is a special kind of contract. More than a contract "It is a partnership in all science; a partnership in all art; a partnership in every virtue, and in all perfection" (RF III 359). For Burke, there exists no contract, somehow prior in time to the formation of society, taken in isolation. Yet there is a sense in which the individual is prior, that society exists to aid in the moral perfection of the human person—the person does not exist for society. Man is prior in the order of final causality. The individual, though, is not prior as antedating society and arbitrarily conceiving of and constructing society. True, society is a convention, hence an artifice of man. But this does not make society a product of the will, rescindable at man's pleasure, for "art is man's nature." The individual is not historically prior to society, but he is metaphysically prior in that society exists to aid in his moral perfection. Instead, man is born into society.

The Jacobin view of society is antithetical to a teleological conception. The Jacobins tend to elevate the individual and his desires, as distinct from his objective goods rooted in a common human nature, above that of the state. They insist on enumerating lists of rights as a check list for governments to meet. The result is a radical individualism, isolating individuals from community, risking anarchy and followed by tyranny. Russell Kirk correctly details the end result: "Infatuation with abstract right in the political concerns of government must end in anarchy, in a fiery and intolerant individualism. Even parliaments cannot endure if the doctrinaires of natural right are triumphant, for any form of representative government is in some degree an invasion of 'absolute liberty.' "[6] Burke's use of terms such as "natural rights" illustrates his concern for society as a living organism, and also his concern for our duties and obligations to civil society as well.[7] These duties, if fulfilled, make for a happier society both in the whole and in its parts than would otherwise be the case. Consequently, civil society is natural to man; more than that, it is demanded by man's nature in order to attain the purposes and ends for which it exists.

In this regard, as Stanlis has correctly concluded, the state as the political expression of society is a divine instrument for man's "social salvation."[8] The state has a moral purpose: to facilitate the perfection of the human person. The political arrangements of the state exist for social ends, and "it is a moral and virtuous discretion," Burke advises, "which keeps governments faithful to their ends."[9]

In concert with the utilitarians Burke aims to make "government pleasing to the people." But there is a standard for bringing pleasure to the people, one that towers over gratifying their changing fancy—that standard being "the limits of justice."[10] His notion of justice will be shown later as part of the argument for natural law as a component of his metaphysics.

Elsewhere the purpose and aim of man and society are further marked off by Burke, who reveals the telic nature of reality as a component of his metaphysics. Teleology as an element of his metaphysics further underscores the reasonableness and the intelligible structure of reality. When speaking, for instance, of Parliament he declares it to be "a *deliberate* assembly of *one* nation, with *one* interest, that of the whole—where not local purposes, not local prejudices, ought to guide, but the general good, resulting from the general reason of the whole."[11] The end to be sought for society is that of the common good, wherein individual man finds fulfillment of his personal good. And the common good which is man's end both individually and corporately is a reasonable end. It is reasonable in that it is conceived and willed by God, and that it meets the rational, social, and emotional needs of man and society.

Man's telos as included in the common good entails a choice. Man must exercise the freedom that is essentially his. The exercise of that freedom must be lawful and must be in accordance with virtue. Man's telos is a moral one, and virtue must mark the path toward its realization. What is the telos of liberty and virtue? What purpose does liberty serve, taking virtue, especially prudence, as a guide?

Liberty aids individuals and society in perfecting their nature. To be deprived of liberty is to be reduced below the level of one's humanity. Liberty is not the exclusive province of any class of society. Liberty, Burke writes, "is the portion of the mass of the citizens; and not the haughty license of some potent individual, or some predominant faction."[12] For order to prevail in society, liberty must exist. And since society is the condition for "the perfection of which [man's] nature is capable," where liberty and order do not obtain, society becomes divided against itself (RF III 448). Without order and peace, the common good, through the virtuous state, cannot be achieved. Burke is not simply speaking of happiness, for happiness is more likely to come to the good man than the bad; it is more likely to be a permanent staple of his life than the transitory, futile pleasures of the corrupt.

But happiness is not achieved without virtue. We are first of all obliged to a life of virtue, the meeting of our obligations, and the courageous commitment to those we love and to those life has placed in our company. As Burke writes in a letter to his son, Richard, in 1791: "Most assuredly it will be wise in us to conform ourselves to that State of things which providence is pleased to direct or permit. To act otherwise is not to make sacrifices to our principles but our passions" (C VI 439).[13] Our lives are filled with all manner of duties, yet these same burdens make for a meaningful, fructuous life, and lend to the cohesiveness of the community. We are at liberty to do good, and that which we do is not counted good unless freely chosen. We choose our social bonds because they affirm our essential humanity.

Liberty does not spell chaos. Rather, liberty, conjoined with virtue, is at the basis of society. Burke explained himself on this point to the electors of Bristol prior to his election from that city: "But the liberty, the only liberty, I mean is a liberty connected with order: that not only exists along with order and virtue, but which cannot exist at all without them. It inheres in good and steady government, as in its substance and vital principle."[14]

Why does liberty require order? Wilkins provides an answer stating that for Burke "man is not wholly rational"; therefore, he needs both "social discipline and self restraint."[15] This may sound like the medicine of the intransigent conservative, one who seeks only the preservation of the current order, whatever the price. Such a vision of Burke does not stand up against a close reading of his *Works* or scrutiny of his life. Recalling that Burke was a Whig, a member of the Rockingham opposition, should be sufficient to remind us of the struggle continuing between the Crown and Commons as pursued by the Whigs. Burke stood shoulder to shoulder with Charles James Fox in his qualified opposition both to the imposition of Grenville's Stamp Act in America and the war being waged against the colonies. I say "qualified" in that for America and Ireland he wished them both to remain within the imperial rule of Britain. This was not simply for a jealous protection of colonial hegemony, but because he felt the strong tradition of liberties vouchsafed to the British peoples would best be preserved within the umbrella of British heritage and protection. Other enemies, Burke feared, loomed to confront a disjoined empire, especially France for Ireland. Also, he pushed hard for the economic reform of the civil list and, in doing so, forfeited his own potentially vast emoluments that would have accrued to him as Paymaster General, an office he acquired when the Rockingham Whigs came to the head of the administration. Burke's politics appear at one moment revolutionary and at another moment reactionary. Regardless, his principled politics are evident in his conception of an ordered social liberty. And virtue, assisting in the flowering of liberty, through her discretionary comportment sees to the fidelity of government to its designs.

Burke values virtue as conducive to the perfecting of human nature. The spirit of all virtue is the spirit of moderation. It is a powerful, ordering virtue whose rein within society makes for a firm, cohesive social structure. Writing to Depont in 1789, Burke claims that "Moderation . . . is the virtue only of superior minds. It requires a deep courage, and full of reflection, to be temperate when the voice of multitudes . . . passes judgment against you" (C VI 49). In addition, exercising the virtue of moderation is required for the attainment of freedom, as Burke declares in a private letter: "Men must have a certain fund of natural moderation to qualify them for Freedom, else it become noxious to themselves and a perfect Nuisance to everybody else" (C VI 10). Turning to the French Revolution, Burke saw many aspects of this monumental event which did not square with his view of politics, Whig or otherwise, not the least of which were the overthrow of the monarchy and the notion of universal suffrage, together with an atheistic attack upon the entire religious foundations of Western civilization. These were immoderate positions that broke much too radically with French traditions, which threatened, in the extremity of the change urged, to overthrow the essence of the nation itself.[16] Consequently, as a restraining, moderating principle, virtue in man helps to preserve the nature of things, as it is lawful in its essence.

Liberty is essential to morality. Burke's growing despair after a long and rather unsuccessful fight over the East India Company, followed so closely by the havoc occurring in France, had clouded his optimism concerning the future of an ordered, social freedom. Still he knew what liberty was and what it was not, and he did not fail to note its relationship to morality, as he did in the *Reflections*: "In some people I see great liberty indeed; in many, if not in most, an oppressive, degrading servitude. But what is liberty without wisdom and without virtue? It is the greatest of all possible evils; for it is a folly, vice, and madness, without tuition or restraint" (RF III 559). Here liberty, the freedom that belongs to man, reveals its lawful, social, reasonable quality, and also the ever present danger of evil which demands the restraints on our passions to preserve order. How do man's fallible nature and the problem of evil affect the ends of society?

Burke's philosophy of human nature avoids a facile philosophical optimism about society. If the purpose of civil society is the perfection of the human person's nature, then there is much in the very heart of man to obstruct this occurrence. Burke refers to "the ignorance and fallibility of mankind"—not totally depraved, yet marked with imperfection (RF III 562). No plans of government, regardless of the care with which they are drawn, will be enough to overcome man's inherent fallibility, which impedes the desired progress of nations. Burke indicates that all we can do is to make sure things do not become worse, given the imperfect ways of man. This does not call forth gloom or despair. Though no utopian, Burke does see the real possibility of improvement, but for every step forward, there is the risk of two steps backward. Yet the good is within reach, leading Burke to write the "there is nothing that God has judged good for us that He has not given us the means to accomplish, both in the natural world and the moral world."[17]

What is the good spoken of here? It is not simply the will of the people expressed at any moment in history. Rather, it is the will of the people expressed within the identity they have achieved through deep ancestral linkage with the generations and wisdom of the past. It is a good achieved by prescription and presumption. Burke argues that

> It is a presumption in favor of any settled scheme of government against any untried project, that a nation has long existed and flourished under it. It is a better presumption even of the *choice* of a nation,—far better than any sudden and temporary arrangement by actual election. Because a nation is not an idea only of local extent and individual momentary aggregation, but it is an idea of continuity which extends in time as well as in numbers and in space. And this is a choice not on one day or one set of people, not a tumultuary and giddy choice; it is a deliberate election of ages and generations; it is a constitution made by what is ten thousand times better than choice, it is made by the peculiar circumstances, occasions, tempers, dispositions, and moral, civil and social habitudes of the people, which disclose themselves only in a long space of time. It is a vestment which accommodates itself to the body [SC VII 94–95].

The will of the people is an outgrowth of all the nation is and has come to be. Furthermore, their will must not abrogate their nature. Instead, it must be compatible with the natural law, and natural law is itself a metaphysical category in Burke's thought.

Classical Conception of the Natural Law

In order to place Burke's conception of the natural law in context, I will review the classical conception of this law as developed by Aristotle, Cicero and Aquinas.

While Aristotle does not work out in detail a natural law doctrine, he nonetheless provides elements for a doctrine especially in the *Rhetoric*, the *Politics*, and the *Nicomachean Ethics*.[18] The emergence of a natural law doctrine occurs in the *Nicomachean Ethics* in the context of a discussion on natural and legal justice. "Of political justice part is natural, part legal,—natural, that which everywhere has the same force and does not exist by people's thinking this or that."[19] Aristotle elaborates, claiming "that which is by nature is unchangeable and has everywhere the same force. . . ." For a more specific statement of a natural law doctrine, though, one must turn to Aristotle's *Rhetoric*: "We may describe 'wrong doing' as injury voluntarily inflicted contrary to law. 'Law' is either special or general. By special law I mean that written law which regulates the life of a particular community; by general law, all those unwritten principles which are supposed to be acknowledged everywhere." Aristotle clarifies the matter thusly: "Universal law is the law of Nature." Furthermore, "the principles of equity are permanent and changeless, and . . . the universal law does not change either, for it is the law of nature, whereas written laws often do change." For Aristotle this is the bearing of the lines in Sophocles' *Antigone*, in which Antigone pleads that in burying her brother she had broken Creon's law, but not the unwritten laws

> Not of to-day or yesterday they are,
> But live eternal. . . .[20]

As Aristotle does not construct an elaborate natural law doctrine, one may ask how one goes about determining what human actions are consistent with nature, and hence with the natural law? Clearly, Aristotle holds that all natural beings possess a nature (*physis*), one that is ordered to some determinate end (telos). To determine what is one's proper end, it is best to observe the normal functioning of such a being. This normal functioning, which is the same everywhere, should disclose the nature of the thing. Consequently, nature and end are related in Aristotle's teleological deliberations.[21] Still, as Yves Simon notes, there are gaps in Aristotle's understanding of the natural law which may be governed by his metaphysical uncertainty over the relation of the world to God.[22]

For Cicero, the natural law is reflected in the harmony obtained between right reason and nature. "True law," Cicero has Laelius argue in *The Republic*, "is right reason in agreement with nature; it is of universal application, unchanging and everlasting; it summons to duty by its commands, and averts from wrongdoing by its prohibitions."[23] The natural law for Cicero is grounded in nature; it is intelligible, and human right reason participates in it through apprehending its content. Natural law is not parochial, but it is true for all people, all places, and all times—past, present, and future. Furthermore, it cannot be altered, repealed or abolished. It is not, therefore, adaptable to the subjective intrigues of the human will. Its ground in the nature of things stems from the fact that God is the author of this nature, and hence of the law. He is also, for Cicero, the law's "promulgator, and its enforcing judge."[24] To attempt to disobey this law is, in effect, to try to flee from oneself, and to deny one's own human nature. At last, it cannot be done without severe consequences.

St. Thomas Aquinas is, of course, one of the central expositors of the natural law tradition. Concerning the nature of law itself, it exists "as a rule and measure of acts, by which man is induced to act or is restrained from acting; for *lex* is derived from *ligare* (to bind), because it obliges (*obligare*) one to act." Aquinas continues, holding that "the rule and measure of human acts is the reason, which is the first principle of human acts . . . for it belongs to reason to direct to the end. . . ."[25] When law is applied to human action in its proper social context, Aquinas makes it clear that all particular action is lawful as it is in conformity with the common good. Thus, "Law is simply any reasonable ordinance that is promulgated for the common good by the one who has charge of a community."[26]

Now the natural law is a participation by man in the eternal law. The eternal law reflects God's own creative ideas of things and their proper ends, and, therefore, entails a Divine Providence. "Hence the eternal law is nothing else than the plan of the divine wisdom considered as directing all the actions and motions of creatures."[27] For Aquinas, God's conception of things in their essence is not subject to the erosion of time; hence his law is eternal and, furthermore, it is one with himself.

The eternal law thus imprints itself upon the human person and this imprint shapes the nature of the person and informs it with certain inclinations and tendencies. Again, this participation of the eternal law in the rational creature is called the "natural law." Obviously, man cannot grasp the eternal law in its oneness with God's essence. Therefore, in order to grasp the natural law man must reflect upon his natural tendencies experientially revealed to him in order to realize the principles governing their proper fulfillment. This reflection leads to the enunciation of the universal precepts of the natural law which governs human actions, dictating, through right reason, the good to be pursued and the evil avoided. The natural tendencies from which the precepts are gleaned are not themselves the natural law, but rather are grounded in human nature itself, which, as a dynamic principle, is oriented towards its own natural good. Hence, the basic precept of the natural law is to seek the good and shun the evil.

From this general precept of the natural law, Aquinas discloses an ordering of precepts as a result of reason reflecting on nature. These precepts reveal that existence is to be preserved, that man must propagate his own kind and educate his young, that truth is to be sought, and that life is to be ordered correctly within society. Aquinas concludes that "to the natural law belongs everything to which a man is inclined according to his nature"; and "since the rational soul is the proper form of man, there is in every man a natural inclination to act according to reason, and this is to act according to virtue."[28] So, all acts of virtue are prescribed by the natural law.

The classical conception of the natural law therefore entails several components. There is a definite human nature which is constant, and received from God. This nature requires virtuous actions in order to realize its potential for good and achieve perfection. The law governing human actions is human nature itself, which becomes the norm of morality. The objects of human acts that are good enrich and realize human nature, and those that are evil corrupt our nature. As Henry Veatch reminds, "the very essence of any natural-law ethics is that there should be a veritable natural end, or natural perfection, or natural telos, of human life. . . ."[29] All human law is just insofar as it facilitates the perfection of human nature. Consequently, all human law has a standard by which it can be judged, by which it stands or falls. This standard, this natural law, is capable of being recognized by right reason, although divine revelation increases our insight, revealing to the human mind for assent aspects of that law that escape natural reflection, or correcting human reason's penchant for error.

Burke's Conception of the Natural Law

Recent writers on Burke have recognized the classical natural law foundation of Burke's political philosophy.[30] There is not, however, unanimity among current scholars on the importance, if any, of the natural law for Burke. Among those current writers who continue to place Burke in the utilitarian camp and dismiss the natural law as an important element of his philosophy is Frank O'Gorman. O'Gorman considers Burke's reference to, and use of, the concept of natural law as being "usually a polemical technique."[31] O'Gorman maintains that Burke is too suspicious of abstract ideas, too unsystematic in the elucidation of his thought, and too pragmatically concerned with the pressing political events of the day to give articulation to the concept of the natural law.[32]

It is my contention that the concept of the natural law is an integral part of Burke's metaphysics and therefore foundational also to his political theory. I will show that the natural law is a law reflective of God's will and justice. Additionally, it is necessary to show that the principles of the natural law reflect both an abiding and changing aspect, making it the same law, yet universally applicable in different historical epochs and societies. Furthermore, the natural law is reasonable, and as a reflection of God's being, it is a part of the objective structure of reality and, at least in its essence, capable of being apprehended by the human mind. As opposed to O'Gorman, I maintain that Burke does not have recourse to the notion of the natural law for sheer polemical purposes. Rather, this concept is a crucial component of his metaphysics.

First, an overview of Burke's philosophy of law is in order to better comprehend his natural law position. An early, but unpublished, work of Burke, the *Tract on the Popery Laws* (1765), sets out what he takes to be the basis of law. The *Tract* was written in response to the conditions of Catholics in Ireland at the time. Throughout this work his arguments are grounded in a natural law conception of human nature. Burke identifies two requisites for the establishment of the law: first, a competent authority, able to declare and, when necessary, modify the law; second, a constitution, equitable in its essence, which the authority shall have the right to make binding on its citizenry (TPL VI 321). If these comprise the requisites of law, what makes up the foundation?

For Burke, "there are two, and only two, foundations of law; and they are both of them conditions without which nothing can give it any force: I mean equity and utility" (TPL VI 323). Continuing, Burke writes: "With respect to the former [that is, equity,] it grows out of the great rule of equality, which is grounded upon our common nature, and which Philo, with propriety and beauty, calls the mother of justice" (TPL VI 323). Equity is justice grounded in natural law, whereas

> The other foundation of law, which is utility, must be understood, not of partial or limited, but of general and public utility, connected in the same manner with, and derived directly from, our rational nature: for any other utility may be the utility of a robber, but cannot be that of a citizen,—the interest of the domestic enemy, and not that of a member of the commonwealth [TPL VI 323].

As the two foundations of law, both equity and utility are derived from "our rational nature." Equity and utility make certain that the law is grounded in the natural order of things. This order imposes certain duties and secures certain rights for man, for the source of both duties and rights is, as Canavan notes, "The objective, divinely founded moral order. . . ." Canavan continues, "The most basic moral obligations thus rest upon the metaphysics of a created universe and are the source of all subsequent and subordinate obligations. . . ."[33]

Equity, then, signifies a common, rational nature, equally shared by man. Equity ensures in society the real rights of men. Burke sees these rights as the advantages that life in civil society can offer him, and the rights men have of living by law. The equitable society does not view man as simply an individual claimant for personal freedoms and rights. Rather, it sees all men in a partnership with one another, each having equal rights. But as equity is grounded in the nature and order of things it must likewise express a recognition of the order and distinctions among people. Consequently, Burke records, "In this partnership all men have equal rights; but not to equal things" (RF III 309). All rights must be consistent with virtue, especially prudence. Ultimately, rights are to be checked against the standard of practical reason and of what benefits man and society in conformity with nature (RF III 313).

Two points are worthy of note. First, the order of things, an order reflecting divine reason, grounds Burke's notion of equity and provides continuity to the varying historical expressions of equity prudently rendered which afford an application of rights and law befitting the changing circumstances. Second, when we turn to utility, the same ground is discovered as that for equity, namely "our rational nature" as conforming to the order instituted by divine reason. Although the touchstone of utility is our common nature, utility does not allow a uniform application in all circumstances. Law can be adjusted with considerations to what has utility for a nation, yet that utility cannot detract from the "substance of original justice" (TPL VI 323).

Turning from the foundations of law we find that there is a law prior to any human law which itself is permanent.

> We are all born in subjection,—all born equally, high and low, governors and governed, in subjection to one great, immutable,

pre-existent law, prior to all our devices and prior to all our conveniences, paramount to all our ideas and all our sensations, antecedent to our very existence, by which we are knit and connected in the eternal frame of the universe, out of which we cannot stir.[34]

This is an unmistakable reference to the natural law to which everything that is must ultimately submit. In that we comport ourselves with it, there is liberty. When we violate its precepts we can no longer shelter ourselves in it, but must reconcile ourselves to it.

All human law possesses, as was anticipated earlier, a telic quality. Burke claims that the "law is a mode of human action respecting society" (TPL VI 323). This activity, as for the activity of individuals themselves, must be governed by the eternal rules of equity. Whatever the law, one thing in particular is required of it: all law must be made for the common good.[35] This, indeed, was the major thrust of Burke's concern as he wrote the *Tract*. The Catholics constituted the majority of the population of Ireland, although the country was ruled by the so-called Protestant Ascendancy, a ruling faction which had successfully curried the favor of the British Crown. It was the goal of the faction to stop at nothing short of totally extirpating Catholicism from Ireland. Two methods were being employed within a legal framework, and one method implied the other. First, penal laws were written to punish even the practice of the Catholic faith. Second, laws were written barring all Catholics from holding any public office. On the level of natural feelings, this constituted a violation of one's *sense* of justice. On the level of principle, it violated all rules of law, forever etched in the eternal framework for all law: that is, the natural law.

Burke maintains that no faction of a community, especially a minority, can legislate in its own interest, particularly when this legislation renders an injustice to the rightful interests of the majority. This underscores his position that the essence of law requires that it exist for the common benefit: "Partiality and law are contradictory terms" (TPL VI 325). The type of "partiality" Burke has in mind is one that does violence to the preexistent law, that is, the natural law. There can be a *just* partiality, one that benefits the social order and enhances virtue and liberty—

in short, a partiality which reflects the natural order of things. This point is confirmed by the following statement Burke makes concerning the economic reform of government: "Law, being only made for the benefit of the community, cannot in any one of its parts resist a demand which may comprehend the total of the public interest."[36] Implied within this remark is a justification of the partial curtailment of the individual's liberties if it is in the interest of the whole.

It is in the order of things that certain privileges and concomitant obligations are due to each station of society, from aristocrat to peasant, and that these privileges and obligations are dissimilar. Burke affirms this when, as noted above, he writes, "All men have equal rights; but not to equal things" (RF III 309). But it is not in the order of things that law should grant a liberty to one faction of society that would destroy the liberties of another, for such destruction would likewise be destructive of the common good. Here, the principles of right embodied in the natural law allow us to discriminate concrete instances of threats to the common good.

Burke maintains that it is absurd to find a rule of justice in constitutions, or to believe "that laws derived their authority from the statutes of the people, the edicts of princes, or the decrees of judges. If it be admitted that it is not the blackletter and king's arms that make the law, we are to look for it elsewhere" (TPL VI 322–23). From where and from whom, then, are laws derived? Burke identifies a superior law, the principles of which no subsequent law can abrogate, and "which it is not in the power of any community, or of the whole race of man, to alter,—I mean the will of Him who gave us our nature, and in giving impressed an invariable law upon it" (TPL VI 322). Not only is the law of God superior, but its extension appears to reach all spheres of law, even down to the laws of business. In an essay which contains his philosophy of economics, Burke warns us not to break the laws of commerce because in doing so we break the laws of nature, and thereby, the laws of God.[37]

Only God is above the law, not as being outside the law, but as the source of all law. The law itself is an expression of God's being. Thus, God is the supreme metaphysical principle as the cause and foundation for all other principles and of all reality. It is in his abiding, unalterable nature that one of the two chief principles we have identified, stability, receives its ground. And the natural law, itself as an element of Burke's metaphysics, likewise finds it source and ground, as Burke notes, in the existence of God (ANW IV 205).

We see in this chapter a further elaboration of Burke's metaphysics through the components of teleology and natural law. Reality as created is not mechanistic in its substance. Rather, it is purposive, giving evidence of design. And there is a natural law, the principles of which the human mind can apprehend. These additional components of Burke's metaphysics complement the ones already elaborated. Both the telic nature of man and the laws governing his existence demonstrate a sameness and continuity throughout man's history. Yet the ends for which man exists are realized in unique ways in concert with the singular moment of his historical epoch. The laws governing his existence, coming as they do from the Creator, are constant in their principles yet flexible enough to find a fresh application to the changing social situation into which each new age is thrust.

NOTES

1. Burke notes the ignorance and fallibility that attend human nature when he writes that those forefathers who helped, over the course of time, give shape to the British constitution "acted under a strong impression of the ignorance and fallibility of mankind. He that had made them thus fallible rewarded them for having in their conduct attended to their nature" (RF III 562).

2. *Speech on Impeachment of Warren Hastings* (February 16, 1788), W IX 453.

3. John Macquarrie, *Existentialism* (Harmondsworth: Penguin, 1976), pp. 220–21.

4. In light of our analysis it is not possible to share Dreyer's conclusion that Burke "pretended to be and belongs in the end to the Lockean tradition of natural-rights individualism." *Burke's Politics*, p. 69. (See also p. 83.)

5. "Burke's social philosophy," writes Francis Canavan, "was teleological; the social contract theory was not." *Political Reason of Edmund Burke*, p. 87.

6. Kirk, "Burke and Natural Rights," *The Review of Politics*, 13, No. 4 (1951), 448.

7. Cf., Peter Stanlis, *Edmund Burke and the Natural Law*, pp. 99 and 210.

8. Ibid., p. 210.

9. *Speech on the Petition of the Unitarians* (1792), W VII 42.

10. *Speech at Bristol Previous to the Election* (1780), W II 421.

11. *Speech at the Conclusion of the Poll* (1774), W II 96.

12. *Letter to Richard Burke, Esq.* (1793), W VI 390.

13. Burke's reference to Providence in this passage refers to the political situation resulting from the French Revolution and Burke's own concern that the Providence of God has permitted this state of affairs and the effort to change the matter is futile.

14. *Speech at his Arrival at Bristol* (1774), W II 87.

15. Wilkins, *Burke's Political Philosophy*, p. 112.

16. Burke's social and political relationships became most strained during the period of the Revolution. Carl B. Cone, a recent biographer, writes that "It was about this time that he began making himself socially disagreeable, disrupting private gatherings by his passionate attacks upon the Revolution. Whether at a meeting of the committee on Johnson's monument or at the Club, Burke made himself unpleasant." Carl B. Cone, *Burke and the Nature of Politics: The Age of the French Revolution* (Lexington: The University of Kentucky Press, 1964), pp. 302–3.

17. *Speech on the Plan for Economical Reform* (1780), W II 357.

18. See Paul Sigmund, *Natural Law in Political Thought* (Cambridge, Mass.: Winthrop, 1971), pp. 9–12; Yves R. Simon, *The Tradition of Natural Law: A Philosopher's Reflections*, ed. Vukan Kuic, (New York: Fordham University Press, 1965; rpr. 1992), pp. 27–30; and A. P. d'Entreves, *Natural Law: An Introduction to Legal Philosophy* (London: Hutchinson University Library, 1960), pp. 8–10. My remarks on Aristotle are influenced by these authors.

19. Aristotle, *Nicomachean Ethics*, trans. W. D. Ross, in *The Basic Works of Aristotle*, ed. Richard McKeon (New York: Random House, 1941), V, 7, 1134b 17–20, 25–26, p. 1014.

20. Aristotle, *Rhetoric*, trans. W. Rhys Roberts in *The Basic Works of Aristotle*, ed. Richard McKeon (New York: Random House, 1941), I, 9 (1368b7–10), 13 (1373b6), I, 15 (1375a31–33, b1–2).

21. Sigmund, *Natural Law in Political Thought*, p. 10.

22. Simon, *Tradition of Natural Law*, p. 27.

23. *The Republic*, III, 22, in Marcus Tullius Cicero, *De Re Publica, De Legibus*, XVI, trans. Clinton Walker Keyes, The Loeb Classical Library (Cambridge: Harvard University Press, 1928), p. 211.

24. Ibid.
25. *Summa theologica*, I–II, 90, 1.
26. Ibid., I–II, 90, 4, c.
27. Ibid.
28. Ibid., I–II, 94, 3, c.
29. Veatch, *Human Rights*, p. 56.
30. The works by Canavan, Wilkins, and Stanlis mentioned throughout this study are most prominent. Also see Stanlis, "The Basis of Burke's Political Conservatism," *Modern Age*, 5 (1961), 263–274.
31. O'Gorman, *Edmund Burke: His Political Philosophy*, p. 19.
32. Ibid., p. 13. For a more detailed critique of O'Gorman's interpretation of Burke and the natural law see the present writer's review of O'Gorman's book, "The Case Against Burke: A Review of Frank O'Gorman's *Edmund Burke: His Political Philosophy*," *Modern Age*, 19 No. 4 (Fall 1975), 431–32.
33. Francis P. Canavan, "Burke on Prescription of Government," *The Review of Politics*, 35, No. 4 (October 1973), 458.
34. *Speech on Impeachment of Warren Hastings* (February 16, 1788), W IX 455.
35. Here the telos of law is that of human nature as well.
36. *Speech on the Plan for Economical Reform* (1780), W II 329. In this passage Burke goes on to suggest an important criterion for all law, stating that "no law can set itself up against the cause and reason of all law." And before this he says that "if the barriers of law should be broken down, upon ideas of convenience, even of public convenience, we shall have no longer anything certain among us." This should help to show that human law seeks the good of the people when ultimately gauged against the most fundamental law of nature, and that it is not simply the will of the people as voiced at any particular time.
37. *Thoughts and Details on Scarcity* (1795), W V 157.

6
Concluding Reflections: Metaphysical Nihilism and Radical Individualism

IN THIS FINAL CHAPTER I wish to offer some reflections on the problem of nihilism and radical individualism in the light of Burke's realist metaphysics. Burke believed that French revolutionary thought was grounded in principles of philosophic atheism. He warned of the "spirit of atheistical fanaticism" (RF III 435) inspired by the writings of the revolutionaries, and he claimed that "The most horrid and cruel blow that can be offered to civil society is through atheism."[1] The spirit of atheism and its connected spirit of destruction were for Burke the driving force of revolutionary thought.

Such revolutionary thought entailed, of course, its own metaphysics. It is not my purpose, though, in this concluding chapter to introduce new material for, as mentioned earlier, Burke himself generalized about revolutionary thought under the rubric of "Jacobinism." My concern is not the correctness of his generalizations, but his insight into metaphysical nihilism which, I believe, characterizes the greater part of our modern, secular temperament. This is clearly manifest by the intellectual and cultural impact of the geniuses of our time, the so-called "masters of suspicion," by whom I mean Nietzsche, Marx and Freud. Alasdair MacIntyre, in his recent work *After Virtue*, disparagingly pronounces Nietzsche to be "*the* moral philosopher of the present age."[2] These shapers of the modern mind are avowedly atheistic, and that their thought should be so crucial to an understanding of our age would be no surprise to Burke. Without engaging specifically these thinkers, I will construct a depiction of nihilism that reflects Burke's own generalizations of revolutionary atheism; weigh its consequences for a radical humanism;

and demonstrate how a Burkean metaphysics constitutes a ringing rebuke and challenge to what I shall call metaphysical nihilism. Further, I will show that such radical humanism destroys true individuality, and that Burke's metaphysics restores and preserves authentic humanism and individualism.

Since God, for Burke, is the absolute perfection of being, and the created world in all of its manifestations and gradations is dependent on God for existence, then the denial of God constitutes a profound metaphysical nihilism. Of course the term "nihilism" was not used by Burke, and in fact the term did not emerge until well into the nineteenth century. Nonetheless, using "nihilism" to refer to an atheistic denial of God makes the term appropriate to refer to Burke's own understanding of French revolutionary thought and its destructive spirit. The consequences of this nihilism introduces a vacuum that atheistic humanism tries to fill. The flavor for Burke of this humanism is the glorification of man as being essentially free, possessing natural rights which entail a radical political democratization of society. Beyond duties and virtues, this humanism posits a radical freedom at the foundation of its politics. Therefore, this brand of humanism asserts the radical freedom of the human person which of necessity entails the denial of God. Why is this the case? Nihilism by its nature is the negation of being, and being finds its ontological ground for the classical metaphysics of Burke in the existence of the supreme being, God. There are reasons for this denial of God, whether they are epistemological, moral, social, or other. But the primary reason for the denial of God in this depiction is the emergence and glorification of man. God must die in order that man might by glorified. But why must this be?

To answer this question is to point to the celebration of human freedom as seen by the nihilists. To celebrate such freedom in conjunction with God's denial is to assume that man is oppressed. The liberation of man is, therefore, tied to the death of God. Since, according to nihilism, God does not exist save as a projection of man's consciousness, and since this projection reduces man to a servile state, he can only overcome the alienation of his state by becoming the independent and free individual he is by nature. Perhaps no motive sustains the revolutionary fervor more than the desire for the unrestrained freedom of the individual, and no greater obstacle lies in the path of this fervor than the avowed claim of God's existence.

Again, it may be asked, why is this the case? Society finds its reason for being in the designs of Providence. For Burke, God wills the state, wills man's social nature, wills the subordination of the various elements of society for the purpose that the state might aid man in obtaining virtue, so that he may fulfill his duties towards his fellowman, thereby promoting order and harmony in the state. Human life is meant to be social, lawful, and orderly; man's freedom is achieved and secured by the rule of law. Now the ground of all law, especially the moral law, is God. For the nihilism of the revolutionaries, God serves to secure the status quo, since social authority flows from God's own law for man. Yet the experienced order of the state for the revolutionary is oppressive; it requires of him to limit his will, to be obedient, law-abiding, and this he finds restrictive. To enjoy the freedom that is natural to man, it is necessary for God to be denied.

It is in an abstract conception of freedom, namely, that of man in his natural condition as free, able to make of himself what he is to be to the extent that he has the requisite strength of will, that freedom is posited and seen as opposed by God's existence. Such an abstract concept demands a further consequence, that all men are naturally equal and that associations or classifications of men unduly regard the freedoms of certain men at the expense of others. It is necessary in this particular conception of nihilism that all men be treated equally, not simply in terms of their essential nature as human, but in the social realization of that nature. The consequence will be the levelling of social classes and the undermining of various associations. With the levelling of class distinctions, Burke feared that the state would grow into a tyranny because there would be no buffer between the absolute power of the state and the shivering solitude of the individual.

This consequence is of course rooted in a conception of human nature as having a pre-social claim to freedom, rendering man as social only as a result of his choice to combine with others. How does this radical freedom for man resolve itself into an egalitarian view of man as equally dominated by a tyrannical rule? It is because the conception of this freedom lies precisely outside its properly social context, a view of freedom which is abstract and pre-social, not concrete and actual. As an abstraction freedom is complete and yet vacuous—it does not exist.

The nihilist view, though, claims to envision a freedom equal for all and to achieve this through the radical democratization of society. Each person's vote is as important as another's. There is no social differentiation. Egalitarianism and radical democratization are not the claims of all nihilists; nor are theists, deists or other descriptions excluded from these claims. Nonetheless, these are the claims of a nihilism that maintains that all men are by nature free, prior to the social state. It is due to freedom and its natural state for man that society is bound to preserve freedom equally for all and give no manner of persons preference. Certain nihilistic views would seek a preferential treatment and disavow this egalitarian picture. Some would reward those who rise above the masses through a will-to-power. But a political nihilism which finds no inherent reason for the subordination of one class to another aims to achieve freedom equally for all and this attainment results in, at least in theory, a radical democratization of the masses. But two irreconcilable forces come into conflict at this point. The first force is that of egalitarianism and the second is the need the state has for a gradation of authority suffused throughout the state and society. Without such a graded authority we have a mass of individuals, not a society of persons. As the notion of a pre-social freedom is an abstraction, so a thoroughly egalitarian society without graded authority is an abstraction.

In a situation where a state removes all barriers to freedom for every human being, and ensures a radical egalitarianism, then authority, which is necessary for society, must fall into the hands of a tyrant. From an abstract freedom and an abstract notion of equality we move from a "sense" of oppression, which the revolutionaries felt under traditional society, to total oppression under the tyranny that necessarily results from this depiction of a metaphysical nihilism. The end result is the annihilation of man. If all reason for law is removed, then the only law that remains is the law of naked power, for only he who can assert his will to the greatest degree can dominate, can be free. And yet the freedom of the tyrant, as Hegel saw in the *Phenomenology of Spirit*, is only a reflected freedom, a freedom reflected in the obedience of the servile class.

But there is another and more serious move that metaphysical nihilism can make. If the ground of being is denied, then reason is overthrown because reason apprehends being and the result for the intellect is the truth. But if the ground of being is removed, so is the ground of reason, and truth becomes an illusion. If this nihilistic view is the truth, then any assertion of truth as reflecting being is an illusion. Taking this to the extreme, then, man must construct his own truth. But even such constructions can be no more than individual illusions or, more broadly, social illusions. And yet man must have some framework of understanding, some horizon of interpretation. Perhaps, though, all reason has its ground, not in being, but in the irrational. This is nothing more than the inversion of the classical view that being discloses itself to reason, hence is knowable, hence is itself rational. But if the locus of being is transferred from the realm of the rational to that of the irrational, then all subsequent reason emerges out of the irrational and is determined by the irrational. This is the next component of my depiction of nihilism: all reason emerges out of the irrational.

Before exploring the notion of the "irrational," I should note that Alasdair MacIntyre confirms my focus on nihilism by asserting that "The contemporary vision of the world . . . is predominantly, although not perhaps always in detail, Weberian."[3] Allan Bloom arrives at a similar conclusion, wondering as he does in *The Closing of the American Mind*: "Who in 1920 would have believed that Max Weber's technical sociological terminology would someday be the everyday language of the United States. . . ?"[4] Further, MacIntyre holds that "Nietzsche's central thesis was presupposed by Weber's central categories of thought."[5] Again, Bloom evidently concurs: "Although it is even now still insufficiently appreciated, Freud and Weber were both thinkers who were profoundly influenced by Nietzsche, as is obvious to anyone who knows Nietzsche and knows what was going on in the German-speaking world in the late nineteenth century."[6] MacIntrye records that Nietzsche's central thesis is that "there is nothing to morality but expressions of will." In other words, morality cannot be objectively grounded or rationally supported. Why is this so? "All faiths and all evaluations are equally non-rational; all are subjective directions given to sentiment and feeling."[7] Reason seeks to veil the non-rational source of values. Hence MacIntrye refers to "Nietzsche's prophetic irrationalism" as underlying Weber's interpretation of the only viable rational authority in the contemporary world, bureaucratic authority.[8] And yet underlying bureaucratic authority is nothing other than the desire for power. So, at bottom, MacIntrye sustains my thesis that in broad outlines contemporary thought has succumbed to the irrational, that will has ascendancy over reason, that reason serves only the ends of domination, and that the result is morality based on the quest for power, or morality based on passion without rational support.

What is the character of the irrational? It does not really matter for our purposes, but whatever it may be it constitutes the unconscious. It may be the unconscious of the passions, of the libido, of socio-economic factors unknown to empirical consciousness, or the unconscious of the transcendental ego. From this view, reason emerges as veiling its ground in the illusion of truth, but is doomed to failure. Such veiling is an attempt to dominate, and the result is ideology.

In the classical view reason discovers and discloses being and its structure to man. In the nihilistic view reason's emergence is an abrogation of its source, which is the irrational. Yet to abrogate is to dominate and domination is power. Further, the being of nihilism resides in its denial of being, in the dark swirls of the irrational. If nihilism has any metaphysics whatsoever it must be the metaphysics of the irrational, of the absurd. And such a metaphysics is simply a denial of the intelligibility of being, and so of being itself. Yet it is the nature of being that necessarily dominates thought because it is thought that reflects being. So, if all thought emerges from the irrational as being below the realm of reason, as unintelligible, then whatever reason pronounces is, in effect, without reason, unfounded and unreal. All reasoning, all saying, all logic becomes an illusory veil drawn to mask the swirling cauldron of the irrational. The political results of such a metaphysical nihilism must be that knowledge is power, dominance, and violence. Its violence lies in casting a net of coherency over what is in its essence incoherent. Coherency violates the incoherent, and the reason for this violation can only be for the purpose of control. Further, power falls to the one or ones who control political discourse. The discourse of the French revolutionaries was the discourse of rights, but their discourse masked their radical nihilism. And while they spoke the language of "freedom" and applauded the "people," in both concepts they erected only an abstraction compatible with their discourse. Lying beneath the discourse was the "reality" of the irrational and the irrational, which by its nature is chaos, disorder, the Bacchanalian whirl. Now a language reflecting a logical structure which makes claims that are grounded in the irrational is simply replete with contrived abstractions. Unlike Aristotelian abstractions, they are without a ground. Removing the veil uncovers the chaos and disarray of the irrational. Politics becomes for the nihilist a thinly disguised gloss that bears the reason of its construction in the desire for domination. As this politics pursues a logic grounded on the illogical, it must be a politics of violence. And this is what separates the politics grounded in metaphysical nihilism from a politics grounded in a metaphysical classical realism. For the latter, the resulting political discourse which argues for a graded, subordinated ordering of authority and classes in society reflects a hierarchy of being. But a political discourse which imposes a logic grounded on the irrational has no justification for any political scheme save a scheme of each man for himself, solitary and alone. And such a scheme is no scheme at all and collapses necessarily into tyranny. This is what Burke foresaw for the French Revolution and correctly predicted, grounded as it was in the illogical logic of the Jacobins.

And yet it was the revolutionaries who applauded the people and fought for individual natural rights. It was their liberal spirit which announced the freedom of the person as an inviolate right and was willing to dissolve society to achieve it. But who is the true defender of the human person, Burke or the revolutionary?

Burke is often depicted as the conservative sychophant of the aristocratic class, the philosopher of the state, neglecting the individual. This depiction is jejune and simplistic, and fails to address the assumption upon which it rests which, once acknowledged, misconstrues Burke as anti-individual and pro-state. That assumption is that man is not social by nature but only by compact, designed to secure his survival. The state easily comes to be seen as by nature oppressive or, at best sufferable, for it is reduced to a servant of the individual's needs. To picture the state as having its reason for being in terms of its ability to serve the individual seems inviting and appealing. But what are the results? Burke sees an increasing dependence upon the state to meet those needs and expectations. This must be the case the more that society becomes levelled, and each individual is reduced to an equal quantitative unity. As society becomes absorbed into the state, the state gains in stature precisely through its tendency to assume all functions ordinarily assumed by various groupings within society, such as the family, the neighborhood, the community, and the church. These groupings and associations were seen by Burke as vital to the protection of the concrete freedoms the individual actually possessed, and as a buffer against the caprice of the state. The individual's own sense of who he is becomes forged on the anvil of these associations, which are natural, not contrived through the political intent of the state to organize the people. To annul these associations claiming that the associations work against the solitary individual, and violate the radical movement toward democratization, is to miss the social and psychological needs which determine the very being of the person. This goes to the heart of Burke's "anti-metaphysical" fulminations by which he meant the geometrical, mathematizing of society, imposed upon the citizens by the ideological fervor of the revolutionaries, which threatened to strip the individual of his various intermediary associations.

There was no doubt for Burke that in arguing for traditional society grounded in the framework of the existing political and social structure he proposed the preservation of the true individuality that requires society. Again, as Burke claimed, it is the purpose of the state to aid the individual in living a virtuous life, not to live it for him.

And here we come to the dividing line between the modern temperament and the traditional, classical understanding of political and social life. The modern age witnesses a radical ideology which argues for freedom, a freedom ebbing away from the restraints of duty, obligation, and responsibility. A radical individualist would argue for an absolute freedom; his only obligation is towards a utopian future—unrealizable, yet promising perfect freedom and self-realization. The wish for absolute freedom is unhistorical in that such a freedom can never be achieved. It exists out of time in the fertile imaginations of certain radical ideologists.

The classical view affirms the social nature of man, a view that entails social relationships and commitments, duties and responsibilities. Man's sociality is governed by a moral law that is to be realized within the station of life that Providence has placed him. This is not an annulment of freedom but a structuring of freedom, a telic view of freedom which finds its achievement within a hierarchical society reflective of the structure of being and of the Divine Will itself. It does not prevent social change, but gives it order and direction. Burke illustrates these points by claiming that "When we marry, the choice is voluntary, but the duties are not matter of choice: they are dictated by the nature of the situation" (ANW IV 166). So, while we are free to marry or not, we are not free to amend the duties and responsibilities which we assume by marriage, duties reflecting the moral, social, and divine law. Burke illustrates this point further:

> Parents may not be consenting to their moral relation; but, consenting or not, they are bound to a long train of burdensome duties towards those with whom they never made a convention of any sort. Children are not consenting to their relations; but their relation, without their actual consent, binds them to its duties—or rather it implies their consent, because the presumed consent of every rational creature is in unison with the predisposed order of things [ANW IV 166].

We cannot escape these duties and our fulfilling of the same brings with them certain rights that society grants to us precisely for having assumed the duties of marriage. Man is social. He is a debtor as well as being one who is owed something. He is owed the advantages and privileges which society is able to secure for him. The rights and duties are reciprocal between individuals and between the individual and society. After all, society and the state are an extension of the individual, composed of individuals, within a moral framework ordained by God Himself and mediated by the state, its laws and customs. The individual attains his true nature and self-realization only within the state, and the various associations, and obligations that constitute his life. At the very core of the individual's existence, Burke recognized, lay the religion of the Christian faith. Religion is the principle of cohesion, giving life to the social whole, grounding our social relations, legitimizing our duties to one another, and giving purpose and dynamism to the integral whole in which the individual achieves genuine individuality.

My portrait of a metaphysical nihilist probably fails to incorporate entirely any single philosopher of modern times. Yet I believe it succeeds in its broad outlines. It calls to mind the atheistic temper of our times. If God is not denied then He seems certain to be bracketed, or He must await an adequate "God" language, or some such treatment. The metaphysical nihilist claims the temporality of thought, that all our terms emerge from the spatial-temporal sphere, are therefore phenomenally rooted, and cannot be adequate to a non-temporal dimension. Analogical thought, itself the foundation of traditional natural theology, finds little support. The cultural truth of our age is dominated by the anthropological reduction: God is a projection of the human mind and desires, bears His existence in dependence upon man, and must be faced for what He is—nothing.

The nothingness of God is foundational to the thought of pivotal thinkers and movements of our secularized postmodern world, and filling the void left by God's demise, as we have seen, is the right of man to freedom, to not only the necessities of life, but also many of its luxuries which have become necessities. This leads to a narcissistic state, consumed by a sense of "me" over any "we." The self and its own satisfaction has become our god. In fact, the revolutionary demand for freedom seems only elementary; freedom casts about for its object and that object appears in a variety of ways to aim at satisfying the pleasure instincts of the self. Man's quest for freedom becomes a search for the diversions of pleasure. The glorification of the self leads to man's further dissatisfaction, restlessness, boredom, fatigue, alienation, guilt—and yet, these qualities continue to be blamed on everything save their proper source, that very same self-glorification. Man gloats over his newly found independence and moans over his unbearable anguish for the lonely, purposeless, solitude he has gained. And yet he is free, and in bondage to his freedom. His freedom gained, his meaning lost, an unbearable solitude grows within the egalitarian political "haven" he has created.

The clamor for freedom has left man nauseated. It is a tragic error to claim that existence is nausea, save that existence be considered unintelligible and unreal. Being, stripped of intelligibility, and without essence, fails to gain for man the freedom for which he aspires. Man is a conspirator in his own demise. He has conspired to try to elevate what is by nature below, above that which by nature is above. He has inverted the natural order and supplanted God with man, and he is nauseated by this act of deicide. Burke saw clearly this inversion of the natural order in the revolutionary scheme of things and he warned against it. He held that "To make a revolution is to subvert the ancient state of our country; and no common reasons are called for to justify so violent a proceeding" (RF III 451). He saw that man himself would be the loser, because society will not endure for long the reign of disorder and chaos the revolution inevitably would bring. Society will know order, and if the natural order of things is upended, then a perverted, unnatural order will take its place. It will be a tyranny, and man's true, concrete freedoms will be removed. In its place will be a dominion of naked, lawless power.

Burke's metaphysical realism, which grounds a hierarchically structured state and society, reflecting the moral law, provides the framework for an authentic, while imperfect, individualism, or, better, a personalism which is achieved only in a community of other persons in association.

Final Remarks

The main goal in this study has been to demonstrate that Burke's political philosophy is grounded in a realist metaphysics, one that is basically consonant with the Aristotelian-Thomistic tradition. Further, it has been shown that no adequate understanding of Burke's political thought can be achieved apart from an understanding of his metaphysics. Without grasping Burke's underlying metaphysical base, one might mistakenly conclude that he is a pragmatist or a utilitarian. In large part, the thrust of this work has been to make explicit the implicit metaphysical core of Burke's political thought.

Burke's political philosophy is grounded in a metaphysics that discloses order which reveals itself to us through experience. We experience reality as vital, and developing, where change is in constant evidence. The reality with which Burke most concerns himself is the social and political reality of his day. Change in the political realm is a vitalizing, renewing force, but a force that is structured by abiding elements in the realities of the social and political realm. And this fabric, giving evidence of order by way of the elements of change and stability, reflects and expresses nature itself and the designs of God. Consequently, if we are to synthesize Burke's metaphysical elements of change and stability as revealed in his political thought, we must speak of the resultant notion of orderly development. Change, growth, development—all must take place, but within the framework of order.

Burke's metaphysics does not ratify a static world of changeless essences in which becoming is short-changed for being. Rather, in this finite, mutable world, man's existence is most properly realized by and through his becoming. In Burke we see a primacy placed on existence—existence in the concrete historical and social conditions which subjects man's essential human nature to the particularities and modalities of his existence as a social being. Indeed, for Burke, man is being-in-the-world, yet not subsumed completely within a temporal horizon.

Burke in no way falls prisoner to an abstraction. It is this wariness of abstractions and of an abstract metaphysics that thrusts his politics into the concrete world of actual experience. Here, man's longing for freedom is not an ideal to be pined for. It is rather to be achieved within his own time, in response to the traditions, customs, and historical developments that have helped shape the character and nature of the citizens of a nation.

Man is a social being, and his freedom, individual rights, and duties are realized in the context of society.

Lingering confusions in Burke's thought have nevertheless led to misunderstandings of his political thought. These could have been largely obviated if Burke had not recoiled from making explicit his implicit metaphysics. Victor Hamm contends that "Burke would have been a sounder thinker, and perhaps a more influential one, had he based his political philosophy on the explicit formulation of a true metaphysics, and not merely on the repudiation of a false [metaphysics]. . . . His strength is not the absence of this deeper thinking, but rather its latent and implied presence, vitalizing and directing his speech and writing."[9] Such is the wording of so many of Burke's individual tracts and speeches as to make the content ambiguous and misleading. His thought has suffered at the well-meaning hands of his interpreters for the very fact that he refused to be more than the "philosopher in action." The advent of the French Revolution and the need to advance in a more specific fashion the latent underpinnings of this thought caused works such as the *Reflections* to be more philosophical in tone and content. How else was he to counter the penchant for theorizing that spawned and fueled so much of the French political thought that so evoked his wrath?

Perhaps I have pointed up some characteristic differences inherent in the French mind as opposed to the English. The French, as heirs of Descartes, seem more given to ratiocination apart from an adequate experiential basis, whereas the English mind is steeped within the empiricist tradition. And Burke, the Irishman, is quite English in this regard. The empiricist aspect of his thought, however, does not evolve into the sort of empiricism of a Locke or a Hume. The youthful appropriation of the classics, being Burke's early fare in Trinity College, Dublin, was never lost to him. As we have seen, his knowledge of Aristotle, Cicero, and other classical authors permeates his writing, and his studies entail the languishing air of scholasticism.

Nonetheless, we cannot make of Burke what he was not. He was neither an academic metaphysician nor a scholastic. Yet, for whatever reason, Burke's thought is impeded from achieving that clarity and cutting edge which could have been his if he had attended, in greater detail, to the philosophical foundations of his political thought. To do less was to invite the metaphysics he assigned to the French to have full reign in revolutionary times. Yet, for Burke to have done more would probably have meant the abrogation of the title he held and lived most completely, the "philosopher in action."

One must retain a perspective on what the political philosopher may desire of Burke and what Burke's life-circumstances actually were. Edmund Burke was, in his time and to his own mind, a politician, not a political philosopher. Only the disarray and chaos that surrounded him forced him to articulate a philosophy he himself had, in the main, appropriated from the living tradition of the perennial philosophy.

NOTES

1. *Speech on . . . the Relief of Protestant Dissenters* (1773), W VII 36.
2. *After Virtue*, 2nd ed. (Notre Dame: Notre Dame University Press, 1984), p. 114.
3. Ibid., p. 109.
4. (New York: Simon and Schuster, 1987), p. 147.
5. MacIntyre, *After Virtue*, p. 114.
6. Bloom, *Closing of the American Mind*, p. 148.
7. MacIntyre, *After Virtue*, pp. 113–14.
8. Ibid., p. 114 and p. 26.
9. "Burke and Metaphysics," in *Essays in Modern Scholasticism*, ed. Anton C. Pegis (Westminster, Maryland: Newman, 1944), p. 220.

SELECTED BIBLIOGRAPHY

PRIMARY SOURCES

Annual Register. London: Dodsley, 1759—.
The Correspondence of Edmund Burke. Ed. Thomas W. Copeland. 10 vols. Cambridge: Cambridge University Press; Chicago: The University of Chicago Press, 1958–1978.
The Correspondence of the Right Honourable Edmund Burke. Edd. Charles Williams, Earl Fitzwilliam, and Sir Richard Bourke. 4 vols. London: Rivington, 1844.
A Notebook of Edmund Burke. Ed. H. V. F. Somerset. Cambridge: Cambridge University Press, 1957.
Samuels, Arthur P. I. *The Early Life, Correspondence, and Writings of the Right Honourable Edmund Burke*. Cambridge: Cambridge University Press, 1923.
The Speeches of the Rt. Hon. Edmund Burke, in the House of Commons, and in Westminster Hall. 4 vols. London: Longman, Rees, 1816.
The Works of the Right Honorable Edmund Burke. 12 vols. Boston: Little, Brown, 1866.

SECONDARY SOURCES

Bevan, Ruth A. *Marx and Burke: A Revisionist View*. La Salle, Ill.: Open Court, 1973.
Blakemore, Steven. "Burke and the Fall of Language." *Eighteenth-Century Studies*, 17, No. 3 (Spring 1984), 284–307.
Boulton, James T. *The Language of Politics in the Age of Wilkes and Burke*. London: Routledge & Kegan Paul, 1963.
Cameron, David. *The Social Thought of Rousseau and Burke: A Comparative Study*. Toronto: University of Toronto Press, 1973.
Canavan, Francis P., S.J. "Burke on Prescription of Government." *The Review of Politics*, 35, No. 4 (October 1973), 454–74.

———. *Edmund Burke: Prescription and Providence*. Durham: Carolina Academic, 1987.

———. *The Political Reason of Edmund Burke*. Durham: Duke University Press, 1960.

Chapman, Gerald. *Edmund Burke: The Practical Imagination*. Cambridge: Harvard University Press, 1967.

Cobban, Alfred. *Edmund Burke and the Revolt Against the Eighteenth Century*. New York: Barnes & Noble, 1960.

Cone, Carl B. *Burke and the Nature of Politics: The Age of the French Revolution*. Lexington: The University of Kentucky Press, 1964.

Copeland, Thomas W. *Our Eminent Friend, Edmund Burke*. New Haven: Yale University Press, 1949.

Courtney, C. P. *Montesquieu and Burke*. Oxford: Blackwell, 1963.

Deane, Seamus F. "Burke and the French *Philosophes*." *Studies in Burke and His Time*, 10, No. 2 (Winter 1968–1969), 113–37.

Dinwiddy, J. R. "Utility and Natural Law in Burke's Thought: A Reconsideration." *Studies in Burke and His Time*, 16, No. 2 (Winter 1974–1975), 105–28.

Dreyer, Frederick. *Burke's Politics: A Study in Whig Orthodoxy*. Waterloo, Ontario: Wilfred Laurier University Press, 1979.

———. "Edmund Burke: The Philosopher in Action." *Studies in Burke and His Time*, 15, No. 2 (Winter 1973–1974), 121–42.

Fasel, George. *Edmund Burke*. Boston: Twayne, 1983.

Fennessy, R. R. *Burke, Paine, and the Rights of Man: A Difference of Political Opinion*. The Hague: Nijhoff, 1963.

Freeman, Michael. *Edmund Burke and the Critique of Political Radicalism*. Oxford: Blackwell, 1980.

Gandy, Clara I., and Stanlis, Peter J. *Edmund Burke: A Bibliography of Secondary Studies to 1982*. New York: Garland, 1983.

Hamm, Victor M. "Burke and Metaphysics." In *Essays in Modern Scholasticism*. Ed. Anton C. Pegis. Westminster, Maryland: Newman, 1944. Pp. 206–21.

Hampsher-Monk, Iain. "Introduction." *The Political Philosophy of Edmund Burke*. Ed. Iain Hampsher-Monk. London and New York: Longmans, 1987. Pp. 1–43.

Hart, Jeffrey. "Burke and Radical Freedom." *The Review of Politics*, 29, No. 2 (April 1967), 221–38.

Hill B. W. "Introduction: 'The Philosopher in Action.'" *Edmund Burke on Government, Politics, and Society*. Ed. B. W. Hill. Glasgow: Fontana/The Harvester, 1975. Pp. 7–64.

Kilcup, Rodney W. "Reason and the Basis of Morality in Burke." *Journal of the History of Philosophy*, 17, No. 3 (July 1979), 271–84.

Kirk, Russell, "Burke and Natural Rights." *The Review of Politics*, 13, No. 4 (October 1951), 441–56.

———. "Burke and the Philosophy of Prescription." *Journal of the History of Ideas*, 14, No. 3 (June 1953), 365–80.

———. *The Conservative Mind: From Burke to Eliot*. Chicago: Regnery, 1960.

———. *Edmund Burke: A Genius Reconsidered*. New Rochelle, N.Y.: Arlington House, 1967.

Lock, F. P. *Burke's Reflections on the Revolution in France*. London: Allen & Unwin, 1985.

Love, Walter D. " 'Meaning' in the Conflicting Interpretations of Burke." In *Edmund Burke, the Enlightenment, and the Modern World*. Ed. Peter J. Stanlis. Detroit: University of Detroit Press, 1967. Pp. 117–129.

MacCunn, John. *The Political Philosophy of Burke*. London: Longmans, 1913.

Macpherson, C. B. *Burke*. Oxford: Oxford University Press, 1980.

Morley, John. *Burke*. New York: Harper & Brothers, 1879.

———. *Edmund Burke: A Historical Study*. New York: Knopf, 1924.

Murray, Robert H. *Edmund Burke: A Biography*. London: Oxford University Press, 1931.

O'Brien, Conor Cruise. *Edmund Burke, Master of English*. The English Association Presidential Address 1981. Mitcham, Surrey: Harfield, 1981.

———. "Introduction." *Edmund Burke: Reflections on the Revolution in France*. Ed. Conor Cruise O'Brien. Baltimore: Penguin, 1969. Pp. 9–76.

O'Gorman, Frank. *Edmund Burke: His Political Philosophy*. Bloomington: Indiana University Press, 1973.

Osborn, Anne M. *Rousseau and Burke*. London: Oxford University Press, 1940.
Pappin, Joseph III. "The Case Against Burke: Review of Frank O'Gorman's *Edmund Burke: His Political Philosophy*." *Modern Age*, 19, No. 4 (Fall 1975), 430–31.
Parkin, Charles. *The Moral Basis of Burke's Political Thought*. Cambridge: Cambridge University Press, 1956.
Pocock, J. G. A. "Burke and the Ancient Constitution." *Politics, Language and Time: Essays on Political Thought and History*. New York: Atheneum, 1971. Pp. 202–32.
———. "Introduction." *Edmund Burke, Reflections on the Revolution in France*. Ed. J. G. A. Pocock. Indianapolis: Hackett, 1987. Pp. vii–lvi.
Reid, Christopher. *Edmund Burke and the Practice of Political Writing*. Dublin: Gill and Macmillan, 1985.
Smith, Bruce James. *Politics and Remembrance: Republican Themes in Machiavelli, Burke, and Tocqueville*. Princeton: Princeton University Press, 1985.
Stanlis, Peter J. "The Basis of Burke's Political Conservatism." *Modern Age*, 5, No. 3 (Summer 1961), 263–74.
———. *Edmund Burke and the Natural Law*. Ann Arbor: University of Michigan Press, 1958.
———. "Edmund Burke and the Scientific Rationalism of the Enlightenment." In *Edmund Burke, the Enlightenment, and the Modern World*. Ed. Peter J. Stanlis. Detroit: University of Detroit Press, 1967. Pp. 81–116.
———. *Edmund Burke: The Enlightenment and Revolution*. New Brunswick: Transaction, 1991.
———. "Reflections on Dinwiddy on Mill on Burke on Prescription." *Studies in Burke and His Time*, 18, No. 3 (Autumn 1977), 190–212.
Weston, John C., Jr. "Edmund Burke's View of History." *The Review of Politics*, 23, No. 2 (April 1961), 203–29.
Wilkins, Burleigh T. *The Problem of Burke's Political Philosophy*. Oxford: Clarendon, 1967.
Woehl, Arthur L. "Burke's Readings." Ph.D. Diss., Cornell University, 1928.

SELECTED BIBLIOGRAPHY 179

GENERAL SOURCES

Alembert, Jean Le Rond d'. *Preliminary Discourse to the Encyclopedia of Diderot*. Trans. Richard N. Schwab. Indianapolis: Bobbs-Merrill, 1963.
Aquinas, St. Thomas. *Commentary on the Metaphysics of Aristotle*. Trans. John P. Rowan. Chicago: Regnery, 1961.
———. *Disputed Questions on the Power of God*. In *The Pocket Aquinas*. Ed. Vernon Bourke. New York: Washington Square, 1960.
———. *Summa contra gentiles, Book One: God*. Trans. Anton C. Pegis, F.R.S.C. Notre Dame: University of Notre Dame Press, 1975.
———. *Summa theologica*. Trans. L. Shapcote and the Fathers of the English Dominican Province. 3 vols. New York: Benziger Brothers, 1947.
Aristotle. *Metaphysics*. In *The Basic Works of Aristotle*. Ed. Richard McKeon. Trans. W. D. Ross. New York: Random House, 1941. Pp. 681–926.
———. *Nicomachean Ethics*. In *The Basic Works of Aristotle*. Ed. Richard McKeon. Trans. W. D. Ross. New York: Random House, 1941. Pp. 927–1112.
———. *Rhetoric*. In *The Basic Works of Aristotle*. Ed. Richard McKeon. Trans. W. Rhys Roberts. New York: Random House, 1941. Pp. 1317–1451.
Ayer, A[lfred] J[ules]. *Language, Truth, and Logic*. New York: Dover, 1952.
Barker, Sir Ernest. *Essays on Government*. Oxford: Clarendon, 1965.
Bentham, Jeremy. *An Introduction to the Principles of Morals and Legislation*. New York: Hafner, 1948.
Bloom, Allan. *The Closing of the American Mind*. New York: Simon & Schuster, 1987.
Boswell, James. *Boswell's Life of Samuel Johnson*. Edd. Anne H. Ehrenpreis and Irvin Ehrenpreis. New York and London: Sheed & Ward, 1939.
Bourke, Vernon. *History of Ethics*. II. *Modern and Contemporary Ethics*. Garden City, N.Y.: Doubleday Image, 1970.

Buckle, Henry. *The History of Civilization in England.* New York: Appleton, 1882.
Cicero, Marcus Tullius. *De Re Publica, De Legibus.* Trans. Clinton Walker Keyes. The Loeb Classical Library. Cambridge: Harvard University Press, 1928.
Copleston, Frederick, S.J. *Aquinas.* Baltimore: Penguin, 1963.
——. *A History of Philosophy.* I, Part II. *Greece and Rome.* Garden City, N.Y.: Doubleday Image, 1962.
——. *A History of Philosophy.* VI, Part I. *The French Enlightenment to Kant.* Garden City, N.Y.: Doubleday Image, 1964.
Diderot, Denis. *On the Interpretation of Nature.* In *Diderot's Selected Writings.* Ed. Lester G. Crocker. New York: Macmillan, 1966. Pp. 70–87.
Entreves, A. P. d'. *Natural Law: An Introduction to Legal Philosophy.* London: Hutchinson University Library, 1960.
Germino, Dante. *Modern Western Political Thought: Machiavelli to Marx.* Chicago: Rand McNally, 1972.
Gilson, Etienne. *The Christian Philosophy of St. Thomas Aquinas.* Trans. L. K. Shook C.S.B. New York: Random House, 1966.
Greenleaf, W. H. *Oakeshott's Philosophical Politics.* London: Longmans, 1966.
Grimsley, Ronald. *Jean D'Alembert.* Oxford: Clarendon, 1963.
Halévy, Elie. *The Growth of Philosophic Radicalism.* Trans. Mary Morris. London: Faber & Faber, 1928.
Hobbes, Thomas. *Leviathan.* Ed. Michael Oakeshott. Oxford: Blackwell, 1946.
Holbach, Baron d'. *The System of Nature.* Trans. H. D. Robinson. Boston: Mendum, 1853.
Hume, David. *A Treatise of Human Nature.* 2 vols. London: Dent and Sons, 1911.
Kierkegaard, Søren. *The Present Age.* Trans. Alexander Dru. New York: Harper & Row, 1962.
——. *Works of Love.* Trans. David Swenson. Princeton: Princeton University Press, 1946.
Kirk, G. S., and Raven, J. E. *The Presocratic Philosophers: A Critical History with a Selection of Texts.* Cambridge: Cambridge University Press, 1969.

Kors, Alan Charles. *D'Holbach's Coterie: An Enlightenment in Paris*. Princeton: Princeton University Press, 1976.
Laski, Harold. *Political Thought in England*. London: Butterworth, 1932.
Lewis, Ewart. "Natural Law and Expediency in Medieval Political Theory." *Ethics*, 50, No. 2 (January 1940), 144–63.
Locke, John. *An Essay Concerning Human Understanding*. Ed. P. H. Nidditch. Oxford: Clarendon, 1975.
Loux, Michael J. "The Problem of Universals." In *Universals and Particulars: Readings in Ontology*. Ed. Michael J. Loux. Garden City, N.Y.: Doubleday Anchor, 1970. Pp. 3–15.
Lovejoy, Arthur O. "The Supposed Primitivism of Rousseau's *Discourse on Inequality*." *Modern Philology*, 21, No. 2 (November 1923), 165–86.
Lucas, J. R. *The Principles of Politics*. Oxford: Clarendon, 1966.
MacIntyre, Alasdair. *After Virtue*. 2nd ed. Notre Dame: Notre Dame University Press, 1984.
Macquarrie, John. *Existentialism*. Harmondsworth: Penguin, 1976.
Maritain, Jacques. *Existence and the Existent*. Trans. Lewis Galantiere and Gerald B. Phelan. New York: Vintage, 1966.
———. "The 'Natural' Knowledge of Moral Values." In *Challenges and Renewals*. Edd. Joseph W. Evans and Leo R. Ward. Cleveland: Meridian, 1968. Pp. 229–38.
———. *A Preface to Metaphysics*. New York: Mentor Omega, 1962.
Mill, John Stuart. *Utilitarianism, Liberty, and Representative Government*. New York: Dutton Everyman's Library, 1951.
Philosophers Speak of God. Edd. Charles Hartshorne and William L. Reese. Chicago: The University of Chicago Press, 1969.
Plamenatz, John. *The English Utilitarians*. Oxford: Blackwell, 1958.
———. *Man and Society: Political and Social Theory*. I. *Machiavelli through Rousseau*. II. *Bentham through Marx*. New York: McGraw-Hill, 1963.
Quinton, Anthony. *The Politics of Imperfection*. London: Faber & Faber, 1978.
———. *Utilitarian Ethics*. New York: St Martin's, 1973.

Reck, Andrew J. "Being and Substance." *The Review of Metaphysics*, 31, No. 4 (June 1978), 533–54.

Russell, Bertrand. *The Problems of Philosophy*. New York: Oxford University Press, 1959.

Sabine, George. *A History of Political Theory*. 3rd ed. New York: Holt, Rinehart, and Winston, 1961.

Sartre, Jean-Paul. *Being and Nothingness*. Trans. Hazel Barnes. New York: Washington Square, 1966.

Sigmund, Paul. *Natural Law in Political Thought*. Cambridge, Mass.: Winthrop, 1971.

Simon, Yves R. *The Tradition of Natural Law: A Philosopher's Reflections*. Ed. Vukan Kuic. New York: Fordham University Press, 1965. Repr. 1992.

Stephen, Sir Leslie. *History of English Thought in the Eighteenth Century*. 2 vols. 2nd ed. London: Smith, Elder, 1881.

Strauss, Leo. *Natural Right and History*. Chicago: The University of Chicago Press, 1953.

Sweeney, Leo, s.j. *A Metaphysics of Authentic Existentialism*. Englewood Cliffs, N.J.: Prentice-Hall, 1965.

Vaughan, Charles E. *Studies in the History of Political Philosophy Before and After Rousseau*. Ed. A. G. Little. 2 vols. Manchester: Manchester University Press, 1925.

Veatch, Henry B. *Human Rights: Fact or Fancy?* Baton Rouge: Louisiana State University Press, 1985.

Wallace, William, o.p. *The Elements of Philosophy: A Compendium for Philosophers and Theologians*. New York: Alba House, 1977.

Whitehead, A. N. *Adventures of Ideas*. New York: Macmillan, 1954.

Wild, John. *The Challenge of Existentialism*. Bloomington: Indiana University Press, 1955.

Index

Accident, 61, 64, 80, 82, 115
Act, 56–57, 60, 62–64, 93, 95, 150–52; action, 62–63, 89–90, 92, 106, 129, 141, 150–52, 155; divine action, 95; human action, 149, 151–52
Alembert, Jean Le Rond d', 79, 90–93, 100*n*78
Alteration, 79, 92
Analogy, Principle of, 85, 87; Spirit of philosophic, 86
Anti-ontologicality, 93
Aquinas, St. Thomas, Thomistic, Thomism, vii, xv, xvi, 7, 9, 13, 19–21, 22, 26, 30, 39, 46*n*18, 52–60, 62–63, 65–69, 73, 75, 78, 80, 84, 94–95, 97*n*45, 114–15, 125, 149–51
Aristotle, Aristotelian, xiv, xv, xvi, 3, 9, 13, 18–22, 26–27, 52–57, 60, 63, 67–73, 76, 80, 82, 84, 91, 93–95, 97*n*45, 115, 125–26, 149–50, 166, 171–72
Atheism, 83, 102, 105, 119, 160, 169
Ayer, A. J., 58

Bacon, Francis, 70
Barker, Sir Ernest, 68
Beattie, James, 51*n*135
Becoming, 54, 93, 171
Being, 3–4, 6–9, 53–56, 61–63, 65–67, 87, 91, 93, 161, 164–65, 170–71; Act of, 58; Analogy of, 65; Being-for-itself, 122; Being-in-the-world, 171; First causes of, 53; Ground of, 164; Hierarchy, 129, 166; Immaterial mode of, 56; Intelligibility of, 165; Material, 55; Mystery of, 59; Principles of, 13, 64; Science of, 1; Substantial, 57; Transcendentals of, 125
Bentham, Jeremy, 23, 25, 28–29, 31–32
Bloom, Allan, 164
Boswell, James, 98*n*48

Boulton, James T., 11
Buckle, Henry, 23–24
Burgersdijck, Franco, 69–70, 72
Burke, Richard, Jr., 21, 107–108, 145
Burke, Richard, Sr., 108
Burke, William, 13

Cameron, David, 49*n*103, 96*n*4, 97*n*46, 100*n*75, 115, 120
Canavan, Francis P., s.J., vii, xii, 21, 68, 70, 72–73, 95, 102, 106–107, 116, 125, 135*n*7, 154, 157*n*5
Category, 57, 61, 66, 76, 78, 82, 96*n*6
Causality, 20, 42, 65, 116; Principle of, 103; Cause, 76, 102–103, 109; efficient cause, 65, 85; final cause, 65, 143; first cause, 76, 100*n*87; formal cause, 65; material cause, 65; physical cause, 75
Change, xiv, xvi–xvii, 6, 14, 38, 44, 60, 62–64, 67, 76–79, 82–89, 92–95, 102, 114–15, 121, 124, 129, 140, 147, 168, 171; Law of, 77–78; *see also* Development
Chapman, Gerald, 107–108, 135*n*12
Cicero, Marcus Tullius, 21, 27, 45*n*16, 68, 70, 149–50, 172
Circumstances, xv, 6, 9–10, 15–18, 21, 28, 45*n*17, 81, 91, 94, 110, 112, 114, 117, 128, 134, 148, 154
Cobban, Alfred, 29
Condillac, 79
Cone, Carl B., 158*n*16
Conservation, Principle of, 85
Conservative, conservatism, 23, 25–28, 36–37, 77, 87–88, 136*n*35, 146
Constitution, Ancient, 113
Contingency, 14, 21
Contract, 27, 35, 128; Primeval, 141; Social, 34, 143, 157*n*5
Copeland, Thomas W., 69
Copleston, Frederick, 65–66, 70, 76
Cosmology, 141

INDEX

Deane, Seamus F., 90
Depont, M. 123–24, 127
Descartes, 70
Determinism, 107; Historical, 109
Development, 78, 110, 121, 129, 140, 171
Diderot, Denis, 79, 83, 90, 92–93
Dinwiddy, J. R., 32, 48n77
Dreyer, Frederick, 11, 44n2, 45n4, 137n42, 157n4

East India Company, 147
Empiricists, 12, 27, 41, 44, 79–80, 90, 171–72; Empirical, 24, 36–37, 42, 54, 58; Empiricism, 34, 41, 44, 53, 55, 66; British empiricism, 22; Theological empiricism, 33, 41
Enlightenment, 90, 93; French, xiv, xvi, 79, 92; French philosophers of, 19
Ens, 74
Epistemology, 41, 44, 49n87, 55, 80; Sensationalistic, 100n87
Equality, xvi, 6, 102, 121, 124, 126–30, 132, 134, 153, 163; Human, 126; Social, 128; Spirit of, 131–32
Equity, 153–55
Esse (act of existence), 57–58, 60, 63, 94–95
Essence, xvi, 4, 6, 8–9, 21, 54, 57–58, 60, 62–65, 77–91, 93–95, 99n59, 102, 114, 116, 118, 121–23, 129, 133, 141, 147, 151–53, 155, 170–71
Essentialism, 56, 67, 84, 87, 94; Moral, 81, 83, 85
Eternal Law, 151
Ethics, natural-law ethics, 152; Political, 113
Eustachius, 69, 72
Existence, 14, 44, 55–56, 58–60, 62–65, 78, 87, 89, 92, 106, 112, 118, 121, 125–27, 129, 132, 139–40, 151, 155, 157, 161–62, 169–71; Act of, 62, 64, 67; Social, 124; Spiritual mode of, 57
Existentialism, xvi, 52–53, 64, 88, 93–94, 99n71, 131; Authentic, 56; Intellectual, 61
Expedience, expediency, 11, 23–29, 32, 37, 40–41, 68; Political, 33

Experience, 25, 27, 37, 41–42, 44, 55, 66–67, 76, 80, 94, 171; Sense-, 55, 94
Evil, 18, 22, 46n17, 119–20, 125, 140, 147, 151–52; Moral, 32

Faith, and reason, 75; and revelation, 102
Fasel, George, 36
Fitzwilliam, Lord, 106, 108–10.
Form, 2, 54–56, 60, 62–63, 80, 84, 92–94, 125, 151; Subjective, 76; Substantial, 57, 82
Fox, Charles James, 137n45, 146
Francis, Philip, 12
Freedom, xvii, 5–6, 9, 89, 107, 110, 112, 121–24, 127, 133, 137nn44 & 45, 143, 145, 147, 154, 161–64, 166, 168–172; Radical, xvii, 89, 161–62; Social, 123, 124, 136n17, 147
Freeman, Michael, 45n17, 98n53
French Revolution, 51n136, 77, 105, 109, 117, 147, 158n13, 166, 172
Freud, 160, 164

God, xii, xiv, xvi, xvii, 19, 28, 30, 41–43, 46n23, 57, 63, 65, 71, 74, 85–86, 90, 102–10, 112, 115, 116, 118, 120, 125, 127, 139–40, 142, 145, 148, 150–53, 156–57, 161–62, 169–71; Attributes of, 103; Existence of, 12, 20, 103; Natural knowledge of, 59, Philosophy of, xiii, 102, 106, 134; Power of, 12; Wisdom of, 20
Good, 18, 21, 22, 46n17, 71, 119–20, 123, 125, 140, 148, 151–52; Common, 128, 132–33, 140–41, 144–45, 150–51, 155–56; General, 144; Human, 143; Moral, 26, 32; Natural, 151; of the community, 24–25; Personal, 144; Political, 28; Public, 28–29
Gorgias, 1
Government, 1, 10–11, 14, 16, 19, 22–24, 26, 29, 37, 73–75, 126, 130, 133, 141, 143–44, 146, 148, 156
Greenleaf, W. H., 54
Grenville, 146

INDEX

Habit, 78, 112, 114–15, 142
Halévy, Elie, 33–34
Hamm, Victor M., 172
Hampsher-Monk, Iain, 38–40
Hart, Jeffrey, 92
Hartshorne, Charles, 135n8
Hastings, Warren, 137n42
Hegel, 164
Heidegger, 1
Heraclitus, 56, 64, 92–94
Hill, B. W., 49n103
History, historicism, 22, 29–30, 37, 39, 46n23, 79, 107, 109–10, 113–14, 135n15, 139, 148, 157
Hobbes, Thomas, 26, 119, 137n38; Hobbesian, 120
Holbach, Baron d', 79, 90–93, 100n87
Humanism, Atheistic, 161; Authentic, 161; Radical, 160–61
Hume, David, 23, 25–26, 29–32, 34, 41–42, 44, 49n87, 51n135, 80, 172

Idea, 2, 54, 80, 92, 103, 148, 155; Abstract, xi, 15, 18, 80, 152; Creative, 151
Idealism, idealist, 54, 56, 128
Ideology, 37, 45n17, 165, 168; French ideologues, 79
Image, 55–56, 105
Imagination, 80
Individualism, Authentic, 161; Radical, xvii, 25, 27, 143, 160, 170
Inheritance, as political principle, 85, 86
Intellect, 22, 55–56, 58–59, 61, 63, 65, 74, 76, 102, 122; Practical, 19–20, 59; Speculative, 19–20
Intuition, 61
Irrationalism, xvii, 165; the irrational, 164–66

Jacobins, Jacobinism, 105, 117, 126, 129–30, 132–33, 143, 160, 166
Johnson, Samuel, 75, 158n16
Judgment, 111; Existential, 58
Justice, 5–7, 9, 25, 33, 41–43, 46n23, 123–24, 134, 144, 152–53, 155–56; Natural, 149; Legal, 149

Kant, 93
Kierkegaard, 130–31
Kilcup, Rodney, 104, 113
Kirk, G. S., 125, 138n46
Kirk, Russell, vii, 46n23, 135n7, 143
Knowledge, 53–54, 56, 58, 60, 65, 71, 74–75, 78, 90–91, 122; Metaphysical, 1–5, 7–8, 15, 55; Natural, 30; Practical, 107; Scientific, 93
Kors, Alan Charles, 100n87

Laski, Harold, 34, 43, 49n87
Lewis, Ewart, 68
Liberalism, Utilitarian, 23
Liberty, xvi, 6, 74, 89, 102, 121–24, 126, 130, 134, 136n18, 137n44, 142–43, 145–47, 155–56; Absolute, 144; Abstract, 89; Metaphysical, 16; Social, 146
Lock, F. P., 37–38
Locke, John, 20, 26, 29, 55, 61, 79–80, 90, 96n23, 100nn75, 143, 172
Loux, Michael J., 58
Love, Walter D., 99n68
Lovejoy, Arthur O., 120

MacCunn, John, 28
McDowell, R. B., 70
MacIntyre, Alasdair, 160, 164–65
Macpherson, C. B., 35
Macquarrie, John, 142
Maritain, Jacques, 48n66, 52–53, 58–59, 61, 75–76, 88–89, 94–95
Marx, Karl, 160
Materialism, 92, 100n87
Matter, 56–57, 60, 62–63, 90–93, 100n87, 125; Prime, 82
Metaphysics, metaphysical, xii–xv, xvii, 1–15, 17–18, 22, 28–29, 33, 34, 37–40, 41–42, 44, 49n87, 52–53, 56–58, 60, 63, 65–68, 71–73, 75–76, 78, 80, 82–91, 94–95, 102, 121, 124–27, 129–30, 132–34, 139, 141, 143–44, 149, 152–54, 157, 160, 165, 171–73; Deductionistic, 80; Existential, 57; metaphysicians, 16, 19, 52, 58, 73, 76, 131–32, 172; Rationalistic, 94; Realist, 60, 79, 81, 160, 170
Mill, John Stuart, 23, 31, 41

Moderation, 79, 124, 146–47
Moral law, xvii, 20, 26, 108, 162, 168, 170
Morley, John, 23
Motion, 92
Murray, Robert H., 70
Mystery, mysticism, 46n23, 54, 59, 61, 67, 75–76; and problem, 75

Natural Law, xi, xiii, xvii, 30, 34–42, 68–69, 110, 127, 134, 139, 142, 144, 149–53, 155–57
Nature, xii, xiv, xvi, 6, 8–9, 32, 42–43, 48n74, 53–54, 59–61, 67, 74–75, 78–83, 85–86, 89–93, 95, 103–104, 106–10, 112–15, 118, 124, 131, 139, 142, 149–51, 154, 157, 161, 167, 169–71; Common, 121, 127–28, 137n43, 143, 153–54; First, 114–15; Human, xiii, xv–xvii, 7–9, 28, 46n17, 78, 85, 102, 105, 111–18, 120–22, 124, 126–29, 131, 133–34, 137n37, 141–43, 145–48, 151–53, 156–57, 162, 171; Law of, 6, 17, 30, 42, 44, 77, 87, 94, 109–10, 127, 142, 149, 156, 159n36; Laws of human, 28, 30, 32; Metaphysical, 14; Method of, 87; Moral, 114, 128, 141; Order of, 128; Passionate, 108, 126; Pattern of, 85; Political, 112; Pre-social state of, 89; rational, 54, 78, 142, 153–54; Religious, 119; Right of, 68; Second, 39, 112, 114–15, 120, 128, 142; Social, 85, 112, 115, 118, 128–29, 132, 142, 162, 168; State of, 26–27, 33, 42, 68, 120, 130, 133
Necessity, Metaphysical, 16
Newton, Isaac, 90
Nietzsche, Friedrich, 65, 160, 164, 165
Nihilism, 162, 165; Metaphysical, xvii, 1, 160–61, 163–66, 169; Political, 163; Radical, 166
Nisibis, Archbishop of, 124
Nominalism, 93; Empirical, 54

O'Brien, Conor Cruise, 37
O'Gorman, Frank, 34–35, 137n37, 152–53

Opinion, 114, 141
Order, xvii, 40–44, 61, 63–64, 67, 76–79, 83, 86, 88, 95, 102, 104–106, 108, 121, 124, 128–29, 139, 141, 145–46, 154, 162, 168; Divine, 77; Moral, 154; Natural, 133, 154, 156, 170–71; Political, 85; Social, 84–85, 116, 121, 155
Osborn, Anne M., 137n44

Parmenides, 63–64, 93–94
Particulars, 18
Passion, 30, 32, 107, 111, 120–21, 123, 126, 134, 136n32, 137n45, 141, 145, 147, 165
People, The, 24, 28, 81, 83, 148, 156, 159n36, 166–67
Personalism, 170
Permanence, 60, 64–65, 67, 77, 83, 94, 124
Phantasm, 55
Phenomena, 83, 91; phenomenal, 56
Philo, 153
Philosophes, French, 26
Philosophy, Existential, 59
Pitt, William, 106
Place, 94
Plamenatz, John, 32, 34, 38, 73, 76, 79–80, 85
Plato, Platonic, 2–4, 21, 54–58, 63, 67, 84, 93, 96n6
Pocock, J. G. A., 113–14
Popper, Sir Karl, 3
Positivism, Positivist, 44
Possibility, 78
Potency, 56–57, 60–64, 93, 95; Potentiality, 94
Pragmatism, 34, 36–37, 53; Pragmatist, xi
Prejudice, 22, 27, 31–34, 38–41, 105, 114, 130, 135n7, 144
Prescription, of government, 27, 33–34, 40–41, 148
Pre-Socratics, 125
Presumption, 27, 33–34, 74, 148
Principles, xii, 18–21, 25–26, 31, 36–37, 40–41, 44, 54, 63, 66, 73–77, 79–80, 82–85, 104, 114, 125, 145, 149, 151, 155–57; Abstract, 117; First, 102, 150; Greatest happi-

ness, 31; Metaphysical, 36–37, 63, 67, 73, 86, 88, 102, 115, 121, 134, 156; Moral, 30, 68; of reformation, 79; Philosophical, xii, 103; Pleasure and pain, 31; Political, 24; Theological, 28–29
Process, 77, 79, 87, 93, 115; Historical, 108
Progress, 79, 89, 93, 113–14, 148; Social, 22, 25, 45n17
Providence, 21, 46n23, 75, 86, 107–10, 114, 145, 158n13, 162, 168; Divine, 106, 151
Prudence, 9–10, 14, 18, 20, 23, 106, 143, 145, 154; prudential, 15
Pufendorf, Samuel von, 72
Pythagoras, 1; Pythagorean, 125

Quality, 60–61, 80, 91, 94, 103, 139–40
Quantity, 78, 94, 132
Quiddity, 64
Quinton, Anthony, 31, 136n35

Ramus, Peter, 69–70
Rationalism, 4, 72, 90, 95
Rationality, 21, 62, 83, 122, 127
Raven, J. E., 125
Realism, 82, 84; Aristotelian-Thomistic, 13; classical, 13, 95, 166; Metaphysical, xvii, 53, 57–58, 84, 166, 170; Transcendental, 54–57, 67
Reason, xiii, 17, 19, 25, 29–32, 34, 40–41, 44, 49n87, 54–55, 67, 74, 76, 80, 95, 102, 104–105, 111, 117–20, 126–27, 134, 135n7, 136n32, 139, 143, 151, 164–165; Abstract, 20, 30, 40, 117; Calculating function of, 32; Discursive, 20, 30; Divine, 42, 154; General, 144; Human, 30, 58, 116, 118, 150; Logical, 20; Political, 17, 19–21, 40, 118; Practical, 118, 154; Speculative, 19–21, 59, 61, 103–104; Sufficient, 13; abstract reasoning, 13–14; human reasoning, 117; metaphysical reasoning, 17
Reck, Andrew J., 73
Reid, Christopher, 36–38
Relativism, 113

Religion, 16, 34, 43, 105, 112, 119, 130, 169; foundation of civil society, 119
Rights, 11, 15–17, 23–26, 28–34, 39–40, 42–43, 83, 107, 117, 120–21, 123, 126, 130, 142–44, 153–54, 156, 161, 166, 168–69, 172
Rockingham administration, 117; Whigs, 146
Rousseau, 119–20, 143

Sabine, George, 29–31
Samuels, Arthur, 69
Sanderson, Robert, 69
Sartre, Jean-Paul, 56, 122
Scholastics, Scholasticism, 1, 172
Science, Philosophy of, 93
Self, 90, 120, 169
Sensation, 55, 58
Shackleton, Richard 69–72, 104
Simon, Yves R., 150, 158n18
Skepticism, 4, 13, 30
Smith, Adam, 115
Smith, Bruce James, 136n26
Smith, William Cusac, 130
Social compact theory, 68
Society, xii, xiv, xvii, 1, 3–5, 7, 9–10, 19, 22, 25–27, 30, 33, 39–40, 42–43, 46n17, 73–75, 78–79, 82, 85, 89, 105, 107, 111, 113–14, 117, 119–23, 126–34, 139–48, 151, 153–56, 161–63, 166–70, 172; Civil, 143, 144, 148, 154, 160
Socrates, 8
Sophocles, 149
Soul, 56, 61, 90, 111, 151
Space, 54, 56, 81, 122, 148
Stability (permanence), xiv, xvi, xvii, 6, 67, 76–79, 82–85, 87–88, 95, 102, 115, 121, 124, 157, 171
Stanlis, Peter J., vii, 45n13, 68, 111, 136n18, 144, 159n30
State, 3–4, 6, 9–10, 28, 32, 46n17, 48n74, 78, 81, 85–86, 109–10, 131, 137n44, 144–45, 161–63, 166–67, 169, 170; Organicist theory of the, 87
Stephen, Sir Leslie, 27
Strauss, Leo, 46n18, 68
Substance, xvi, 57, 59–65, 77–83, 86,

92–95, 99n59, 100n87, 102, 115, 132, 146, 157; Material, 84; Metaphysical, 80

Teleology, 77, 134, 139, 143–44, 157
Temperance, 79
Theory, 3, 15–19, 23, 33, 37, 39–40, 88, 109, 127, 129, 142, 152
Time, 54, 56, 81–82, 87, 122, 148
Tradition, traditionalism, 9, 15–16, 19, 26, 30, 33, 35, 37–39, 41, 43–44, 46n17, 113, 115, 126, 136n35, 171–72; Realist, 80, 82; Utilitarian, 31, 33
Truth, 24, 27, 59, 141, 164; Eternal, 30, 49n87; Necessary, 30; Political, 27

Universal law, 149
Universals, xv, 2, 14, 16, 18, 88
Universe, xiv, xvii; Essence of, 77; God-created, 41; Order of, 122, 124, 134; Physical and moral, xiii; Physical and political realm of, 78
Utilitarian, Utilitarianism, xiii–xv, 12, 22–24, 26–29, 31–38, 40–44, 48n85, 53, 144, 152, 171
Utility, 11, 26, 28–29, 31–33, 35–36, 38–39, 43, 153–54

Vaughan, Charles E., 24–27
Veatch, Henry, 93–94, 152

Webb, D. A., 70
Weber, Max, 164–65
Weston, John C., 113, 135nn15–16
Whigs, 146–47
Whitehead, A. N., 77
Wild, John, 62
Wilkins, Burleigh T., 33, 68–69, 72, 98n54, 134n2, 136n32, 146
Will, 59, 63, 123, 126, 142–43, 148, 162–65; Divine, 168; Free, 124; God's, 107, 112, 152, 156; Human, 150
Wisdom, 53–54, 63, 74–75, 86, 105, 107, 118, 123, 134, 147–48; Ancestral, 105; Divine, 151; God's, 103–104; Human, 126; Practical, 18
Woehl, Arthur L., 69

www.ingramcontent.com/pod-product-compliance
Lightning Source LLC
Chambersburg PA
CBHW031245290426
44109CB00012B/450